Canadian Legal Guide for Small Business

Nishan Swais, LLB

Self-Counsel Press
(a division of)
International Self-Counsel Press Ltd.
Canada   USA

Self-Counsel Press acknowledges the financial support of the Government of Canada for our publishing activities. Canada

Printed in Canada.

First edition: 1999; Reprinted: 2001, 2003, 2005
Second edition: 2008; Reprinted: 2009, 2012; 2017

Library and Archives Canada Cataloguing in Publication

Swais, Nishan, 1963-
    Canadian legal guide for small business / Nishan Swais. — 2nd ed.

ISBN 978-1-55180-798-0

    1. Small business—Law and legislation—Canada—Popular works. I. Title.

KE1658.S97 2008   346.71'0652   C2008-902526-1   KF1659.S97 2008

Self-Counsel Press
(a division of)
International Self-Counsel Press Ltd.

North Vancouver, BC   Bellingham, WA
Canada   USA

Contents

Part III: Ongoing Operations

14 Taxes

15 Professional Advisors

Afterword: The Road to Success 235

Download Kit 236

Checklists

Case Studies

Samples

Notice to Readers

Laws are constantly changing. Every effort is made to keep this publication as current as possible. However, the author, the publisher, and the vendor of this book make no representation or warranties regarding the outcome or the use to which the information in this book is put and are not assuming any liability for any claim, losses, or damages arising out of the use of this book. The reader should not rely on the author or the publisher of this book for any professional advice. Please be sure that you have the most recent edition.

Acknowledgements

I wish to thank my parents; my wife, Masae; and my children for their ongoing support, especially my son Kai, who helped edit the latest edition of this book.

This book is dedicated to my father.

Introduction

In 1892, in London, England, a small-business owner by the name of Aron Salomon took the relatively novel step of suing his own company. Little did he know that in doing so, he would help set a legal precedent that still stands today as one of the basic principles of modern business law.

Before considering exactly what it was that Mr. Salomon did and why, more than a century later, it is important to you as a small-business owner, you should take note of the fact that the owner of a modest, family-run shoe manufacturing business — for that is what Mr. Salomon was — could have such a lasting effect on the law.

a. Business and the Law

Business and the law go hand in hand. Neither develops in isolation. Rather, each shapes the other. Changes in accepted business practices are followed by changes in the law, and changes in the law are undertaken by legislators and the courts with a view to their effect on the business world.

As a small-business owner or as someone planning to start a small business, you should be aware of how the law affects your business and how your business practices can sometimes shape the law.

What is the purpose of a shareholders' agreement? How is a contract formed? Why should you incorporate a company? What happens when you sue? These are just a few of the many legal questions you may encounter in the day-to-day conduct of your affairs.

Yet, as any businessperson knows, it is not always cost-effective or practical to seek a lawyer's advice on matters as general, albeit important, as these. *Canadian Legal Guide for Small Business* was written to answer the question, "What do I — as a small-business owner — need to know about the law in Canada"?

The book opens with a discussion of the sources of law in Canada and how the law affects your small business. The subsequent chapters consider specific issues of importance to anyone owning and operating a small business in Canada, including the following:

* The ways of carrying on a small business in Canada, and the advantages and disadvantages of each

* What every small-business owner should know about company law

* What every small-business owner should know about contract law

* What every small-business owner should know about consumer law

* What every small-business owner should know about resolving disputes

* The types of commercial and related legislation affecting your small business

* Frequently encountered business documents and their significance to you

An understanding of the legal issues associated with owning and operating a small business can form an integral part of its success. The goal of this book is to provide you with that understanding and with a solid grounding in how the law works, who it affects, and what it can do to help you achieve your business goals. That requires an examination of the substantive law itself — that is, the legal rules and regulations that guide the business world — as well as what goes on "behind the scenes" of the law. In other words, we must look at why the substantive law is what it is and how it came to be that way.

This book can then serve as a valuable source of information regarding the law and as a guide to how those who shape the law think about and approach business issues.

b. What Is a Small Business?

To establish a context for discussion, let me define the term "small business" and examine what it means to own and operate one. Who, in other words, is this book written for?

Defining a small business is no simple task. Opinions vary as to what constitutes a small business. Banks have their view. Governments have their view. Small-business owners have yet another view. Still, most agree that to be a Canadian small business, a business —

* must have fewer than 100 employees in the manufacturing sector and fewer than 50 employees in any other sector,

* must have annual revenues of less than $5 million in the manufacturing sector or less than $2 million in other types of business,

* will usually be owner operated, and

* must be located and operated primarily in Canada.

In addition, a small business must, like any other type of business that is not run for a charitable or religious purpose, be run for profit.

If you own a small business (or plan to) or if you operate one for someone else, this book is for you. It is written with your concerns in mind, particularly as they relate to the law and the legal issues your business may face. Much of the information in this book is applicable to medium-size businesses as well.

c. The Law in Canada

But what do I mean by the "law?" Simply this: those bodies of principles, standards, or rules that have been established and are enforced by the state in accordance with the will of its citizens.

At issue here are the laws of not just any state, but of Canada in particular, including the laws of various geographic areas, or jurisdictions, within Canada. Moreover, the laws examined in this book are those that affect small businesses.

To understand how laws are made in Canada, it is important to know that the Canadian legal system is relatively unique in that it actually comprises two legal systems, both of which exist independently in other parts of the world.

1. Common Law versus Civil Law

First there is the common law tradition, which Canada inherited from England and which is currently used in the United States, Australia, and, of course, England, among other places. The common law tradition dates back to feudal times and is distinguished by the fact that its laws are developed through centuries of judgments and decrees of courts based on a body of previous judicial decisions. Common law is, therefore, another way of saying judge-made law, provided one understands that in making laws, judges base their decisions on previous decisions. Each such decision is referred to as a case, and the common law is really a body of case law.

Canada's other legal system was inherited from France, which in turn based its legal system on the Roman tradition. Known as the civil law tradition, it operates throughout most of the western world and, in Canada, in the province of Quebec. Its distinguishing feature is that, unlike the common law tradition, the civil law tradition relies on codification of the law. In other words, judges do not determine legal disputes based on the decisions of previous judges (that is, they don't rely on precedent for their decisions); rather, they appeal to a codified set of laws that they are free to interpret and apply in any given set of circumstances.

Perhaps the best way to illustrate the distinction between common law and civil law is with an example. Suppose two farmers are arguing over which of them owns a particular sheep. In a common law jurisdiction, the court deciding the issue would look to similar disputes that in the past had been brought to court and, by comparing them to and distinguishing them from the dispute in question, would base its decision on the tradition established thus far. If a similar case had been decided in favour of the person on whose land the sheep did most of its grazing, the issue of ownership in the present case would be decided on the same basis.

As you can imagine, the ability to compare and distinguish cases in your favour before a court could be of great benefit to anyone involved in a dispute. Thus, persons skilled in those arts — lawyers — came to acquire a certain importance in the common law tradition, one that survives today.

This is not to say that lawyers aren't important in the civil law tradition. Under that system, ownership of the sheep would be decided based on a codified set of rules or principles that a judge would refer to in coming to a decision. That code might have said (as the common law did) that the issue of ownership must be decided on a basis of where the sheep did most of its grazing. In these circumstances, one of the people involved in the dispute might have sought the assistance of a lawyer to try to persuade the court as to how the phrase "most of its grazing" should be interpreted. Should it be interpreted to mean "where the sheep ate most of its food" or to mean "where the sheep most often ate"? As anyone with even a passing interest in the law knows, such distinctions can determine a dispute.

As you can see, both systems of law can result in a similar outcome when presented with a similar set of facts. Neither has a monopoly on justice. The split between the civil law tradition operating in Quebec and the common law tradition operating in the rest of the provinces, federally, and in the territories may not always be as significant as might first appear.

That said, this book focuses exclusively on the law of the common law jurisdictions in Canada; that is, everywhere in Canada, except Quebec. Though some (or even much) of what is said here may apply to the laws of Quebec, this book does recognize that Quebec operates under a legal system distinctly its own and should for that reason receive independent consideration elsewhere.

2. Sources of Law in Canada

There are two sources of law in Canada: case law and legislation.

(a) Case Law

Case law, as already noted, refers to a body of decisions of courts. Each case itself comprises a specific set of facts relating to a dispute brought before a court. By applying the law to those facts, a decision in the case is rendered and the dispute resolved.

But cases aren't significant in themselves. What makes a case important is the reasons for the judge's decision, the *ratio decedendi*, as it is referred to in legal circles. Those reasons are the basis for any precedent the case might set. (A precedent is a standard or authority that can be used by any future court in deciding identical or similar cases.)

Must a court use a past case as a precedent? In short: yes, according to the Latin principle of *stare decisis et non quieta movere*, or "To adhere to precedents and not to unsettle things which are settled." In practice, this principle operates to make the decision of a higher court in a particular jurisdiction binding on a lower court within the same jurisdiction (see Chapter 13, Resolving Disputes, for a discussion of the hierarchy of courts in Canada). Thus, the *ratio decedendi* of a decision of the Supreme Court of Canada, as the highest court in the land, is binding on every court in Canada from the date that decision is made.

It is through this interplay of *ratio decedendi* and *stare decisis* that Canada has built a body of case law as a source of law.

(b) Legislation

The other source of law in Canada is legislation, the body of laws enacted by the state through its legislatures. Most legislation, when enacted, takes the form of a statute: a declaration of a legislature codifying, commanding, or prohibiting something as law.

There are literally tens of thousands of items of legislation currently in effect in Canada. Many of those cover business issues ranging from the sale of goods to the collection of interest.

In applying statutes to the cases brought before them, judges interpret the provisions of those statutes in much the same way one might do under a civil law system. There is, however, an important distinction in that the common law often develops around legislative provisions and must (where applicable) be used in interpreting statutory provisions.

That said, legislation is often enacted with the specific purpose of changing the common law. When judges resist that kind of change, an interesting tension often arises between the forces of justice, as embodied by the judicial system, on the one hand, and the will of the people, as embodied in the actions of its freely elected legislators, on the other.

When all is said and done, it is those (sometimes competing) interests that are the ultimate source of the law.

d. The Small-Business Owner and the Law

Which brings us back to the case of Mr. Salomon. Why is it significant to you, as a small-business owner? To answer that question, you have to consider what Mr. Salomon did.

Mr. Salomon incorporated a company, to which he then sold his small business. In exchange, Mr. Salomon received a large block of shares and £10,000 worth of debentures. A debenture is simply a written promise to pay back a debt (see Chapter 6, Financing Your Small Business, for a further explanation). In doing this, Mr. Salomon became both the owner and a creditor of his company.

Now it happened that the company, through no fault of Mr. Salomon, could not meet its debts. Having fallen on hard times himself, it occurred to Mr. Salomon that as a creditor, he could sue his company for what it still owed him under the debentures.

Naturally, this did not please the other creditors of the company. They thought they should be the first to be paid what was due them. They argued that because the company both belonged to and was run by Mr. Salomon, it was only fair that he should bear the brunt of any losses. Indeed, the company's creditors went so far as to call Mr. Salomon's company a sham, created simply for the purpose of avoiding his business debts, and reasoned that he was, therefore, personally indebted to them out of his own pocket.

The English Court of Appeal agreed with the creditors. But Mr. Salomon did not give up, and he took his case to the House of Lords, the highest court in Britain.

After a long and bitter battle between Mr. Salomon and his company's creditors, Mr. Salomon prevailed. The court reasoned that Mr. Salomon and his company were not — despite outward appearances — the same thing. Legally, they were as different as if they were two separate persons, and as such, they could sue each other and be sued by each other.

Moreover, as a separate entity from his company, Mr. Salomon was not any more responsible for its debts than he would have been for the debts of anyone else. In short, as a shareholder of an incorporated company, Mr. Salomon had the benefit under the law of limited liability (see Part I, Ways of Carrying On a Small Business, for a further discussion of limited liability).

What, then, can you — a small-business owner — learn from Mr. Salomon?

First, Mr. Salomon's case shows how business shapes the law. Imagine what might have happened to Mr. Salomon had his creditors prevailed. What effect might that have had on others in business? A chilling effect, to be sure. Many people would have been reluctant to invest in business ventures for fear of risking (and possibly losing) their personal property to their business creditors. The economy might then have stagnated for lack of investment capital. Ultimately, this was what was in the judges' minds when they came to their decision.

The court concluded that a legal distinction between Mr. Salomon and his company was needed to ensure that he — and millions of others like him — could risk money in a business venture without at the same time risking everything he owned personally if the venture went bad. In short, the court reasoned that the economic needs of society outweighed the debts owed to Mr. Salomon's company's creditors, and it shaped the law accordingly.

Second, Mr. Salomon's case shows how the law shapes business. By incorporating a company, Mr. Salomon sought to take advantage of the limited liability this step could afford him personally. Both Mr. Salomon and the creditors of his company wished to test the strength of the law granting him that limited liability by fighting the matter in court. The court ultimately decided in favour of Mr. Salomon and thereby set a precedent that has been accepted in Canada as good law (both in legislation and at common law). As a result, people such as you and I may, in pursuing our business ventures, rely on this precedent, confident of the risks we are assuming.

Finally, Mr. Salomon's case illustrates that business law is about real people and real businesses in real situations. Today, much of what businesspeople are forced to undergo at the hands of lawmakers seems, at first glance, arbitrary or irrelevant. What you will discover as you read this book, however, is that everything that happens in the law happens for a reason. Every law affecting your business serves a purpose, sometimes social, sometimes purely commercial.

As a small-business owner, it is incumbent on you to know and understand these laws and the purposes behind them. That alone can help you conduct your business affairs, confident that the law is on your side.

❦ ❦ ❦

This book addresses both start-up issues and ongoing concerns in the life of your business. The focus throughout will be practical in nature, with the goal of providing you with useful information you can use on a day-to-day basis in your small business.

Part I (Chapters 1 to 3) explores the different ways in which you can carry on a small business: as a sole proprietorship, partnership, or corporation. Part II covers start-up issues. Chapters 4 and 5 deal with the legal issues of naming your business and obtaining licenses and permits. Chapter 6 considers what financing you might need and the legal issues associated with obtaining it. The final start-up related issue — your insurance needs as a small-business owner — is contained in Chapter 7.

Part III looks at the various legal issues associated with operating a small business successfully. Chapter 8 examines how to protect your copyrighted works, trademarks, patents, and other intellectual property. Chapter 9 focuses on writing and interpreting business contracts. Chapter 10 suggests guidelines for ensuring good consumer relations. And Chapter 11 helps you to ensure that you get paid for what you do by exploring the legal aspects of billing and collecting your accounts. Chapter 12 takes up the legal issues involved in finding, hiring, and firing employees.

In Chapter 13, we consider the resolution of legal disputes. Going to court is only one — and not necessarily always the best — option.

Chapter 14 looks at the taxes relevant to small businesses, while Chapter 15 offers insight into the professional services of accountants, bankers, and lawyers, and considers what you can and should expect from them as a small-business owner.

Finally, bonus chapters on the download kit consider the advent of the Internet age and how online commerce affects your small business, as well as privacy issues.

This book closes with a few concluding remarks. By this point, you will have come to better understand the legal issues affecting your small business. As Mr. Salomon has shown, your success as a small-business owner depends on it.

A final word about this book. The breadth and scope of the law in Canada make it impossible to account for every development or contingency that may affect the law in your area. As such, the contents of this book are provided to you for general information purposes only and should not be taken to be a complete statement of the law or any aspect of it. Views expressed in this book are for assistance only and should not be considered as binding on any court, government agency, or organization. A qualified lawyer should be consulted in connection with any action you take in relation to a legal issue facing you or your small business.

Part I
Ways of Carrying On a Small Business

There are three ways for you to carry on a small business in Canada. You can operate as a sole proprietor. You can carry on business in partnership with another person (or persons). Or you can incorporate a company.

Each of these ways of doing business has advantages and disadvantages. The purpose of Part I is to help you determine which business form is best suited to meet your particular needs and expectations.

1
Sole Proprietorship

The simplest and least expensive way to carry on a small business in Canada is the sole proprietorship.

As its name implies, a sole proprietorship means one person in business for himself or herself. As a way of carrying on a small business, sole proprietorship has proven especially popular with students, homemakers, and people who are just starting up a business or are already employed full time in some other enterprise.

Typical examples of businesses that are sometimes conducted as sole proprietorships are —

* a student mowing lawns in his or her neighbourhood;

* an employed person who supplements his or her income by spending weekends making pizzas at home, freezing them, and then selling them to neighbourhood restaurants; and

* a house painter who does not necessarily require much equipment or overhead and, for the most part, can do the job alone or with minimal help from others.

These examples share an important similarity, one that defines the very essence of a sole proprietorship; namely, as a sole proprietor, you are the business.

a. Setting Up a Sole Proprietorship

Because, as a sole proprietor, you are the business, no special legal steps are needed to set up a sole proprietorship. As soon as you do business for yourself — that is to say, as soon as you engage in some sort of commercial activity — you are doing business as a sole proprietor. Thus, the term "sole proprietorship" does not refer to any formal legal structure; it merely designates that you are involved in a commercial activity.

It is worth noting that you are nonetheless required to obtain licenses or permits to engage in certain types of commercial activity. For example, you may operate a plumbing business as a sole proprietor; however, to do so legally, you must be licensed by the municipality in which you plan to carry on that business. (See Chapter 5, Licenses and Permits, for a further discussion of license and permit requirements relevant to your small business.)

As a sole proprietor, you may carry on business under a name other than your own. For example, a house painter by the name of Fred Green can, if he wishes, carry on business under the name "The Happy House Painter." That means he can advertise to the public under that name, list his business in the telephone book under that name, enter into contracts as "The Happy House Painter," and do anything else in connection with his business under that name that he can legally do under the name Fred Green.

Note, however, that anyone who carries on business under a name other than his or her own name is required to register that name with the relevant government authority. This is necessary to ensure that both the government and the public can determine who, in a given instance, is carrying on business under a particular business name. (See Chapter 4, Choosing a Business Name, for a further discussion of business name registration requirements.)

b. Advantages and Disadvantages

To determine whether you should operate your small business as a sole proprietorship, consider some of this structure's advantages and disadvantages.

1. Advantages

There are several advantages to operating your small business as a sole proprietorship:

(a) *You can start doing business right away.* You don't need to do anything to set up a sole proprietorship. Your sole proprietorship is established when you begin whatever business activity you plan to carry on.

(b) *It is inexpensive compared to other ways of carrying on a small business.* This is because no special legal steps need to be taken to conduct business as a sole proprietorship.

(c) *Though most sole proprietors carry on business alone, a sole proprietorship can have employees.* Being able to hire employees means you can spread the workload among several people. This is useful if the job you do requires you to be in several places at once or for work that can't be done by one person alone, such as moving furniture. An employee is also capable of filling in for you when you are sick or otherwise unable to work. (See Chapter 12, Employees, for a further discussion of employment matters.)

(d) *All the benefits of the business belong to you personally.* That means the assets and income of the business are yours to do with as you please. For example, if you carry on business fixing small appliances in your basement on weekends, the tools you buy all belong to you personally. If you decide to stop doing business, the tools remain yours. As you will see, this is not necessarily the case with other business forms. In addition, any money you earn in your business becomes part of your personal income: your business profits are your profits.

(e) *Business losses may reduce your personal income tax.* Because any income your business earns becomes part of your personal income, it is added to any other income you earn (for example, as an employee of another business) and taxed at the individual rate set under the federal *Income Tax Act.* Depending on your financial circumstances, this may not be an advantage. However, if your business creates losses — that is, if the costs you incur in your business exceed its revenue — those losses may be used to reduce your personal income tax and possibly place you in a lower tax bracket. (See Chapter

14, Taxes, for a further discussion of tax matters.)

(f) *Because there is nothing involved in setting up a sole proprietorship, there is nothing involved in winding one down.* Your sole proprietorship ends when you stop doing whatever work you were performing as a sole proprietor.

2. Disadvantages

As you might expect, there are disadvantages to sole proprietorships:

(a) *Just as the benefits of the business belong to you personally, so too do the obligations.* If, as "The Happy House Painter," you have a telephone line installed in your basement, the cost of installation and any telephone bills become your personal obligations. That is because you are the business. Any debts or liabilities you incur in conducting your business are your debts and liabilities. As you can see, the knife cuts both ways.

(b) *Your liability for things you do in the course of operating your business is unlimited.* In other words, not only are the obligations of the business your obligations, but there is also no limit on the amount for which you may be obligated. Moreover, your business obligations can be satisfied by recourse to your personal assets. If you agree to paint someone's living room and, while doing so, accidentally splash paint on their Renoir painting, not only are you obligated to repair or replace that Renoir but you may also be required to use your personal assets (e.g., dip into your savings account) to satisfy that obligation.

The risk associated with unlimited liability is the single biggest deterrent to carrying on business in the form of a sole proprietorship. To avoid that risk, you must either incorporate a company and do business that way (see Chapter 3, Corporation) or procure adequate insurance against any possible mishaps. In some cases, your insurance coverage may be all that stands between you and personal bankruptcy (See Chapter 7, Insurance, for a further discussion of insurance matters affecting your small business.)

(c) *Though you can employ others, you cannot employ yourself.* While employing oneself might seem a little strange, being able to employ oneself — as is possible when you carry on business in the form of a corporation — may result in tax savings.

(d) *In Canada (to the chagrin of many), individuals are taxed at progressively higher rates than corporations.* A sole proprietor cannot take advantage of the more favourable tax treatment afforded incorporated businesses.

(e) *The federal government and certain provincial governments have established grant and loan programs as well as other small-business assistance measures that often apply only to incorporated businesses.* Therefore, these programs are not available to sole proprietorships.

(f) *Certain types of business arrangements will not allow you to carry on your small business as a sole proprietorship.* For example, if you want to carry on business as a franchisee of a pizza chain, it is likely that the franchisor will require you to incorporate a company in order to operate that franchise.

(g) *There is a (misguided) perception that a sole proprietor may not be as serious about his or her business as is someone who does business in the form of a corporation.* This can raise problems where you require a loan from a bank or credit from a supplier.

(h) *When you stop doing business, the sole proprietorship ceases.* It does not continue without you. The business cannot be passed on after you die, if that is your intention. That is not to say you cannot pass on the assets that make up the business, but it means that the person to whom the business is passed will have to start his or her own business with those assets or make them part of a business that he or she already operates.

c. Is a Sole Proprietorship Right for You?

The ideal candidates for carrying on a small business in the form of a sole proprietorship will have a special skill or talent that they wish to use in earning income. They will also be capable of running the business substantially on their own.

Checklist

If sole proprietorship seems right for you, before starting business, remember to do the following:

✓ Register any names under which you plan to carry on business.

✓ Obtain the necessary licenses and permits to legally allow you to do what you do.

✓ Obtain appropriate insurance coverage.

---

d. Summary

Many successful small businesses are run as sole proprietorships. In addition, many large businesses started out as sole proprietorships and were incorporated only after the business itself became too much for one person to handle. In short, sole proprietorship remains the basis of many a great entrepreneurial beginning.

2
Partnership

Another way to carry on a small business in Canada is in partnership with one or more other persons.

Partnership refers to the relationship between two or more persons who carry on business together with a view to making a profit. In many ways a partnership is similar to a sole proprietorship and, for practical purposes, can be thought of as a sole proprietorship operated by more than one person.

Similarities between a partnership and a sole proprietorship include the following:

❦ The partners carry on the business of the partnership directly (i.e., the partners, taken together, are the business).

❦ The benefits and obligations of the partnership are those of the partners personally.

❦ A partnership can have employees.

There is one major distinction between a sole proprietorship and a partnership. Whereas the person who owns and operates a sole proprietorship must be an individual, the partners comprising a partnership may either all be individuals, all

be corporations, or be a mixture of any number of individuals and corporations.

Two forms of partnership are typically used to carry on a small business in Canada. In a general partnership, the distinguishing feature is that the liability of each of the partners for the debts and obligations of the partnership is unlimited. That means you — as a partner in a general partnership — are personally responsible for any partnership obligations incurred by any other partner. By contrast, under a limited partnership arrangement, the liability of only certain of the partners is unlimited.

Discovery

Nowadays it is common for business-people to speak of their businesses "partnering" with another to carry out some specific project or enterprise.

However, using the term "partnering" suggests that the businesses are in a legal partnership arrangement, with all of the liabilities that entails. If that is not what you intend, it is better to avoid using the term "partnering" loosely and rely instead on some other term of association.

---

a. General Partnership

As noted, any partnership involves an arrangement whereby two or more persons — meaning either individuals or corporations — carry on business in common with a view to profit. Further, the defining feature of a general partnership is that the liability of the partners for the debts and obligations of the general partnership is unlimited. In practical terms, that means that each partner is personally responsible and can be held accountable for any obligation of the partnership, including any obligation that another partner might incur on behalf of the partnership. Even so, for the reasons discussed later in this chapter, a general partnership is the partnership arrangement most often used in carrying on a small business.

Indeed, there are numerous examples of persons who might carry on business in the form of a general partnership, including the following:

* Three friends who operate a neighbourhood window washing service

* Two people skilled in technical matters who operate a computer repair service out of a small office

* A group of people who take tourists on white-water rafting excursions

* Two or more professionals, such as chartered accountants, lawyers, or architects (groups of professionals may also do business in the form of a limited liability partnership. However, that type of business structure is highly specialized and therefore outside the scope of this book).

* Two corporations, one manufacturing pinball machines and one manufacturing video games, that operate a chain of amusement arcades

Like a sole proprietorship, in each case the partners are the business.

1. Setting Up a General Partnership

General partnership arrangements are covered in each province by partnership legislation. That legislation makes it relatively easy and inexpensive to establish and maintain a partnership relationship. The need for a partnership agreement (discussed in section a. below) will, however, add to your start-up costs.

Under the relevant legislation (and similar to a sole proprietorship), no special legal steps are needed to set up a general partnership. As soon as you and one or more other persons carry on business together with the intent of making a profit, you are doing business in partnership. This is so regardless of what you agreed to among yourselves or whether or not you have taken any other steps to formalize your relationship (e.g., by entering into a written partnership agreement). If there is a dispute among the partners or between the partnership and any third party, a court will look to the intent of the parties to determine whether or not a partnership existed. Thus, both to protect yourself and make clear your intent, it is important that you enter into a partnership agreement before you begin doing business.

(a) The Partnership Agreement

As its name suggests, a partnership agreement is a contract setting out the terms of your partnership arrangement. Although a written agreement is not required for you to carry on business in the form of a partnership, it is strongly recommended that you and your partners enter into one before beginning business. Among other things, a partnership agreement will —

* provide concrete evidence of the existence of a partnership arrangement,

allow you to set out, in writing, your rights and obligations as a partner (and those of the other partners),

✤ provide for matters such as the partnership name and how the partnership can be dissolved (i.e., brought to an end), and

✤ allow you to amend the legislative default rules governing partnerships.

At the end of this chapter, you will find a sample partnership agreement you can use in establishing your own partnership arrangement. As you review that agreement, note the issues it addresses and consider whether or not they apply to you. If not, you should draft language that better meets your needs.

You may also use the sample partnership agreement to highlight some of the issues you will need to consider in creating your general partnership. Be sure to take into account any matters not found in the agreement that apply to your circumstances.

A partnership agreement determines your rights and obligations in terms of both your partners and the partnership and ultimately concerns your livelihood. It is important, therefore, that you obtain competent legal advice when preparing to enter into a partnership arrangement to ensure that you get exactly what you bargained for.

If there is no agreement, the rights and obligations of the partners are governed by partnership legislation and the common law. You should contact a lawyer to determine precisely what that entails for you and your small business.

(b) The Partnership Name

A partnership must be carried on under a partnership, or firm, name. This is a result of partnership legislation, which provides that a partnership name must be registered with the relevant governmental authority before the partnership engages in business.

Discovery

Many partnerships choose to do business under the partners' names. For example, two consultants may do business under the name "Smith & O'Donohue." In some jurisdictions, it is not necessary to register a partnership name if the partnership name is composed of the names of the partners.

What you choose to call your general partnership is up to you. "Holmes and Watson, Detectives" is an example of a partnership name, as is "The Kootenay Group." A general partnership can legally carry on business under either of these names, provided the name is registered and no one else is using it. Again, registration ensures that both the government and the public know who they are dealing with in any given instance.

Discovery

A partnership agreement should provide that a partner's name, if used in the name of the partnership, should be removed from the partnership name on the date that the partner ceases to be partner. Otherwise that partner might find his or her name continuing to be associated with a partnership to which he or she no longer belongs.

(c) Other Matters

As with a sole proprietorship, carrying on certain types of commercial activity in partnership may require a license or permit.

2. Advantages and Disadvantages

To determine whether or not you should operate your small business as a general partnership, consider some of the advantages and disadvantages.

(a) Advantages

The advantages of carrying on a small business in the form of a general partnership include the following:

(a) *You can start right away.* As with a sole proprietorship, your partnership begins whenever you and your partners begin to carry on business. You don't need to take any formal legal step before starting. However, it is strongly recommended that you enter into some type of written partnership agreement. Of course, you must also register your partnership name.

(b) *It's relatively inexpensive.* Apart from the costs of registering your partnership name and obtaining legal advice in preparing the partnership agreement, there are very few other expenses you will likely incur in setting up a partnership.

(c) *A partnership, like a sole proprietorship can have employees.* (See Chapter 12, Employees, for a further discussion of employment matters.)

(d) *All benefits of the partnership belong to the partners personally.* That means that each partner has a right to a portion of the profits of the partnership based on whatever distribution formula had been agreed to by all. However, it does not mean that property contributed to the partnership or otherwise acquired by it is the partners' property. That property belongs to the partnership, and no partner has a right to simply take that property for himself or herself. In the absence of any agreement to the contrary, the partners have the right only to the proceeds of the sale of the property on the dissolution of the partnership, after all the debts of the partnership have been satisfied.

(e) *The income earned by the partnership is attributable to the partners personally.* Thus — as in a sole proprietorship — your earnings from the partnership are added to any other income you earn (e.g., as an employee of another business) and taxed at the individual rate set under the federal Income Tax Act. Again, depending on your financial circumstances, this may not necessarily be an advantage. However, if the partnership creates losses, those losses can be used to reduce your personal income tax.

(b) Disadvantages

The disadvantages to carrying on a small business in the form of a general partnership include the following:

(a) *Any partner acting on behalf of the partnership legally binds all the other partners.* Thus, if one partner enters into a contract on behalf of the partnership, all other partners are bound by that contract. This is often seen as the greatest risk of doing business in partnership; you cannot always control what the other partners do in the name of the partnership. That, of course, opens the door to abuse by unscrupulous partners who may not always act in the best interests of the partnership.

(b) *Just as the benefits of the partnership belong to each of the partners personally, so too do the obligations.* Each partner is, together with the other partners and by himself or herself (i.e., jointly and severally), liable for the debts and obligations of the partnership. That means you can be called on by a creditor either alone or with the other partners to satisfy any debt or obligation of the partnership.

(c) *Your liability as a partner is unlimited.* As with a sole proprietorship, your personal assets — such as your car, cottage, and Rembrandt — can be seized by the courts to satisfy any debts of the partnership. As any partner can legally bind all the other partners, the risk of unlimited liability can present a major barrier to choosing to do business in the form of a general partnership. To overcome that barrier, you should, at a minimum, ensure that the partnership is adequately insured.

(d) *A partnership cannot employ any of the partners.* Again, this precludes certain tax advantages that might otherwise be available if doing business as a corporation.

(e) *The partnership is not subject to tax; however, the partners are.* Any partnership income is therefore taxed, in the case of partners who are individuals, in the hands of those individuals at the individual rate set under the Income Tax Act.

(f) *A partnership may not be eligible for certain federal and provincial grants and loans.*

(g) *Dissolving a partnership — bringing it to an end — is not always a simple matter.* In most cases, dissolution will require the agreement of the partners. If the partners don't agree, the legislation provides for certain circumstances in which a partnership may be dissolved. These include the death or insolvency of a partner, and a partner giving notice to the other partners of his or her intention to dissolve the partnership.

Before dissolving the partnership, the partnership debts must be paid out. It is worth noting here that a former partner will still be responsible for any debts of the partnership incurred while he or she was a partner.

3. Is a General Partnership Right for You?

A general partnership may be right for you if —

* you plan to go into business with one or more persons,

* your potential partners are persons you can trust, and

* you and your partners want to take a hands-on approach to your business and exercise direct control over your business activities.

Checklist

If a general partnership seems right for you, before beginning business, remember to:

✓ Enter into a written partnership agreement.

✓ Register the partnership name.

✓ Obtain the necessary licenses and permits to legally allow the partnership to conduct the partnership business.

✓ Obtain appropriate insurance coverage.

A general partnership is a suitable business structure for two or more persons who have faith in each other's integrity and business skills. Because a partnership is much less difficult than a corporation to establish, maintain, and dissolve, it is ideal for those seeking to enter into some common enterprise that requires their direct involvement. Anyone desiring a hands-off approach or less direct involvement should consider forming a limited partnership.

b. Limited Partnership

A limited partnership is a special kind of partnership arrangement that provides limited liability to certain of the partners. Those partners are called the "limited partners." The general partner(s) does not have limited liability. However, by law, only the general partner is allowed to be involved in the conduct of the business of the limited partnership or to contribute services to the partnership. The limited partners are forbidden to do so. If a limited partner does become involved in the operation of the business, he or she loses limited liability status.

Typical examples of persons who might carry on business as a limited partnership include —

❧ three individuals, two of whom have money available for investment and a third who is skilled in the art of theatre production, who wish to produce a musical; and

❧ two small recording companies that plan to join forces to pursue a new business venture.

1. Setting Up a Limited Partnership

Every limited partnership is made up of some combination of general and limited partners. (A partner can be an individual or a corporation.)

A typical limited partnership arrangement involves a general partner, usually a corporation, that carries on the business of the partnership, and several limited partners, all of whom generally function as little more than passive investors. At the end of this chapter you will find a chart setting out the structure of a typical limited partnership. You may wish refer to it as you read this section.

As might be expected, setting up a limited partnership is no simple matter when compared to setting up a general partnership.

To begin with, a limited partnership, unlike a general partnership, does not simply arise when two or more people carry on business with a view to profit. To set up a limited partnership, you must meet the requirements of the relevant legislation, and that means — among other things — filing the appropriate documentation with the relevant government authority. The documentation requires you to set out the name of the partnership, whether a partner is general or limited, and the type of business the partnership intends to conduct. Any changes in that information must be filed as they occur.

A written partnership agreement is recommended as part of the establishment of a limited partnership. An agreement can help to clearly define the rights and obligations of the various parties, especially regarding the division of the partnership profits. A limited partnership agreement is difficult to prepare and will require the assistance of a good lawyer. However, if there is no agreement, the partners' relation will be governed by legislation and the common law.

If the general partner is going to be a corporation, that corporation will need to be incorporated (see Chapter 3, Corporation) as part of the establishment of the limited partnership. In most instances, the general partner is a corporation since the limited liability associated with carrying on business as a corporation can be used to offset the unlimited liability of a general partner. However, the time and expense of setting up a corporation must be calculated into the costs associated with setting up a limited partnership.

Remember that the general partner conducts the business of the limited partnership. If the general partner is a corporation, the directors of the general partner are ultimately responsible for the conduct of that business. The establishment of a limited partnership includes determining how many directors of the general partners there are going to be and who they will be. Of course, the directors can be the limited partners (or some of them), thereby placing some control back into the hands of the limited partners; but, as you can see, things begin to get complicated, especially where issues of limited liability arise.

In sum, anyone considering doing business in the form of a limited partnership should give serious consideration to the time, cost, and effort involved in setting one up.

2. Advantages and Disadvantages

To determine if a limited partnership is the business form best suited to your needs, you should evaluate its advantages against its disadvantages.

(a) Advantages

The advantages of operating your small business as a limited partnership include the following:

(a) *Limited liability.* As a limited partner, your liability is limited to the extent of your contribution to the partnership.

(b) *The option, as a limited partner, to be involved in a business enterprise only as a passive investor.* The actual operation of the partnership business is left to someone else.

(c) *The option to have employees.*

(d) *Potential tax benefits.* The income earned by a limited partnership is attributable to the partners in accordance with the partnership agreement. Limited partners who are individuals are taxed at the individual rate set under the federal Income Tax Act. That can reduce the taxes you have to pay.

(b) Disadvantages

The disadvantages to carrying on a small business in the form of a limited partnership include the following:

(a) *Hassle.* Setting up and maintaining a limited partnership is an expensive, complicated, and time-consuming process.

(b) *Circumscribed involvement.* Your limited liability comes at the expense of not being allowed to provide services directly to the limited partnership. In other words, to retain your limited liability status, you cannot take a role in the operation of the partnership business. You must remain a passive investor.

(c) *Limits to limited liability.* A limited partner's liability may not be limited in a province in which the limited partnership was not established. For example, if you establish your limited partnership in BC and the partnership then carries on business in Newfoundland, the liability of the limited partner is not necessarily limited in Newfoundland, even though it is limited in BC.

(d) *Obligation to renew.* A limited partnership must be renewed every few years (usually five) or risk being administratively dissolved.

(e) *Lack of access to types of funding.* A limited partnership may not be eligible for certain federal and provincial grants and loans.

(f) *Difficulty in dissolving the partnership.* As is the case with a general partnership, dissolving a limited partnership is not a simple matter. Among other things, it requires filing dissolution papers with the relevant government authority.

3. Is a Limited Partnership Right for You?

For the reasons discussed above, few people choose to carry on their small business in the form of a limited partnership. However, there may be circumstances in which a limited partnership is right for you:

❦ You plan to go into business with one or more persons but primarily as a passive investor

* You can afford the costs of setting up and maintaining a limited partnership, including the costs of setting up and maintaining a corporate general partner

* You want to take a hands-off approach to operating your small business

A limited partnership is the ideal arrangement for people interested in trading control over their small business for the right to invest in that business on a limited liability basis. This is not the typical small-business owner profile, and so a limited partnership is not the most frequently used way of carrying on a small business.

However, this is not to say that no small business should be carried on as a limited partnership. The arrangement may be appropriate in situations where a mix of people — some who want to be passive investors and others who want direct control over what they do — are interested in becoming involved in some common business enterprise.

c. Summary

Carrying on business in partnership with others can be a rewarding experience, especially if each partner has something unique to contribute, whether in the form of skills or money.

Inevitably, partnerships, when successful, amount to more than the sum of their parts. The key to a successful partnership is using your business judgment to determine whether your prospective partners are capable of living up to your expectations and you are capable of living up to theirs.

Checklist

Before starting business as a limited partnership you should do the following:

✓ Enter into a written partnership agreement.

✓ Incorporate and organize the general partner (if, as likely will be the case, it is going to be a corporation).

✓ File the required documents.

✓ Obtain the necessary licenses and permits to legally allow the limited partnership to conduct the partnership business.

✓ Obtain appropriate insurance coverage.

Sample 1
Partnership Agreement

PARTNERSHIP AGREEMENT

THIS PARTNERSHIP AGREEMENT, made as of the _____ day of _____,
20____

A M O N G :

_____, a corporation incorporated under the laws of the
(partner name)   Province of [*Ontario*],

OF THE FIRST PART

- and -

_____, an individual residing at _____;
(partner name)

OF THE SECOND PART

- and -

_____, an individual residing at _____;
(partner name)

OF THE THIRD PART

WITNESSES that, in consideration of the mutual covenants and agreements contained in this
agreement, the parties hereby agree as follows:

1. DEFINITIONS

1.1 In this agreement **"Partners"** means collectively [*name each partner*] and any other person admitted as a partner under this agreement; and **"Partner"** means any one of them.

2. CREATION OF PARTNERSHIP

2.1 The Partners agree to carry on business in partnership on and from the _____ day of _____, 20____, and the partnership shall continue until terminated by the Partners in the manner and subject to the terms and conditions provided in this agreement.

3. NAME

3.1 Until changed by partnership resolution, the firm name of the partnership shall be _____. A Partner shall not enter into any agreement on behalf of the partnership except in the firm name, unless authorized by the Partners.

4. PRINCIPAL OFFICE

4.1 The principal office of the partnership shall be located at _____ or at such other place or places as may be determined by the Partners.

5. BUSINESS

5.1 The business of the partnership shall be that of providing consulting services to persons engaged in [*the airline and travel industry*], and related businesses and such other business or businesses as the Partners may decide.

6. FISCAL YEAR

6.1 The fiscal year-end of the partnership shall be on _____ in each year during the currency of the partnership or such other day as may be determined by the Partners.

7. BANKING

7.1 The bankers of the partnership shall be such banks or trust companies as shall from time to time be determined by the Partners. All monies received from time to time on account of the partnership shall be paid immediately into the bank or trust company for the time being of the partnership, to the credit of the partnership, in the same drafts, bills, cheques, or cash in which they are received. Cheques and other orders for the payment of money, unless otherwise determined by the Partners, shall be signed by at least [*two*] persons authorized by the partnership.

8. CONTROL AND VOTING

8.1 Except as otherwise provided in this agreement, all decisions with respect to the affairs of the partnership shall require [*the unanimous*] approval of the Partners.

8.2 Decisions concerning a matter of policy or expenditure or otherwise in connection with the partnership business; decisions with respect to allocation of the partnership's profit and loss distributions, including decisions respecting admission of new Partners, removal of a Partner, and mergers with other firms and office relocations; and all other decisions with respect to the partnership or the partnership business shall be made at a meeting of Partners duly called or by written instrument signed by all Partners.

8.3 Meetings of Partners may be called at any time by any Partner by giving not less than 72 hours' written notice of the meeting to all Partners, stating the time, place, and purpose of the meeting. Meetings of Partners may be held at any time if all Partners are present and waive notice. The quorum required for meetings of Partners is a majority in number of the Partners present in person, or if there are less than [*three*] Partners, the quorum is all Partners.

9. AUTHORITY AND DELEGATION

9.1 Each Partner may take part in the management of the partnership business. The Partners may at any time and from time to time delegate to any one or more of the Partners the right to manage the affairs of the partnership and to determine any one or more matters that might otherwise be determined by the Partners pursuant to Article 8.

10. RIGHTS AND DUTIES OF PARTNERS

10.1 Each Partner shall devote substantially all his or her ordinary working time to carrying on the business of the partnership.

10.2 Any contract or liability entered into or incurred by a Partner in contravention of any provision of this agreement shall be for the separate account of such Partner who shall indemnify the other Partners from and against all costs, claims, damages, liability, loss, and expenses that such Partners may at any time incur, suffer, or be required to pay in respect of such contract or liability incurred in contravention of this agreement.

11. LIABILITY OF PARTNERS

11.1 If at any time a Partner is required to pay or becomes personally liable for more than one-third of the partnership debts, such Partner shall have as against the other Partners, a right of recovery of the proportionate share of such payment or indemnification against such liability, and such Partner shall have, on becoming liable for such debt, a first lien or charge on the capital and all other interest or interests of the defaulting Partners in the partnership.

12. CONTRIBUTIONS OF PARTNERS

12.1 The Partners shall contribute a total of $_____ in cash, in proportion to their respective partnership shares, to the start-up capital of the partnership by no later than _____.

12.2 If at any time capital is required for carrying on the business of the partnership, such capital shall be advanced by the Partners in proportion to their partnership shares or as otherwise agreed.

12.3 If at any time the capital contributions to the partnership of the Partners are unequal, the portion of the contribution of one Partner which is in excess of the contribution of the other Partners, shall as among the Partners for all purposes of division of the profits of the partnership and the dissolution of the partnership be deemed to a loan by the Partner contributing such excess, shall be repayable at any time when the affairs of the partnership will permit in priority of payment and distribution of profits and/or assets of the partnership among the Partners.

12.4 No interest accrues on a Partner's capital contributions to the partnership in proportion to his partnership share. However, if a Partner makes an additional payment or advance for the purpose of the partnership beyond his or her partnership share, he or she is entitled to _____% per annum interest from the partnership on that additional payment or advance until refunded by the partnership.

12.5 Subject to 12.6 hereof, all capital and assets of the partnership from time to time shall belong to the Partners in proportion to a Partner's partnership share.

12.6 An individual capital account shall be maintained in the records of the partnership for each Partner which account shall in each case be:

(a) credited with the Partner's capital contributions to the partnership and share of the partnership's net profit; and

(b) debited with the Partner's share of the partnership's net losses, withdrawals, or returns of capital and distributions to the Partner.

12.7 No capital may be returned or repaid to any Partner without the prior written consent of [all] the Partners.

13. BOOKS OF ACCOUNTS

13.1 Proper books of account shall be kept, and entries shall be made in those books of all such matters, transactions, and things of the partnership as are usually written and entered in books of account kept by persons engaged in concerns of a similar nature, and all books, securities, letters, and other things belonging to or concerning the partnership shall be kept at the place of business where the partnership is being carried on, and a Partner shall have free access at all times to inspect, examine, and copy them, and shall at all times furnish to the other Partners correct information, account, and statements of and concerning all such transactions. Statements of the business and affairs of the partnership shall be prepared on a monthly basis unless otherwise determined by the Partners and shall be in such form as the Partners shall agree.

14. TERMINATION

14.1 The partnership may be dissolved at any time by a Partner giving notice in writing to the other Partners of the Partner's intention to dissolve the partnership, in which case the partnership is dissolved as from the date mentioned in the notice as the date of dissolution.

14.2 The partnership shall not be terminated or dissolved by the withdrawal, death, mental incapacity, insolvency, bankruptcy, or other disability of a Partner; by the admission of any additional Partner; or as the result of the assignment, transfer, or other disposition by a Partner of all or any portion of his or her interest in the partnership or otherwise, except in accordance with this agreement.

14.3 On dissolution of the partnership, subject to any contrary agreement binding the former Partners and their estates and after making any necessary adjustments in accordance with generally accepted accounting principles to allow for any debit balances in the Partners' separate capital accounts, the partnership business shall be promptly liquidated and applied in the following order:

(a) To pay the debts and liabilities of the partnership

(b) To refund any outstanding additional advances, together with accrued interest

(c) To distribution of the credit balances of the Partners' separate income accounts

(d) To distribution of the credit balances of the Partners' capital accounts

(e) To distribution of any residue to the Partners in proportion to their respective share in the partnership

15. NOTICES

15.1 Any notice required to be given in this agreement shall be deemed to be given to the person to whom it is intended to be given or shall be sent by post, addressed to him or her at his or her usual or last known residence address and, if sent by post, shall be conclusively deemed to have been given on the third business day after the date of mailing.

16. ARBITRATION OF DISPUTES

16.1 Any dispute between the Partners arising out of or related to this agreement and any amendments to it, whether before or after dissolution of the partnership, shall be referred to and settled by a single arbitrator agreed upon by the Partners or, in default of such agreement, to a single arbitrator appointed pursuant to the legislation governing submissions to arbitration in the jurisdiction whose laws govern this agreement. The decision of the arbitrator is final and binding on the Partners with no right of appeal.

17. AMENDMENT TO AGREEMENT

17.1 This agreement may only be amended in writing signed by all the Partners, and such amendment shall be binding upon each of the Partners and shall have the same force and effect as and from the date of the signing thereof as if it had originally formed part of this agreement.

18. SEVERABILITY

18.1 Every provision of this agreement is intended to be severable. If any term or provision of this agreement is illegal or invalid for any reason whatsoever, such illegality or invalidity shall not affect the validity of the remaining terms and conditions of this agreement.

19. HEADINGS

19.1 Headings preceding the articles of this agreement have been inserted for ease of reference only and do not affect the meaning, construction, or effect of this agreement.

20.   ENTIRE AGREEMENT

20.1   This agreement constitutes the entire agreement between the Partners pertaining to the subject matter of this agreement.

21.   GOVERNING LAW

21.1   This agreement shall be governed by and construed in accordance with the laws of the Province of [*Ontario*] and the federal laws of Canada applicable in that province.

22.   SUCCESSORS AND ASSIGNS

22.1   This agreement binds and benefits the Partners and their respective heirs, executors, administrators, legal representatives, committees, successors, and assigns as the case may be.

IN **WITNESS WHEREOF** the parties hereto have set their hands and seals as of the day, month, and year first above written.

```
                                    )
                                    )
_____            )    Per: _____
(Witness)                           )
                                    )
_____            )    Per: _____
(Witness)                           )
                                    )
_____            )    Per: _____
(Witness)                           )
```

Limited Partnership Structure

LIMITED PARTNERSHIP STRUCTURE

LIMITED PARTNERSHIP

General Partner

- Unlimited liability
- Usually a corporation
- Operates business partnership

Limited Partner

- Limited liability
- Passive investor/not involved in operation of partnership business

Limited Partner

- Limited liability
- Passive investor/not involved in operation of partnership business

3
Corporation

By far the most popular way to carry on a small business in Canada is in the form of a corporation.

A corporation — or company, as it is called in some jurisdictions — is a legal entity, created by statute, that is used to carry on a business and exists separate in law from its owners. By incorporating, you bring that legal entity into existence.

In Canada, a business can be incorporated under either federal or provincial law. The only requirements are that you complete and file the necessary documentation in accordance with the governing legislation (see section a. below).

Once your corporation is formed and the necessary documentation filed, you can use it to conduct your business on your behalf. However, you must first transfer your business (and all the property it comprises) to the corporation in exchange for an ownership interest, which is represented by the number and class of shares or stocks in the corporation you receive in return. You then become a shareholder of the corporation (or a member or stockholder, as owners of corporations are called in some jurisdictions).

As a shareholder, you are now in a position to elect the director(s), who will oversee the business operations of the corporation. In turn, the

directors appoint the corporation's officers — the president, vice-president, secretary, etc. — to manage its day-to-day business affairs. Provided your shares grant you majority voting power, you can use your position as the majority shareholder to elect yourself as the director of your corporation, and then, wearing your director hat, appoint yourself as one or more of the corporation's officers. This allows you to effectively maintain control over your business, even though it now legally belongs to another entity — your corporation.

As you can see, the practical effect of incorporation is to place an intermediary — the corporation — between your business and yourself. The resulting legal structure is one in which you own the corporation (as a shareholder) and the corporation owns your business. Of course, this arrangement is the exact opposite of a sole proprietorship or partnership in which the sole proprietor or partners own their business directly.

Yet, by choosing to carry on business in the form of a corporation, you are able to limit your personal liability for the debts and obligations of your business in a way that a sole proprietor or partner cannot. That is because those debts and obligations now belong to the corporation. This, more than any other factor, accounts for the broad appeal among small business owners of incorporation. There are, however, other advantages, as you will see.

a. Setting Up a Corporation

Setting up a corporation is a three-step process involving incorporation, organization, and maintenance.

It is possible to incorporate, organize, and maintain your own corporation, and there are books available to assist you with this. (See, for example, the province-specific incorporation guides published by Self-Counsel Press). However, setting up a corporation requires a significant investment of time and effort — two things that you may wish to devote to other business start-up issues.

Moreover, incorporation has become such a commonplace service of law firms that most can incorporate and organize a corporation in relatively little time for less than $1,000 (plus disbursements) and provide annual maintenance services for a cost in the low- to mid-hundreds of dollars.

Still, regardless of whether you choose to set up your own corporation or have a lawyer do it for you, it is worth knowing something about the process involved.

1. Incorporation

As noted, incorporation refers to the actual act of bringing a corporation into existence. This process involves several important steps.

(a) Choosing an Incorporating Jurisdiction

The first step to incorporating is to determine whether you wish to incorporate under federal or provincial statutes. Each province has its own legislation regarding incorporation. Further, in some provinces, a corporation is referred to in the governing legislation as a company. (Indeed, it is common in ordinary conversation to use the words "corporation" and "company" interchangeably, as I will do here.)

Because of the differences among the various provincial corporate statutes, it is difficult to say what advantages or disadvantages, if any, there are in incorporating a company under the federal act rather than a provincial one. In general, however, the only real advantage to incorporating a company federally rather than provincially is that it allows you to engage in business anywhere in Canada without having to register in each province in which you do business. This is not the case with a provincially incorporated company; you will have to register it in every province (other than its home province) in which it carries on business.

That said, the documentation and costs associated with extra-provincial registration are usually not very high. Moreover, as most small businesses carry on business almost exclusively in their home province, there seems little reason to incorporate federally; hence, few businesses do.

Most small-business owners incorporate their company under the legislation of their home province, and unless there is some compelling reason for you to do otherwise, incorporating provincially is recommended.

(b) Determining a Share Structure

As noted earlier, the shares you hold determine your ownership rights in your corporation. Specifically, they establish whether —

* you have a right to vote at shareholders meetings on issues affecting the corporation,

* you are entitled to a dividend (a payment to shareholders out of the profits of the company) when declared by the directors, and

* you are entitled to share in the distribution of the corporation's property when its affairs are wound up and it is dissolved.

Thus, in being issued a share, what you acquire is a bundle of rights in the company.

When setting up your company, you must decide what kinds of bundles of rights you will create and how many of those bundles will be created. In so doing, you determine the authorized capital of your company.

In most cases, the authorized capital of a small business will consist of an unlimited number of only one class of shares — that is, one type of bundle of rights. These are generally called common shares and include the right to vote at shareholders meetings and share in the distribution of the corporation's property on its wind-up and dissolution.

For example, your corporation may "issue and allot" you (i.e., grant you ownership of) 100 common shares in the company in exchange for your business assets. If those are all the issued shares in the capital of the corporation (otherwise known as the issued capital), you, as their holder, effectively have full control over the affairs of the company. As the sole shareholder, you can elect the directors, appoint the officers, and vote your shares in whatever way you wish on whatever matter arises regarding the company and its affairs. Needless to say, this is the share structure favoured by many small-business owners.

But not every small business will be run by a sole shareholder. Nor is one class of shares — that is, one type of bundle of rights — always sufficient.

At the end of this chapter, you will find two case studies involving multiple shareholders and the use of preference shares. You will also find a list and brief explanation of the rights that may be attached to shares.

Determining the share structure of a corporation is never a task to be taken lightly. Sound legal advice is the key to ensuring that every class of shares created accurately represents the needs of the corporation and meets the expectations of current and potential shareholders.

(c) Preparing and Filing the Incorporating Documentation

Once you have decided on a jurisdiction in which to incorporate your company and determined your authorized capital, the next step is to prepare and file the incorporating documentation with the relevant government authority. Depending on the jurisdiction you have chosen, documentation to be filed will usually include —

(a) *Articles of Incorporation.* In some jurisdictions, these are also known as the Memorandum of Association. The articles of incorporation — or "articles" — establish the basic structure of the corporation. Among other things, they set out —

❧ the name of the corporation;

❧ the address of the corporation's registered office;

❧ the names and addresses of the corporation's first director(s) (in some jurisdictions, if a change of directors takes place, a special form of notice must be filed with the relevant government authority);

❧ what, if any, restrictions there are on the types of business the corporation can carry on or things it can do;

❧ the classes and number of shares the corporation is authorized to issue and any rights or restrictions associated with those shares (see below); and

❧ whether there are any restrictions on the right of the shareholders to transfer the shares.

Once the articles are complete and have been accepted for registration, they become the basis on which your company is founded. They also become a matter of public record, available to the public for inspection.

(b) NUANS *report*. The acronym NUANS stands for "newly upgraded automatic name search." This report consists of a list of names similar to the one you have chosen. Its purpose is to help both you and the ministry in charge of incorporation in your jurisdiction determine whether or not you can incorporate your company under the name you have chosen for it (See Chapter 4, Choosing a Business Name, for a further discussion of the NUANS report).

(c) *Notices and consents*. In some instances, it may be necessary to file certain notices and consents, including a notice of registered office and notice of directors and consent of directors to act as directors.

In addition to the above, you will have to pay an incorporation fee at the time of filing. This is usually payable by cheque and runs between $300 and $800.

Once documentation has been filed and the fee paid, a Certificate of Incorporation (or similar document) will be issued by the government authority, declaring that your company now exists under the laws of the jurisdiction under which it was incorporated and setting out the date of incorporation (usually the date of filing).

The incorporation process is now complete.

2. Organization

Organizing a company involves attending to the administrative requirements of the law and interested parties, such as shareholders, officers, and directors.

(a) By-Laws

A company's by-laws establish the procedures to be taken in the company's ongoing operation. On incorporation of a company, a general by-law is typically prepared to provide for matters such as —

* number of directors the company will have and the procedures relating to their removal and replacement;

* place and manner of meetings of directors;

* types of officers (e.g., president, secretary, treasurer) to be appointed, the manner of their appointment, and the procedures relating to their removal and replacement;

* place and manner of meetings of shareholders; and share-related matters, including the manner of issuing and allotting shares to shareholders;

* date of the financial year-end of the company; and

* persons who are authorized to sign documents on behalf of the company.

To be effective, any by-law must be adopted by resolution of the shareholders and passed by the directors. Of course, by-laws can be repealed or amended and new by-laws adopted at any time during the corporation's existence. For example, your company may be required by a bank to pass a by-law relating to the company's right to borrow money.

(b) Directors First Meeting

Corporate legislation often requires that within a set period following incorporation, the company's directors must attend to certain matters relating to the organization of the company, including —

* making by-laws,

* adopting the form of share certificates to be used by the company,

* authorizing the issuance and allotment of the shares to the shareholders,

* appointing the officers, and

◆ making any banking arrangements, such as choosing the company's bank.

Resolutions relating to the above matters may be passed at a directors meeting, but most corporate legislation provides that as long as all the directors consent, the directors may pass such resolutions in writing, rather than hold a meeting. This latter option is favoured by most small-business owners.

(c) Shareholders First Meeting

After the directors have had their meeting (or passed their resolutions), the shareholders are also required by law to meet to, among other things, confirm the election of the directors named in the articles or elect new directors and adopt the by-laws passed by the directors.

Again, providing all the shareholders consent, these matters can be dealt with by a resolution in writing signed by the shareholders.

(d) Minute Book

The minute book of a company is essentially a binder in which all the company's records are kept. It is usually maintained by the corporate secretary and contains —

◆ articles of incorporation and any amendments to the articles;

◆ by-laws;

◆ resolutions;

◆ blank share certificates;

◆ ledgers containing the names and addresses of the company's directors and officers, together with the dates on which they started and stopped serving in those capacities;

◆ a ledger containing the names and addresses of the company's shareholders, together with information on the number and classes of shares they hold and the

dates on which they became and ceased to be shareholders;

◆ a ledger recording the issuance, allotment, and any subsequent transfer of shares in the company; and

◆ any other document of relevance to the company, including financial statements, major contracts, loan documentation, and government filings.

The minute book should be maintained at either the company's head office or some other safe place.

(e) Share Certificates

Each shareholder of the company should be issued a share certificate evidencing the number and class of shares he or she holds. The certificate must be issued and allotted in accordance with the governing legislation and the company's by-laws.

(f) Shareholders Agreements

As its name implies, a shareholders agreement is an agreement among some or all of the company's shareholders regarding their rights and obligations with respect to each other and the company.

Although not required by law, there are several reasons why shareholders agreements are advisable. These include dispute resolution, share-transfer control, and corporate planning.

(i) Dispute resolution

A shareholders agreement can provide for mechanisms to resolve disputes between the shareholders. This becomes especially relevant in situations where there are only two shareholders, each owning 50 percent of the voting shares in the company. In such circumstances, a shareholders agreement can provide that any deadlock be resolved by a third party (e.g., a particular officer or an accountant) and be binding on the shareholders.

(ii) Share-transfer control

Subject to the relevant corporate legislation and what is contained in the company's articles, shareholders are usually free to transfer their shares to whomever they wish, whether by sale, gift, or otherwise. You could, as a result, find yourself in the unhappy situation of having a shareholder of whom you approved be replaced by someone with whom you would rather not be involved. A shareholders agreement can reduce the likelihood of this happening by setting out certain share-transfer restrictions. These may include either or both of the following mechanisms:

* *Right of first refusal.* First refusal grants shareholders the right to match any outsider's offer to purchase another shareholder's shares. Thus, current shareholders can decide whether someone who is not at present a shareholder may become one.

* *Buy-sell arrangement.* Such an arrangement grants any shareholder the right to offer to buy the shares of another shareholder and, if that shareholder refuses to be bought out, to require that shareholder to buy out the offering shareholder on the same terms as the original offer.

(iii) Corporate Planning

What happens if a shareholder dies or becomes mentally incompetent and cannot handle his or her own affairs? What happens if a shareholder becomes bankrupt? Should a shareholder be able to transfer shares to a spouse? To the shareholder's offspring? To a company that is wholly owned by the shareholder? What restrictions, if any, should there be on the ability of a shareholder to vote his or her shares in whatever way he or she wishes on certain issues? What level of shareholder approval should be obtained before certain actions can be taken by the corporation, such as borrowing large sums of money? What obligations does a shareholder have to make loans to the company? Under what circumstances must a shareholder transfer his or her shares to the other shareholders — when a shareholder resigns from the board of directors? When a shareholder breaches the shareholders agreement? How are his or her shares to be valued? Who among the shareholders has the right to buy those shares? In what proportion relative to the other shareholders? These are just some of the issues that may arise and which you may wish to address in a shareholders agreement.

A shareholders agreement is typically drafted to be binding on any new shareholders in the company, regardless of how those shareholders acquire their shares. Becoming a party to the shareholders agreement is usually a condition of acquiring any shares in the company.

In companies with several shareholders, it is not uncommon to find agreements among specific shareholders who have a common interest and who may, as a result, agree to vote their shares in a certain way on various matters facing the company.

When a shareholders agreement is made among all shareholders of a company, it is called a "unanimous shareholders agreement." In some jurisdictions, a unanimous shareholders agreement allows the shareholders to assume powers that would otherwise at law belong to the company's directors.

As you can see, entering into a shareholders agreement as part of the incorporation and organization of your company can help you establish mechanisms to deal with any issues that may arise affecting you or your business. However, it is recommended that you obtain the services of a qualified lawyer in drafting your agreement. Not only can a lawyer alert you to the types of issues that may arise, but he or she will also understand the legal means available to address those issues.

Checklist 1
Shareholders Agreement Checklist

The following is a list of issues to consider when preparing a shareholders agreement. It can save you both time and money to have the answers to these questions ready before you meet with your lawyer.

1. **NATURE OF AGREEMENT**

   ❑ Will the shareholders agreement be a unanimous agreement (i.e., made among all shareholders of the corporation) or will it be an agreement among only certain shareholders?

   ❑ Is the agreement intended to address only certain issues that may arise among the shareholders?

2. **DATE**

   ❑ On what date do the provisions of the shareholders agreement take effect?

3. **PARTIES**

   ❑ What is the name and address of each shareholder, whether an individual or a corporation, who will be a party to the agreement?

   ❑ What is the name and address of the corporation? Adding the corporation as a party to the shareholders' agreement is important to ensure "privity" — that is to say, important for ensuring that the corporation is legally bound by any obligations to which it might be subject under the agreement.

4. **SHAREHOLDERS RIGHTS**

   ❑ How many shares of each class will each shareholder hold?

   ❑ What will constitute a quorum at a shareholders meeting?

   ❑ Who — if anyone — will have a second or casting vote at shareholders meetings (i.e., to break any deadlock)?

   ❑ Will minority shareholders have a right of veto in respect of any matter(s)? If so, what matters?

   ❑ Will shareholders have a right to encumber their shares (e.g., by offering them as security for a debt)?

5. **CORPORATE GOVERNANCE**

   Directors

   ❑ Who will serve as the corporation's directors? Will there be a chair of the board?

   ❑ What, if any, restrictions will there be on the directors' exercise of their powers?

   ❑ How will any deadlock occurring at a board meeting be broken? Will the chair have a casting vote?

   ❑ How will any vacancies on the board be filled?

Officers

❏ Who will serve as the corporation's officers?

❏ Who will manage the day-to-day operations of the corporation? (Usually it is the president.)

❏ What are the other officers' responsibilities?

❏ Who will be entitled to sign a contract or issue a cheque on behalf of the corporation?

6. **MANAGEMENT OF THE CORPORATION'S BUSINESS**

❏ What is the nature of the corporation's business? Are there any restrictions on the kinds of business the corporation can carry on? If so, what are they?

❏ Which, if any, shareholders are allowed or required to work in the business of the corporation? In what capacity?

❏ Will the corporation be required to provide monthly or quarterly financial reports to shareholders in addition to annual financial statements?

❏ Will profits be distributed among the shareholders? If so, in what manner?

7. **FINANCING OF THE CORPORATION**

❏ How will the corporation be financed initially (e.g., shareholder loans, equity, other forms of debt financing)?

❏ How will the corporation be financed on an ongoing basis?

❏ How will a shareholder loan be secured? Will a shareholder be required to subrogate his or her loans to some other form of financing, such as a bank loan?

❏ Are the shareholders obligated to personally guarantee loans by third parties (e.g., a bank) to the corporation?

8. **SHARE TRANSFERS**

❏ Will the shareholders (or any individual shareholder or class of shareholders) have a put right? A put right gives a shareholder the right to have the corporation repurchase its shares from the shareholder and can be exercised either at any time or after a specified period. In effect, a put right acts as an escape valve for the shareholder exercising it. Commonly encountered issues include how the shares are to be valued and their price set, and how payment for the shares is to be made by the corporation (e.g., all at once or within 30 days of the exercise of the right).

❏ Will the shareholders (or any individual shareholder or class of shareholders) or the corporation have a call right? A call right gives a shareholder — or the corporation itself — the right to purchase the shares of another shareholder. In effect, a call right is a mechanism for forcing a shareholder out of the corporation. Again, that right can be exercised either at any time or after a specified period.

❏ Will the shareholders (or any individual shareholder or class of shareholders) have a right of first refusal? If a shareholder wishes to sell his or her shares to someone who isn't a shareholder, do the other shareholders have a prior right to purchase those shares? If so, in what proportion and on what terms?

❑ Will the majority shareholder(s) have a drag-along right? By exercising a drag-along right, the majority shareholder(s) can force all other shareholders to sell their shares to a third-party purchaser on the same terms that the majority wish to sell their shares to that third party.

❑ Will the minority shareholder(s) have a piggyback right? A piggyback right allows minority shareholders to have their shares bought by any third party wishing to purchase the shares of the majority shareholders.

❑ Will the agreement contain a take-over bid provision? For example, if a shareholder receives an offer from a third party to purchase all (but not less than all) the issued and outstanding shares in the corporation, will that shareholder have the right to require any shareholder who does not wish to sell his or her shares to purchase all shares of those who do wish to sell? (That shareholder [or those shareholders] would have to purchase those shares on the same terms as the third-party offer.)

❑ Will the agreement contain a shotgun buy-sell provision? Such a provision allows a shareholder to submit an offer to buy the shares of the other shareholders. If the other shareholders reject that offer, they are required to buy the offering shareholder's shares on the terms of the original offer (i.e., on the terms on which the offering shareholder was prepared to purchase their shares).

9.   DEATH OR INCAPACITY OF A SHAREHOLDER

❑ On the death or incapacity (e.g., for reasons of mental health) of a shareholder, will the corporation or the remaining shareholders have a right to purchase the interest of the deceased or incapacitated shareholder? Will the corporation or the remaining shareholders have an obligation to do so? At what price?

10.   DEFAULT

❑ Are there any "events of default" (e.g., personal bankruptcy) that would entitle either the corporation or the other shareholders to purchase the shares of a defaulting shareholder? How will the purchase price for the shares be set, and what are the terms of sale (e.g., how will the purchase be financed)?

11.   GENERAL

❑ Will there be any restrictions on what a shareholder can do in connection with the corporation's customers, suppliers, or employees after he or she ceases to be a shareholder? For example, will he or she not be allowed to contact any of those people to solicit business? Will a shareholder be prevented from entering into a competing business for a certain period?

❑ Are the shareholders bound by any confidentiality requirements obligating them to remain silent about the affairs of the corporation or any matters relating to the other shareholders?

❑ What means will be used to resolve any disputes among the shareholders regarding matters arising out of the shareholders agreement? For instance, will any dispute first have to be submitted to arbitration, mediation, or some alternative form of dispute resolution?

❑ When does the agreement terminate? On a specific date or event (e.g., the departure of the majority shareholder[s])?

Any shareholders agreement must be tailored to meet your specific requirements. The shareholders agreement checklist, Checklist 1, will assist you in identifying those requirements. Use the checklist to take stock of the issues you want your shareholders agreement to address and then present the results to your lawyer. Remember that because each shareholder's interests are potentially in conflict with the interests of the other shareholders, each should obtain independent legal advice regarding the terms of the agreement before signing it.

3. Maintenance

Corporate maintenance refers to the things you need to do — usually on an annual basis — to ensure both that the company continues to subsist under the governing legislation of the jurisdiction in which it was incorporated, and that the records of the company remain up-to-date and in order. These include —

* holding meetings or passing resolutions, usually on an annual basis, relating to the ongoing affairs of the corporation, including the election of directors, the appointment of officers, the approval of the financial statements, and the transacting of any significant business;

* having annual financial statements prepared for the company;

* making any required governmental filings; and

* ensuring that the minute book is kept current.

b. Advantages and Disadvantages

A corporation is fundamentally different from a sole proprietorship or partnership, and offers unique advantages and disadvantages.

1. Advantages

Following are some advantages of a corporation:

(a) *Personal protection*. You and your company are separate legal entities at law, even if you are the sole shareholder of the company. And because you run your business through your company, the obligations of your business belong to your company and not to you personally. A creditor of the business cannot come after you personally to satisfy any debts or liabilities of the business; the creditor's only recourse is to the assets of your company.

(b) *Limited liability with maximum flexibility*. As a shareholder of a corporation, your liability is limited to the value of the cash and property you contributed to the company (usually in exchange for your shares). At the same time, the shareholders, through the exercise of their voting power, direct the affairs of the corporation and ultimately determine how it carries on business. The corporate business form thus represents the best way for a small-business owner to maximize participation in his or her business while limiting personal liability.

(c) *Potential personal tax benefits*. Just as the obligations of the business belong to the company and not to you personally, so too do the benefits. While at first glance that may seem to be something of a disadvantage, a closer look reveals that is not necessarily the case. For example, if the company turns out to be extremely profitable, the value of your shares increases. You are not, however, taxed on that increase until you sell those shares or otherwise dispose of them. You are then taxed on the increase in value, but based on the lower capital gains rate as opposed to the personal income rate.

(d) *Option of employment with your own company*. Not only can your company have employees but you can be an employee of your company as well. The company can, among other things, hire you to perform services on its behalf and pay you a salary (and, if you wish, a bonus). This may, in turn, create personal income tax savings for you.

(e) *Versatility*. You can structure your company's authorized capital to allow for different ways to participate in your business. For example, you — as the holder of all of the common shares in your company — can maintain full control over your company's affairs while at the same time granting to your spouse — as the holder of a class of non-voting dividend-earning shares — the right to earn dividends out of any profits of the corporation. Of course, you can own some of the same preferred shares yourself and thereby participate in two fundamentally different ways in your own business.

(f) *Multiple business names*. A corporation can do business under one or more business names, provided that those names are registered in accordance with the relevant legislation. Thus, a corporation incorporated by Jack Jones under the name "1234567 Ontario Inc." can carry on business as "Jack's Thumbtacks," "The Tack Man," "Tacks International," "Stickies," or any other business name the company can legally register.

(g) *Potential corporate tax benefits*. Corporations qualify for various types of favourable tax treatment.

(h) *Transfer of business to others*. A company exists until it is dissolved. Unlike a sole proprietorship or partnership, it is not the same entity as its owners and therefore does not live and die with them.

The advantage is that this allows for the company — and, hence, the business — to be easily transferred among different persons and from generation to generation.

2. Disadvantages

Following are some disadvantages of a corporation:

(a) *Expense*. A corporation is relatively expensive to set up, organize, and maintain compared to the cost of setting up a sole proprietorship or partnership. If a shareholders agreement is required, that cost increases.

(b) *Annual documentation*. You must file forms, notices, and other documents on an annual basis, often to ensure that your company continues to maintain its existence under the governing legislation. This can be something of an administrative burden for those who would rather not spend their time filling out forms.

(c) *Potential liability*. While a corporation does offer the prospect of limited liability, recent years have seen a growing number of cases in Canada in which directors and officers have been found by courts to be personally liable for the obligations of their company. The grounds for liability cover everything from unpaid wages to environmental contamination. As a countermeasure, many companies now obtain insurance for their directors and officers, protecting them from liability. There is, of course, a cost associated with obtaining such insurance.

(d) *Difficult dissolution*. Just as setting up a corporation is no simple matter, winding up its business affairs and dissolving it is equally difficult. Among other things, the required documentation must be filed (including articles of dissolution); the company's debts must be satisfied; the appropriate consents from various government agencies must be obtained (including the relevant taxing authorities); fees must be paid; and the assets of the corporation distributed in accordance with the governing legislation, the articles, and the rights of any shareholders. Once dissolved, a company can be revived, that is, brought back into existence. However, this action requires filing articles of revival as well as jumping through a number of other administrative and legal hoops.

c. Is Incorporation Right for You?

A corporation is the business form under which you should carry on your small business if —

❋ your business will be your primary source of income and you expect the income from that business to be substantial (e.g., more than $30,000 a year),

❋ the type of business you do suggests a strong need for limited personal liability,

❋ you want the option of participating in different ways in your small business,

❋ you want to be employed by your business, or

❋ you want your business to survive you so that, for example, you can pass it on to your children.

By choosing to operate your small business as a corporation, you can take advantage of the benefits associated with the independent legal status granted corporations under the law. As a shareholder in that corporation, perhaps the greatest benefit is that you can participate directly in the affairs of your business while at the same time having only limited liability for

its debts and obligations. This advantage, more than any other feature, has made incorporation the business form of choice in Canada for small-business owners.

Checklist

Along with the incorporation and organization of your new business, don't forget to do the following:

✓ Enter into a written shareholder agreement with any other shareholders.

✓ Register any business names of the corporation.

✓ Obtain the necessary licenses and permits to legally allow the company to conduct its business.

✓ Obtain appropriate insurance coverage for the company and any directors or officers.

Discovery

The Franchise

Nowadays, it is common for a small business to operate as a franchise. A franchise is not a business form in the proper sense of the term but is rather a license granted by a license-holder (the "licensor" or "franchisor") to a corporation, partnership, or individual (the "licensee" or "franchisee"). The license or franchise effectively bestows on the franchisee the right to use the franchisor's name, trademarks, and other identifying business marks in connection with the franchisee's business, usually in a pre-established geographic area and for a limited period. For example, a franchisee can sell its hamburgers under the name McDonald's and decorate its premises with golden arches. In return, the franchisee is usually required to pay the franchisor a pre-determined franchise fee and a monthly portion of the franchisee's profits, known as a royalty.

Because a franchisor has a vested interest in ensuring the continuation of its good name, most franchisors exercise strict control over how the franchisee can conduct its business. A franchisor will typically determine such matters as the hours of operation of the franchisee's business, the goods and services the franchisee can offer to consumers (and in what manner they can be offered), from whom the franchisee can purchase its supplies, and in what geographical area the franchisee can solicit business. If you are planning to obtain a franchise, be sure to thoroughly investigate any prospective franchisor and determine — with the assistance of your lawyer — whether a particular franchise is right for you.

d. Summary

Whether you choose to carry on your small business as a sole proprietor, in partnership with someone else, or through a corporation, you should now be familiar with some of the advantages and disadvantages associated with each of these business forms. Your task is to determine your particular business needs and expectations and to consider which of these forms is best suited to meet them.

Case Study 1
Share Structure

Two siblings, Krista and Stephen, each contribute some property and start-up funds to the establishment of their new bakery, which they plan to incorporate. Krista contributes money and property worth $60,000, and Stephen contributes money and property worth $40,000. Because they are both making a contribution to their business, they each want a say in its affairs. They also both want a right to a portion of the property of the business when it is wound up and dissolved. To achieve those ends, they each take back a number of common shares in their new corporation. The corporation thus has two shareholders, entitled to vote on its affairs and receive its property on its wind-up and dissolution. But matters don't end there.

Because Krista has contributed more to the business than Stephen, she wants a proportionately larger say in the affairs of the company. (After all, she has more to lose if the business fails.) Accordingly, the company issues its shares to them in proportion to their contributions. That is, it issues 60 common shares to Krista and 40 to Stephen. (See the discussion below on proportionate distribution of shares.) The effect, of course, is to grant a majority voting interest to Krista, which she can exercise in controlling the affairs of the corporation. (For example, she could choose to vote her shares to elect whomever she wishes as director.) It also gives her the right to a proportionately larger share of the distribution of the company's property on its wind-up and dissolution.

It is not uncommon for small-business owners to find themselves in Krista's and Stephen's position. It is worth briefly considering what their circumstances entail:

1.   The obvious outcome of our example is that Krista is the majority shareholder in the company. She effectively controls the handling of the company's affairs (by controlling who sits on the board of directors). As noted, Krista's majority status is meant to reflect her proportionately larger contribution to the business.

      But suppose Krista and Stephen had each contributed the same amount to the corporation. They would then, presumably, be 50-50 shareholders in the company and have an equal say in the handling of its affairs. This is also quite common and really presents a problem only when there is a deadlock. To provide for a mechanism to deal with deadlock, shareholders sometimes enter into a shareholders agreement.

      A shareholders agreement can also be used to deal with control issues when, as in the case of Krista and Stephen, shareholdings are not equal. Suppose Krista needed Stephen's contribution to run the business; without that contribution, the business could not be successful. This puts Stephen in a position of some power. Accordingly, Krista and Stephen agree that although Krista will remain the majority shareholder, they will enter into a shareholders agreement to provide for, among other things, an equal say in how the business is operated (again, with a mechanism for dealing with deadlock). It could also provide for the right of Krista or Stephen to buy each other out in case, for example, they find they can't get along. In this way, the difference in shareholdings can be modified to more accurately reflect the relation of the shareholders.

2.   Krista and Stephen were issued 60 and 40 common shares respectively in exchange for their contributions. In so doing, the company attributed a purchase price of $1,000 to each share. Nothing, however, would have prevented the company from issuing and allotting only six shares

to Krista and four shares to Stephen, or, indeed, 1,200 shares to Krista and 800 shares to Stephen for their respective contributions. The only thing those distributions would affect is the purchase price attributable to each share. Of course, what is important is that regardless of the number of shares issued, the distribution of shares must proportionately reflect Krista's and Stephen's respective contributions. In other words, any issuance and allotment of shares must reflect a 3:2 contribution split.

Let's assume, for the sake of argument, that Krista and Stephen received 60 and 40 common shares respectively in exchange for their contributions. As noted, the value attributable to each of those shares is $1,000. Suppose, however, that a few years have passed, and the company has become so successful that after any liabilities were accounted for, $100,000 in profits has been added to the initial $100,000 contributed to the company by the siblings. If the company were dissolved, it would have $200,000 worth of cash and property to distribute to its shareholders. And because the company has only one class of shares entitled to partake of a distribution of assets on dissolution (i.e., the common shares) and each share issued carries that right, any distribution would have to be divided equally over the number of shares issued. The result is that each share has now increased in value from the $1,000 originally paid for them to the $2,000 they are now worth.

Now if Ronnie, the siblings' mother, wants to contribute $30,000 in exchange for some common shares, she will receive only 15 shares in exchange for her contribution, as each share is now worth $2,000. If she were able to obtain shares in the company at their original cost of $1,000 she (and the company) would be "diluting" the shareholders' equity in the company. Specifically, she would be unfairly reducing the value of each of the siblings' shares. To understand how she would do so, consider that if Ronnie were able to buy 30 shares in the company at $1,000 each, the company would then have $230,000 of cash and property to allocate over 130 shares. The resulting value of each share would, as a result, dip to about $1,769 per share. Thus, by virtue of Ronnie's "contribution," Krista and Stephen would each have lost — through dilution — some $31 off the value of their respective shares.

The point to take from this is that, in most cases, the value of a share is not static. It rises and falls with the performance of the company. To determine the value of the shares at any given time requires the assistance of an accountant. It is an accountant's job to take stock of the assets and liabilities of a company and assign the company a value. That value can then be allocated to the various classes of shares issued and an individual share value determined.

3. Now suppose the company decided to issue 101 new common shares to Ronnie (for their fair market value), such that there were now 201 common shares issued and outstanding in the company. This time, it is the existing shareholders' voting rights (and hence control in the company) that are diluted, rather than their equity. For now, Krista is no longer the majority shareholder.

Even together, Krista and Stephen cannot out-vote their mom. To prevent this kind of dilution, it is not uncommon for existing shareholders to either vote their shares to elect directors who will not issue shares contrary to the existing shareholders interests (which usually means voting themselves in as directors) or place restrictions in the articles of the corporation, shareholders agreement, or some other agreement that effectively bars the company from issuing additional shares without the consent of the existing shareholders.

4. Note that most corporate legislation requires that certain major changes involving a corporation — such as the sale of its business — must have the approval of at least two-thirds of, and in some cases all, the shareholders. Holding 60 percent of the voting shares of a corporation does not, therefore, put you in a position of absolute power over the corporation's affairs, even in the absence of a shareholders agreement providing for power sharing.

5. Even if Krista held a much larger percentage of the issued shares, say 90 percent (and was capable of meeting a two-thirds majority), the "oppression remedy" provided for in most corporate legislation forbids a majority shareholder to use his or her power to unfairly prejudice a minority shareholder. In this case Stephen could sue Krista for exercising her power in a way that unfairly prejudices Stephen's interests. So again, while Krista might hold the lion's share of power in the corporation as the majority shareholder, that power is not absolute.

These are just a few scenarios that may occur when a company has more than one shareholder.

Case Study 2
Share Structure

Kai and Julia contribute, respectively, $80,000 and $20,000 in start-up funds to the establishment of their new video store, which they plan to incorporate. However, Julia does not want a say in the handling of the business; she'll leave that to Kai, who is experienced in this type of enterprise. What Julia wants is the right to receive dividends from the profits of the business when declared by the directors and to rank ahead of Kai in the distribution of any property on the wind-up and dissolution of the company.

To achieve that end, two classes of shares are required. First, a class of common shares is needed. All the issued shares of this class will be held by Kai, thereby granting him control over the affairs of the corporation.

As well, a second class of "preference shares" is needed, which are so called because of the preferential rights they bestow on the holder. These will be issued to Julia and, to reflect that Julia will have no say in the affairs of the corporation, will be non-voting. However, her preference shares will grant her the right to receive a dividend, if and when declared, by the directors. They will also grant her the right to stand first in line, ahead of Kai, when the property of the corporation is distributed on its wind-up and dissolution.

The ability to offer different types of bundles of rights in a company (by creating and issuing different classes of shares) presents a great opportunity for people with various expectations and capabilities to play different roles in the success of a small business. In this case, because of the different classes of shares available, Kai can use his experience and Julia can contribute her money to what will most certainly be a mutually beneficial enterprise.

Rights that Can Attach to Shares in a Corporation

A share represents a "bundle of rights" in a company. The following is a list of some of the rights that can attach to shares. In each case, it is up to the person preparing the constating documents of a company (e.g., the articles of incorporation) to determine the rights that will attach to a particular class of shares.

1. COMMON SHARES

Common shares generally carry two types of rights:

- *Voting rights.* A voting right entitles the shareholder to vote at meetings of the company shareholders on matters affecting the company. For example, it would entitle a shareholder to vote on who will serve as the company's director(s). Common shares are usually drafted to grant one vote per share.

- *Participation on dissolution.* Common shares generally carry the right to participate in the distribution of assets upon the dissolution, liquidation, or winding-up of the company.

In some cases, common shares also carry the right to a dividend when declared by the Board of Directors of the company. A dividend is a portion of the profits of the company.

2. PREFERENCE SHARES

Preference (or "special") shares are often referred to in the constating documents of a company by class (Class A Shares, Class B Shares, etc.). In some cases, preference shares often include the same rights as common shares. Most often, however, preference shares do not carry voting rights unless they relate to certain specific matters involving the company. Among the rights that a class of special shares will typically carry are:

- *Participation on dissolution.* Preference shares often carry the right to participate in the distribution of assets upon the dissolution, liquidation, or winding-up of the company. If a company's common shares and preference shares both carry this right, the constating documents usually provide that one of these classes is entitled to distribution in priority over the other class.

- *Dividends.* Preference shares also usually carry a dividend right. Again, the issue is whether the preferred shares rank in priority over the common shares with respect to the payment of dividends. (They usually do.)

- *Redemption.* Preference shares may carry a right of "redemption"; that is, a right to be redeemed by the company. That means that the shareholder may, in accordance with the redemption terms set out in the company's constating documents, require the company to purchase the shareholder's preference shares at any time (or at a specified time) for a pre-determined purchase price per share.

- *Exchange.* Some classes of preference shares allow you the right, in particular circumstances and subject to the terms attaching to those shares, to exchange shares of one class for shares of another. For instance, preference shares that do not carry a right to a dividend may be exchanged for the same number of shares that do.

3. SUMMARY

The rights attached to any class of shares can be further defined. For example, a right to a dividend could be a right to a cumulative dividend, non-cumulative dividend, or set at a fixed dividend rate. In addition, there are stock dividends that effectively entitle the holder of a share to receive another share of the same or another class as a dividend rather than money or property.

With respect to the redemption of shares, the constating documents can provide that certain events must take place before those rights can be exercised.

To ensure that you can participate in the ownership of your company in a way that best suits your needs, discuss the various share rights, restrictions, privileges, and conditions available to you with your lawyer before incorporating your small business.

Part II
Start-Up Issues

Once you have decided how you wish to carry on your small business — that is, as a sole proprietorship, in partnership with others, or through a company — the next step is to consider the start-up issues. These involve matters that must be settled before you actually open your doors for business and include choosing the appropriate name for your business, obtaining the necessary licenses and permits, and insuring your business against the inevitable mishap. Perhaps most important, start-up also means obtaining the necessary financing. By taking care of these issues up front, you can better ensure your business's success in the long run.

4
Choosing a Business Name

It is important that you choose the right name for your business. After all, what you call your business can say a lot about the type of work you do and the approach you take to doing it. This chapter considers some of the legal and practical issues associated with naming a business.

a. What Is the Purpose of a Business Name?

A business name serves several important purposes. First, it identifies your business. This may seem obvious, though it is not always well understood. Many small-business owners forget that identifying their business means, first and foremost, identifying their business to consumers — and consumers do not like to have to jump through hoops to know with whom they are dealing. Your business name should reflect that reality. A name such as "J. Jay & H.P. Herbs, Grades 5, 6, and 7 Tutoring and Advanced Learning Academy" is both cumbersome and difficult to remember. Even for those who could remember that name, looking it up in the telephone book would still be a problem. When choosing a business name, remember to approach it from the perspective of the consumer and what he or she is likely to be able to readily call to mind.

Second, a business name should distinguish your business from other businesses. Not only is it important for consumers to be able to identify your business, it is also important for them to be able to distinguish your business from your competition. One way consumers will most certainly do so is to rate you on the quality of your work. Once you've shown them that you're the best, you don't want to confuse them with whether it was "Norma's Garage" or "Nora's Garage" — which just happens to be down the street — where they received such excellent service.

Your business name should also convey information about your business. Consider the difference between a bakery operating under the name "Marla's Bakery" and one operating under the name "Marla's Old Fashioned Cookies and Baked Goods." Clearly, the latter is a more descriptive name and can make a difference in helping people decide if your business is likely to meet their needs. This is particularly relevant when you are just starting out and people may not be familiar with the goods and services you can offer them.

Finally, your business name should convey a certain image. "Café Paris" conjures up images of chequered tablecloths, croissants, café au laits, and belles chansons. "Joe's Coffee" suggests donuts, cigarette smoke, and Styrofoam cups. Either name may accurately describe your small business. The point is that your business name is often the first impression your business makes, and — as everyone knows — you never get a second chance to make a first impression.

Remember that your business name should serve the needs of consumers. Choose one that's easy to recall, look up, write down, and mention to others by those doing business with you. Don't choose a business name that will confuse the public. There is no good reason to identify yourself as "The Lincolnshire Pub" if down the street someone is doing business as "The Lancashire Pub."

Let your business name say something about your business. This can be as simple as "Jones and Rasmussen Consultants," although most people would agree that "Jones and Rasmussen Environmental Consultants" is much better. Also be certain that your business name is one that will make a good first impression on the public. A teenager looking for the latest hairstyle (assuming teenagers are your target clientele) is more likely to enter a salon doing business as "The Groovy Hairstylist" than "Bob's Barbershop."

Discovery

Choosing a Business Name: Dos and Don'ts

- ❦ Don't confuse the public with your business name.

- ❦ Do choose a business name that says something about your business.

- ❦ Do choose a business name that will make a good first impression on the public.

b. The Business Form

Once you have settled on a name, you must meet the legal requirements to do business using that name. What those requirements are will depend on the business form under which you operate.

1. Sole Proprietorship

A sole proprietor can carry on business under his or her own name, under a business name (also known as a business style or trade name), or under his or her own name and a business name. This means that you, as a sole proprietor, can do business as "Fred Green" (i.e., use your own name), "The Happy House Painter," or both.

If you do business simply as Fred Green, no filings or registrations with any government authority are required to legally do business as Fred Green. That means anything your business can legally do, you can do in your name. For example, you can advertise as "Fred Green, house painter," you can enter into contracts as "Fred Green," and you can sue (and be sued) for the work you do as "Fred Green."

If you do business under a name other than your own — for instance, "The Happy House Painter" — then to do so legally you must meet certain registration requirements. This is true regardless of whether or not you also carry on business under your own name (i.e., regardless of whether or not you paint houses under the name "Fred Green" and "The Happy House Painter").

In general, each jurisdiction in Canada has business names legislation requiring that anyone doing business under a name other than his or her own must register that name with the appropriate government authority, usually a provincial ministry of consumer and commercial affairs. The records of the agency are available for inspection by the public, which allows the public a means of identifying the person behind the business name. That way anyone who wishes to do so will be able to determine that "The Happy House Painter" is really a person named Fred Green.

There are several legal requirements associated with registering a business name, some of the more important of which are —

* *Name search.* You cannot use a business name that somebody else is using. You will have to ask a representative at the ministry to conduct a search of its files to determine whether the business name you have chosen is available for use. This can usually be done at the time you register your name.

* *Documentation.* You must fill out the appropriate form. Among other things, the form will ask for your name, your business address, the type of business you conduct, and, of course, the business name under which you plan to operate.

* *Fee payment.* You must pay the fee associated with registration or renewal of a business name.

You must register the business name before you actually use it. Failure to register your business name can have serious repercussions if discovered by authorities, including the payment of fines and penalties. Your registration lasts only for a certain period (usually about five years) and must be renewed; otherwise someone else may adopt it.

2. Partnership

If you carry on business in partnership, the name under which you plan to do business — the partnership, or firm, name — is usually decided by the partners in the partnership agreement.

(a) General Partnership

Business names legislation, and in some cases partnership legislation, often requires that the name of a general partnership be registered with the relevant government authority. Worth noting is that (different from a sole proprietor) the individual partners cannot do business in their own names on behalf of the partnership. The business of the partnership can be carried on only under the registered name.

Registration of a partnership name is undertaken in the same manner as the registration of a business name by a sole proprietor: the relevant form must be completed, the fee paid, and the partners identified to the public. (See section b.1. above.)

As with a sole proprietorship, the failure to register a partnership name can lead to fines and penalties.

(b) Limited Partnership

Legislation requires that a limited partnership file a declaration stating, among other things, the limited partnership's name.

As is the case with a general partnership, none of the partners — whether general or limited — can do business on behalf of the limited partnership in their own names. In fact, for a limited partner to do so could negate that partner's limited liability. (See Chapter 2, Partnership, for a discussion of limited liability in the partnership context.) For this reason, limited partnership legislation prohibits the use of the surname or a distinctive part of the corporate name of a limited partner from appearing in the name of the limited partnership. So, if you, Peter Proctor, are a limited partner in a limited partnership, be sure that the partnership does not include "Proctor" in its name.

Filing a declaration requires you to complete the relevant form, pay the applicable fee, and file the names of the limited and general partners. There are fines and penalties associated with failing to file a declaration. As with a business name registration, a declaration lasts for a limited time only (usually five years) before it must be renewed, at which time a renewal fee is applicable.

3. Corporation

Choosing a name for your corporation is an essential part of the incorporation process. (See

Chapter 3, Corporation, for a discussion of the incorporation process.) There are two ways to select a corporate name. The first is simply to select a name of your own choosing. The second is to have a numerical name assigned to your corporation by the relevant government authority when you file the articles of incorporation. In addition to your corporate name, you may also do business under a business name. These matters will be addressed in more detail below.

(a) Choosing a Corporate Name

Incorporating a company, whether federally or provincially, requires that you prepare and file articles of incorporation. The articles, in turn, require that you designate a name for your corporation. For the most part, what you choose to call your company is up to you. There are, however, specific requirements that must be met if your name is to be accepted by the government ministry responsible for incorporation. These requirements vary by jurisdiction but share the following similar features:

🍁 *The name of your corporation cannot be the same as or deceptively similar to that of any other entity, regardless of whether that other entity is another corporation or sole proprietorship, partnership, or individual.* For example, you cannot call yourself "Sherlock Homes Developers Inc." if someone else is doing business under that same name or under a name such as "Sherlock Homes Housing Development Ltd." However, it is always a question of fact whether or not a name is deceptively similar to another name, and therefore a NUANS report usually must be filed along with the articles of incorporation. The NUANS report provides a list of names similar to the one you have selected. It will help both you and the ministry determine whether or not you can incorporate under your chosen name.

🍁 *Corporate names need not be formed purely from the letters of the alphabet.* Elements of punctuation (e.g., commas, hyphens, periods) and numbers may also form part of your corporate name. Note, however, that each element of your corporate name is an essential element. For example, if your business is called "Sherlock Homes Developments, Inc.," then precisely that, and not "Sherlock Homes Developments Inc." (i.e., without the comma), is your legal name. This is especially worth remembering if abbreviations such as "Mfg." and "Intl." form part of your business name, or if numbers are spelled out (e.g., "Six Village Greenery Inc." is not the same as "6 Village Greenery Inc.," though, admittedly, they are deceptively similar).

🍁 *Your corporate name cannot consist of certain words and phrases that are prohibited by legislation.* You cannot call your company by such names as "World Health Organization Foods Inc." or "RCMP Clothing Ltd." Clearly, the words "World Health Organization" and "RCMP" could mislead the public as to with whom they are doing business. If you are concerned that you may be using a prohibited word or phrase, consult your lawyer.

🍁 *Your corporate name must end with either "Limited," "Corporation," or "Incorporated" or their respective abbreviations, "Ltd.," "Corp.," or "Inc."* These terms can be used as part of a corporate name only; they cannot be used in a business name or partnership name.

🍁 *In most provinces, your corporate name can have an English form, a French form, or an English and French form.* Name forms that are not in English or French or both are not permitted under Quebec law. In Quebec, a corporate name must have a French form. Either the French form or the English form of a corporate name is its legal name. Your corporate name cannot contain any obscenities in any language.

Since NUANS searches are conducted on a provincial basis, it is important that you conduct name searches in each of the provinces in which you wish to carry on business so as not to run into obstacles in other provinces once your name has been established at home.

(b) Obtaining a Numerical Name

If you are unable to decide on a corporate name or simply do not want to be bothered with choosing one, your corporation will be assigned a number name when the articles of incorporation are filed (e.g., "1234567 Alberta Ltd." or "7654321 Ontario Inc."). The number name will then be the legal name of your company. As the number name is assigned by the relevant government agency, no NUANS search is required.

(c) Choosing a Business Name

In addition to a corporate name, a corporation can also do business under a business name. However, you must register the business name under the relevant legislation just as you would for a sole proprietorship: the form must be completed, the fee paid, and the corporation identified to the public. Once you have done so, you are allowed to use your business name (as well as your corporate name) to answer your phone, advertise, and otherwise identify yourself to the public.

By adopting a business name for your company, you are not changing or otherwise affecting your corporate name. If your corporate name is "1234567 Alberta Ltd.," it will remain "1234567 Alberta Ltd." regardless. By adopting a business name — for example, "Kai's Yummy Cookies" — you are simply taking on another name in addition to your corporate name under which you can legally do business.

Nevertheless, your legal name remains "1234567 Alberta Ltd." In other words, this is the name under which you must enter into any contracts or fill out any government forms. Your business name is merely another name under which you can legally do business. The distinction is subtle but worth bearing in mind.

Finally, depending on the type of business you carry on or the industry sector in which you operate, it is sometimes necessary to obtain approval for the use of your business name from the organization or association governing your industry. These organizations or associations are often responsible for the public trust in or perception of the industry and its members, and therefore wish to ensure that a trade name does not mislead the public. Thus, a real estate broker operating and doing business in Ontario must obtain the approval of the Registrar of Real Estate and Business Brokers for a particular business name before trading under that name.

c. Changing Your Name

The law allows you to change your corporate name, partnership name, or business name at any time, provided you meet the relevant legislative criteria. But before you take that step, there are some things you should consider.

The first is that your name has value. That value comprises part of the goodwill of your business and is not easily quantifiable. However, it is very real. Think about the value of doing business under names like IBM, Canadian Tire, or McDonald's. These names carry a weight in the business community that is not easily matched. You should consider whether or not your corporate/business/partnership name also carries weight. Has it come to be associated with quality goods or service in a particular trade or industry? Has it acquired a good reputation among consumers and suppliers? If so, will a name change detract from that reputation by confusing others as to whether or not they are doing business with the same entity? If the answer to that question is yes, a name change may not be the best course of action. Perhaps adding a business name, or even simply leaving things just as they are, is more appropriate. Of course, this makes your initial choice of a name that much more important.

Second, a name change must be done legally, by filling out the appropriate forms and paying the applicable fees. In the case of a corporate name, you will need to prepare and file articles of amendment, as well as obtain a new NUANS search. This will easily cost you hundreds of dollars.

In addition to filing fees, you may incur costs for —

* notifying customers and suppliers of your name change;

* changing telephone book, association, and other listings;

* changing letterhead, signs, and other advertisements; and

* changing all your bank accounts.

There may be restrictions on what you can change your name to. A partnership agreement may provide that the name of the partnership can be changed only with the consent of all partners. Similarly, an updated NUANS search might prevent you from adopting the new corporate name of your choice.

If none of the above is an issue for you or if they are outweighed by your need or desire to change the name of your business, it is simply a question of filing the appropriate forms. In most cases, a name change can be obtained on the spot.

d. Summary

Choosing a name for your small business is not a task to be taken lightly. To get a sense of whether or not the name you propose will have the desired effect, run it by friends and perhaps others in your industry to see how they respond. When it comes to names, you'll be surprised at how honest people can be.

5
Licenses and Permits

It is one thing to own a small business; it is quite another to be legally entitled to operate it. For that, you must obtain the necessary government licenses and permits. Failure to do so can put you on the wrong side of the law.

a. Licenses and Permits: What Are They?

The distinction between a license and permit is a difficult one to make and not always relevant. The terms are often used interchangeably to refer to a right granted by a government or other authority to do something over which that authority exercises regulatory control, such as operating a certain type of business.

It is important to note that licenses and permits can apply to several aspects of your small business, including the following:

* *You as the owner.* For example, some provinces provide that a certain share of a pharmacy must be owned by a licensed pharmacist. The same goes for real estate brokerages: a certain ownership stake must be held by a licensed real estate broker.

* *Your employees.* Certain jobs may be carried out only by people duly licensed to perform these jobs (e.g., operating certain types of construction equipment).

* *Your equipment.* Some equipment may produce hazardous waste or present other problems in need of regulation. As such, permits to own and operate such equipment may be required.

* *Your business itself.* Most businesses require some sort of license to operate. This is true whether you drive a cab or run a hotel.

b. What Is the Purpose of a License or Permit?

Licenses and permits serve several purposes, the most important of which is to allow for government regulation and control of the industry. By requiring you to obtain licenses and permits, governments can monitor and control the number of people or businesses operating within a certain industry, establish standards to be met by those in that industry, and ensure quality control. Licenses and permits also allow governments to gain valuable information about your industry with a view to better serving both the industry and the public at large.

c. What Kinds of Licenses and Permits Do You Need?

The licenses and permits you need will ultimately depend on the type of business you plan to operate. A small retail sales business will not require the same variety or number of licenses as a manufacturer of hazardous waste producing chemical compounds. The key is to find out what licenses you will require in connection with your small business and what you should do to obtain them.

Your best sources of information are others in your industry. If you plan to open your own restaurant, speak to other restaurateurs to discover which licenses and permits are required to serve liquor, provide live entertainment, or set up a sidewalk patio. You should also speak to a lawyer who has experience with the type of business you are operating.

The government is also a good source of information about the licenses and permits you may need, but it will not always be clear which government agencies you should contact to make your enquiries. Start with the most obvious — for example, a liquor license agency if you plan to operate a bar — and ask for its help in directing you to other agencies that might be relevant.

While trying to determine which licenses and permits you need, keep in mind that every level of government must be canvassed to discover what, if anything, is required by them. For example, a municipal or local license may be required by certain types of tradespeople such as plumbers and electricians and in connection with certain types of businesses such as restaurants, taxi cabs, masseurs, and driving schools.

Discovery

Choosing a Location for Your Small Business

Unless you plan to operate a hot-air balloon shuttle service, the location of your business can be as important as what you do. After all, opening your children's clothing boutique in the middle of Nightclub Alley might not be the best way to attract customers or get their attention. It's important that you find a location suited to your business needs. Consider accessibility (both to you and your customers), cost (either to buy or lease your premises), neighbouring businesses (both those that complement and those that compete with your business), and business climate (whether the area is a friendly environment to which people will go without reservation). Finally, be aware that municipal by-laws and zoning regulations play an important role in determining where you can set up business. It is unlikely that you'll be able to locate your pneumatic-drill testing station immediately adjacent to a retirement home. Be sure to consult with your lawyer before coming to any final decision about where to establish your business.

Provincial licenses and permits are required for — among other businesses — personnel agencies, car dealers, real estate brokers, pharmacies, radiology clinics, and securities dealers.

Federal licenses and permits are sometimes required for inter-provincial carriers and businesses involving the use of aircraft, including sight-seeing tours and commercial airlines.

d. How Do You Obtain the Necessary Licenses and Permits?

Obtaining a license is rarely as easy as just filling out a form. In fact, there are usually several steps involved in obtaining any sort of license or permit. These include the following:

(a) Determining the licenses and permits you need to operate your business. This should be done as soon as possible and certainly before you open for business. Few licenses issue (i.e., take effect) on the date of application, and there is nothing worse than opening for business only to find that you're breaking the law on your first day.

(b) Determining what requirements you must fulfil to obtain the licenses and permits you need. For example, do you need to have completed special courses or training? Does your place of business need to comply with special standards and specifications? Must you obtain certain consents or compliance letters from other government agencies?

(c) Filling out the relevant applications and attending to whatever other matters are required in connection with the application (e.g., obtaining the necessary accompanying materials and paying the required application fees).

(d) Waiting until your license issues.

(e) Being advised that your license or permit has been issued.

To illustrate this process, here are some of the steps involved in obtaining a new liquor license for a restaurant in Ontario. You must —

(a) complete and submit the required application and pay a fee;

(b) obtain proof of compliance from the Ontario Minister of Finance regarding payment of retail sales tax;

(c) arrange for and obtain inspections and approval letters from the building department, fire marshal, and public health department;

(d) enclose with your application a résumé of the person who will be supervising the licensed premises (that person must have the relevant food and beverage industry experience or must obtain that experience before the license will issue);

(e) wait for a prescribed period, during which time a notice of your application is published and submissions from the public are requested;

(f) obtain and submit floor plans of your premises;

(g) undergo an inspection of your premises by a liquor license board inspector; and

(h) wait for liquor license board approval before the license issues.

The entire procedure can take up to three months.

e. Summary

Failure to obtain the appropriate licenses and permits can lead to fines and penalties. Moreover, if you operate your business without them and are caught doing so, you may not be granted those licenses or permits in the future. It isn't worthwhile to risk your business and livelihood in that way, considering the little bit of legwork needed to determine and fulfil the license and permit requirements applicable to your small business.

6
Financing Your Small Business

You will need money, or financing, to start and run your small business. There are two ways to obtain that money: through a loan (debt financing) or through equity (non-debt financing).

This chapter considers why you might need financing, what is meant by debt and equity financing, and how you can determine which is most likely to meet your business needs.

a. Why Do You Need Financing?

There are any number of reasons why your small business might need financing. A few of these could be lack of money to —

* start the type of business you wish to operate,

* continue operating your business in the way you want or need to for it to be a success,

* purchase a piece of equipment or property, or

* expand your business or take it in a new direction.

Whatever the reason, you must remember that obtaining financing from someone other than yourself almost always comes at a price. Rarely will someone simply give you the money you want or need for your business; you have to give something in return. What you give depends on the type of financing — debt or equity — you choose.

b. Equity Financing

"Equity" refers to your right of ownership in your business. That right is granted to you in direct proportion to the amount of money or property you have contributed to the business. If your contribution comprises all your business's money and property, you alone hold the equity in it. Accordingly, equity is usually reflected in your ability to control the business and profit from its success.

In equity financing, a contribution of money or property (i.e., a capital contribution) is made to your business — by you or someone else — in exchange for a right of ownership. Depending on the business form under which you operate, that right can mean becoming a partner in your partnership or receiving shares in your company. Whatever the case, equity financing grants the person making the contribution — the financier — the right to participate in what he or she anticipates will be the ongoing success of your business. The financier becomes an investor in your business.

Discovery

Buying a Small Business

Rather than start a small business from the ground up, you may wish to purchase one that is already in operation. Among the advantages of doing so is that you already have a sense of how the business is faring and what you can do to improve it once it is in your hands. When buying a small business, be sure to thoroughly investigate all matters relating to it. You must know what assets the business owns (and which you want or need to purchase); what debts and liabilities the business has (and how you can ensure they are satisfied by the current owner or, alternatively, how you can avoid inheriting them); and what contracts the business is bound by (including property and equipment leases, supplier contracts, purchase orders, and service agreements) and how you can terminate or continue these contracts. You should also be certain you understand why the business is being sold and whether the asking price is a fair one. A good indicator of profitability is the business's financial statements. Be sure to have your accountant review the financial statements covering as many periods of the business's operations as are available to you. Then, in consultation with your lawyer and after you are convinced that you are getting a good deal, submit your purchase offer.

1. Sources of Equity Financing

Several sources of equity financing are available to your small business:

* *Yourself*. In many cases, you will be the primary source of equity financing for your business because you, more than anyone else, are likely to invest in your vision of the business. The advantage of being your own primary financier is that it allows you to maintain the primary right of ownership over your business. In other words, you pay the piper, you call the tunes. But before dipping into your personal savings, remember that money and property that has been contributed to a corporation belongs to the corporation and, as noted in Chapter 3, creditors of the corporation can look to that money and property to satisfy its debts.

* *Friends and family*. These people are another common source of equity financing. Sometimes friends and family may even "gift" money or property to your business, asking nothing in return. Of those that do ask for something in return, few may demand any right to actually participate in the operation of your business. In that case, you can structure the ownership rights in your business to allow friends or family to participate in some other way, such as by granting them a right to a share of the profits.

* *Other businesspeople*. There are people who, despite never having met you, may be willing to invest in your business out of a desire to "get in on the ground floor" of something big. This can happen if you have a particularly good business idea or strong track record of making a success of what you do. Investors of this sort are usually sophisticated businesspeople who rely on research to direct them in their business affairs. You can be assured that

such people will do their homework: they will ask you and others (your bank, former business partners, customers, suppliers) about everything they need to know to assure themselves that investing in your business will benefit them. In some cases, such people will be passive investors, content to let you carry the ball. In others, they may wish to participate in the operation of your business, either directly or through a nominee.

There are several ways to obtain equity financing from individual investors, including advertising or simply being introduced to them by mutual acquaintances. You should know, however, that securities laws in Canada prohibit you from making public offerings of securities (including shares in a company or any investment contract) unless you comply with the applicable registration and prospectus requirement. (See Section b.3. below.)

✤ *Institutions*. Banks, finance companies, and venture capital investors may be willing to invest in your business for much the same reasons an individual businessperson would. They will also subject your business to the same vigorous investigation and likely demand some say in its operation. Again, there are several ways to obtain equity financing from institutional investors, including approaching them yourself.

✤ *Government*. Both federal and provincial governments have programs offering different types of equity investments to small businesses — provided they meet the relevant criteria. (See Section d. below.)

Note that when you obtain equity financing from someone other than yourself (or friends and relatives), you are essentially allowing strangers to buy into your business. It is important, therefore, when obtaining equity financing, to know

with whom you are dealing, what rights in your business these investors or institutions will have as a result of their contribution, and whether you can tolerate sharing your business (or some aspect of it) with others.

2. Types of Equity Financing Arrangements Available

The types of equity financing arrangements available depend both on the business form under which you operate and the demands of the financier.

If you carry on business as a sole proprietor, anyone interested in financing your business with equity capital will probably ask you to enter into a written agreement that allows him or her to participate in some way in your business. For example, the financier might ask for a certain percentage of the profits. Of course, there is a danger that you and the financier might be construed as carrying on business together, that is, in partnership with each other. As noted in Chapter 2, such an arrangement would make the financier jointly liable with you for the debts of your business. Financing a sole proprietorship with equity capital can therefore present a risk to the financier.

The situation is much the same for a partnership. Anyone contributing equity capital to your partnership may wish to become a partner. It is up to you and your partners to decide what that entails in terms of a right to participate in partnership affairs; a partnership agreement will help to establish that.

Note again that someone who does not want to join the partnership or otherwise be actively involved in its business runs the risk, at law, of being considered a partner if he or she can be said to be carrying on business in common with the others. For that reason, a limited partnership is better suited to passive investors than a general partnership. As discussed in Chapter 2, a limited partnership comprises (usually) one general partner and (usually) more than one limited partner.

The limited partners enjoy limited liability for the obligations of the partnership (i.e., to the extent of their contribution), which allows them to invest in the business of the partnership without running the same risks as a partner in a general partnership. Again, the partnership agreement will set out the basic rights and obligations of the various limited partners.

However, it is a corporation that allows the most flexibility in structuring equity financing arrangements because share ownership determines equity (i.e., determines ownership rights in the corporation). And shares, you'll recall, are merely bundles of rights. Since you can create as many different bundles of rights — as many classes of shares — as you wish, you can structure ownership of the corporation to meet the needs of even the most obscure investment demands.

For instance, in exchange for equity capital contributions, a company can offer any combination or permutation of some of the following bundle of rights:

* Common voting shares

* Non-voting, non-redeemable, dividend-bearing preference shares

* Non-voting, non-redeemable preference shares, convertible to common shares

* Non-voting, redeemable, dividend bearing, non-convertible shares, with a right to rank ahead of any other class of shares on the wind-up and dissolution of the company

The issue is, what type of investment does the financier want to make in the company? If no class of shares satisfies the financier's particular needs, one that will can be created.

A company can also issue share warrants or options. These give the purchaser (i.e., the person who acquires them in exchange for an equity capital contribution) the right to buy certain classes and numbers of shares at some future time for a price determined at the time the warrants or options are sold. The advantage to the investor is that the shares may increase in value during the life of the warrant or option, effectively allowing the investor to purchase those shares at a discount.

Another attractive aspect of investing in a corporation (as opposed to any other business form) is that the shareholders (the people with an equity interest in the business) can enter into a shareholders agreement. Not only can a shareholders agreement be used to define the rights and obligations of the various shareholders but it can also provide for matters relating to the handling of the actual affairs of the company, such as which class(es) of shares has the right to elect members to the company's board of directors and how officers will be remunerated.

The versatility of the corporate business form makes it the most efficient way for a small business to raise equity capital.

3. Securities Legislation

As noted, securities legislation restricts your ability to offer securities for sale to the public. The term "security" has a broad definition. Securities include the following:

* Any share in a company

* Any share warrant or option

* Any investment contract

* Profit-sharing agreements

* Anything commonly known as a security

Clearly, the definition of security covers most types of equity financing arrangements and therefore has a direct bearing on your ability to raise equity capital for your small business, especially if you operate it as a corporation.

(a) The Private-Company Exemption

Securities legislation restricts your ability to offer your securities for sale to the public. Accordingly, if you do not propose to offer your securities to the public and your company's articles contain the relevant private-company restrictions set out in securities legislation, you are exempt under that legislation from its registration and prospectus requirements.

In brief, the private-company restrictions require that —

* the right to transfer the shares of the company be restricted;

* the number of shareholders in the company be (with certain exceptions) no more than 50; and

* the company cannot invite the public to subscribe for shares.

The problem is that the term "public" is not defined in the legislation, so it is not entirely clear what public designates. Public should, therefore, be given its ordinary meaning. Accordingly, if you incorporate a company and issue shares either only to yourself or to yourself and one or more others with whom you are acquainted, it is not, for the purposes of securities legislation, a sale of shares to the public.

As a consequence, the private-company restrictions can be found in the articles of most small businesses run through a corporation. The fact is, the restrictions do little to hinder a small business from raising the kind of equity capital it usually requires. Moreover, the restrictions allow a company to maintain the tax benefits associated with private-company status (see Chapter 14, Taxes) and avoid the registration and prospectus requirements of securities legislation.

(b) Private Placement

But what happens if you require a large amount of equity capital and wish to raise it by offering securities — for instance, a certain class of shares in your company — to the public? To comply with securities legislation, you must either —

* be registered as an issuer under the securities act of the jurisdiction in which the securities are to be sold and file a public prospectus, or

* fall within a statutory exemption from the registration and prospectus requirements.

A prospectus is a publicly available disclosure document that provides prospective investors with "full, true, and plain disclosure" of all information material to the investment in which the securities are being offered for sale. Among other things, a prospectus details the history of the business; the identity and qualifications of directors, officers, and other key business personnel; the nature of any material contracts; and the purpose for which capital is required.

A prospectus is not an easy document to prepare and usually requires significant input from a variety of professionals, including lawyers and accountants. The purpose of securities legislation in requiring a prospectus is, however, clear: investors should have a solid foundation of objectively verifiable facts on which to base their investment decisions.

That said, securities legislation recognizes certain situations in which the registration and prospectus requirements would be both burdensome and inappropriate. It acknowledges that a detailed disclosure document would be redundant in circumstances in which, for example, the prospective purchasers were all sophisticated investors or in which the offer to buy securities was made to a limited number of people (usually no more than 50) and an actual sale to no more than 25 took place. In those circumstances, securities legislation provides for certain private placement exemptions, exempting companies (and others trading in securities) from the registration and prospectus requirements relating to the public sale of their securities.

An offering of securities — for example, shares in your company — can be made through a private placement provided you still advise investors of the information material to the investment. This is done by way of an offering memorandum, which is a document much like a prospectus in that it requires "full, true, and plain disclosure" of all material information relating to the investment. However, an offering memorandum is usually not as detailed as a prospectus and, perhaps more important, does not have to be made publicly available. In most cases, you need only present it to prospective investors. This is a significant advantage where privacy is a concern.

In addition, choosing to raise equity capital through a private placement allows you to maintain the tax benefits associated with private-company status.

4. Summary

Equity financing has several advantages. It adds to the value of your business (by increasing its capital); creates a larger capital base against which you can borrow even more capital; and, depending on the arrangement you choose, does not necessarily require you to relinquish control over your business. Perhaps the most important advantage, though, is that equity financing does not have to be repaid the way a loan does.

c. Debt Financing

Debt financing means borrowing money to meet your capital needs. The cost of borrowing involves repaying the amount you borrowed plus some additional amount over a pre-determined period or at the demand of the person who made the loan. That additional amount or interest is usually calculated as some percentage of the amount borrowed. Debt financing thus creates a creditor-debtor or lender-borrower relationship between the financier and your business.

1. Sources of Debt Financing

The sources of debt financing for your business are the same as those of equity financing:

- *Yourself.* You can loan money to your business. Shareholder loans are particularly common, as they can result in tax savings for the lending shareholder (see Chapter 14, Taxes). Also, loaning money to your business makes you one of its creditors, with all of the rights against the assets of the business that entails.

- *Friends and family.* These people are sometimes willing to loan money to you at a low rate of interest or simply provide you with an interest-free loan. Obtaining loans from friends and family has several advantages. First, the terms of the loan can be fairly flexible. You might be granted a generously long period over which to repay the loan. Second, a loan from a friend or family member allows you to obtain capital without either relinquishing control over your business or losing any of your equity in it. Friends and family also probably won't do much in the way of credit checks or require extensive documentation evidencing the loan. Finally, friends and family are unlikely to sue you if you fail to make a payment on time or otherwise have trouble repaying the loan. By the same token, taking a loan from those close to you can damage your personal relationships if, for whatever reason, you are unable to repay it.

- *Other businesspeople.* You may be able to ob-tain a loan from an arm's-length business-person (i.e., one who is not otherwise involved with you or your business). This can usually be arranged through a broker or sought by advertising in newspapers or trade publications. Again, financiers of this type tend to be sophisticated businesspeople and will do whatever credit checks and ask whatever questions they think they need to in order to minimize the risk that their loan (and any interest) won't be repaid. Further, unlike loans from friends and family, arms-length business-people will usually require that the loan be fully evidenced by a variety of different types of loan documentation. They may also ask for the loan to be secured against the assets of your business or by way of your personal guarantee.

* *Institutions*. Banks, trust companies, insurance companies, credit unions, and commercial finance companies all actively compete to loan your business money. Indeed, successful loans and the interest they earn represent a primary source of revenue for these institutions. It can, therefore, sometimes be something of a borrower's market. However, lending institutions will thoroughly investigate your business's creditworthiness before they advance one cent. They will more than likely insist that, among other things, the loan be thoroughly documented, personal guarantees be provided by any owners of the business, and the loan be secured. In addition, lending institutions may place restrictions on how you operate your business.

* *Government*. There are several types of loans available to small business through both the federal and provincial governments (see section d. later in this chapter).

It may be stating the obvious to say that lenders look to maximize their returns while limiting their risks. For that reason, they favour businesses with sound management, low debt, and strong growth potential. Once your business has met those criteria, only two issues remain: the type of loan you require and what you can provide to secure that loan.

2. Types of Loans Available

Two types of loans are available to small businesses: the operating (or working capital) loan and the term loan.

(a) Operating Loan

An operating loan is used to finance the day-to-day operation of your business, including the payment of overhead, wages, and suppliers' accounts for inventory. You will need an operating loan if your business is experiencing cash flow problems. Without an operating loan, suppliers may stop providing you with the things you need when you need them, seriously restricting your ability to run your business.

Four types of operating loans are available to your small business:

* *Revolving line of credit*. As its name suggests, a revolving line of credit allows the borrower to periodically dip into a pool of funds to meet its operating capital needs. The lender usually sets an upper limit on how much the borrower can take from the pool and determines for how long the line of credit will be available. A line of credit is often not large enough to finance any major purchases, and so lenders do not often place restrictions on how the borrowed funds may be used.

* *Non-revolving line of credit*. A non-revolving line of credit does not allow for periodic dips but is made available for a specific purpose. For example, you may need a non-revolving line of credit today to allow you to purchase the latest item of technology for your business as soon as it becomes available (just in case you don't have the money yourself at that time).

* *Inventory loan*. A lender may provide you with a loan for the specific purpose of allowing you to purchase inventory for your business. This type of loan is

particularly important if your business is inventory driven, such as stereo or appliance sales. With an inventory loan, you can be assured that your business always has the stock in hand to meet consumer demands.

❋ *Accounts receivable loan.* Accounts receivable are the unpaid monetary debts owed to your business. Lenders sometimes are willing to provide you with loans based on the value of those debts. In this way, they can be assured that whatever debt you incur through them is balanced by the debt owed to you. Again, there are usually few restrictions on how you can use the borrowed funds.

A lender will help you determine which types of operating loans are available to you. Many small businesses find that a revolving line of credit allows them to meet all their debt financing needs.

(b) Term Loan

Term loans allow borrowers to make specific purchases for use in their business. The need for a term loan often arises when a small business intends to purchase expensive equipment or land or incur some other major expense, such as research and development costs for a new product.

As its name suggests, a term loan matures over a specific period (usually between one and five years), during which the borrower is required to make regular payments of blended principal and interest.

Because a term loan is often granted for a specific purpose, lenders tend to place severe restrictions on how the money can be used. In most cases, lenders will want a detailed account of what the money will be used for and how that use will benefit the borrower's business.

(c) Documents Establishing the Loan Terms

Anyone lending your business money will likely require you to sign a document setting out the terms of the loan. If the lender is a bank or other institution, you can be assured of it. There are two kinds of documents commonly used by lenders for establishing the terms of a loan: the commitment letter (or term sheet) and the loan agreement.

The commitment letter is a letter from the lending institution setting out the terms of the loan. It can be used for both an operating loan and a term loan. The letter will be signed by a representative of the lender with authority to do so, and there will be a place for you, the borrower, to sign in acknowledgment of your acceptance of the terms set out in the letter. Those terms include —

❋ the principal amount of the loan;

❋ the rate of interest to be charged;

❋ payment date(s);

❋ restrictions (if any) on the use of the funds; events of default (such as bankruptcy) that will require the loan to be repaid immediately;

❋ the information the business is required to provide to the lender on a regular basis, such as financial statements, records of accounts receivable, and inventory lists;

❋ any security and guarantees the bank will require (see below); and

❋ restrictions (if any) on how the business is to be operated.

Upon acceptance of the commitment letter by the borrower, it becomes a formal contract between the lender and the borrower.

Though in many ways similar to a commitment letter, a loan agreement is a more formal document. In addition, it tends to be more comprehensive regarding the obligations and restrictions it places on the borrower, and so is almost always used when significant sums of money are borrowed. Not only will a loan agreement address the same matters a commitment letter does, it will also contain extensive representations and warranties from the borrower regarding things such as the borrower's legal identity, financial history and status, and conduct of business. A loan agreement takes the form of a contract with both the lender and borrower named as parties.

Though not common, loan terms may be set out in a licensing, franchise, or other type of agreement. The danger in doing so is that the agreement might be struck down by a court as invalid for some reason entirely unrelated to its loan terms, leaving the lender in a very precarious position.

(d) Documents Evidencing the Debt: The Promissory Note

A commitment letter or loan agreement sets out the terms of the loan. As evidence that the loan has actually been made, a lender will commonly ask a borrower to sign a promissory note, such as the one used in Sample 3.

A promissory note is defined in the federal Bills of Exchange Act as "an unconditional promise in writing made by one person to another person, signed by the maker, engaging to pay, on demand or at a fixed or determinable future time, a sum certain in money to, or to the order of, a specified person or bearer."

Thus, "A promises to pay B $10 on May 5, 2012," when written on a piece of paper signed by A, constitutes a promissory note at law. In this case, A has issued what is called a term promissory note, because it requires A to pay back B at a fixed or determinable future time. A demand promissory note, on the other hand, is payable on the demand of the lender (i.e., B), whenever B chooses to exercise that power.

Of course, the promissory note that a sophisticated lender such as a bank might ask you to sign won't be quite as simple as this example. Lenders recognize that you may not be able to pay a large loan back all at once. The lender may therefore draft the promissory note so that the amount outstanding is payable in instalments over a specified period (e.g., monthly for the next two years). And because time has a devaluing effect on money, promissory notes typically provide for the borrower to pay interest on the principal.

Unless otherwise provided (and subject to certain exceptions), a promissory note is both a negotiable and assignable instrument. As a negotiable instrument, a promissory note is the equivalent of cash. A lender can therefore choose to satisfy a debt of its own by transferring a promissory note to another person. Under the act, transferring a promissory note involves endorsement by the transferor (i.e., the lender) and physical delivery to the transferee, the same as one might do with a cheque. The transferee then becomes entitled to enforce the note against the borrower, and so anyone signing a promissory note should ensure that he or she signs only one copy of it. However, given that in practical terms there is no market for promissory notes, the ability to negotiate one may be less useful than it appears.

Assignment also transfers the right to collect the amounts due under a promissory note (i.e., to the assignee) but does not confer on the assignee all the powers of someone who holds the note through negotiation, such as the power to sue in the transferee's own name. Moreover, the assignor has to notify the borrower that the promissory note has been assigned and that payment under the note should now be made to the assignee. In the absence of notification, the borrower could and should continue to make payment only to the person to whom the borrower is obligated under the note to do so (i.e., the assignor), notwithstanding any claim by the assignee.

Promissory Note

FOR VALUE RECEIVED, the undersigned, _____ (the **"Borrower"**), hereby acknowledges himself indebted and promises to pay or cause to be paid to _____ (the **"Lender"**) or its order, at its office at _____ or at such other place as the Lender may designate in writing from time to time, the principal sum of _____ ($_____.00) in lawful money of Canada (the **"Principal Sum"**).

The Principal Sum shall be due and payable, by way of cash or certified cheque, on July 20, 20--.

Notwithstanding anything to the contrary, the whole of the Principal Sum shall become due and be immediately payable by the Borrower at the option of the Lender in the event that the Borrower makes an assignment or a proposal in bankruptcy or a creditor files a petition in bankruptcy against the Borrower.

No delay or failure on the part of the Lender to exercise any power or right given under this Promissory Note (including, without limitation, the right to declare immediately due and payable the whole or any part of the unpaid balance of the Principal Sum shall operate as a waiver of any right or remedy of the Lender (including, without limitation, the right to be paid under this Promissory Note); nor shall any right or remedy of the Lender under this Promissory Note or under any applicable law be abridged or modified by any course of conduct by the Lender or the Borrower.

The Borrower may prepay the whole or any part of the amount payable under this Promissory Note, at any time and from time to time, without notice, penalty, or bonus.

The Borrower hereby waives demand and presentment for payment, and notice of non-payment and notice of protest and dishonour of this Promissory Note.

If any provision of this Promissory Note shall be invalid or unenforceable, the remainder of this Promissory Note shall nevertheless survive and be binding upon the parties hereto.

Time is of the essence of this Promissory Note.

This Promissory Note shall be governed by and construed in accordance with the laws of the province of Ontario and the laws of Canada applicable therein.

IN WITNESS WHEREOF, this Promissory Note has been made and delivered as of the 20th day of July, 20--.

SIGNED, SEALED AND DELIVERED)
In the presence of:)
)
)
)
)
_____) _____
Witness) [Borrower's Name]

Other documents can evidence the borrower's debt, including debentures, post-dated cheques, bank drafts, invoices, and bonds. However, because promissory notes are both easy to draft and readily enforceable, lenders favour their use in evidencing the borrower's debt.

3. Loan Security

A loan can be either secured or unsecured. A secured loan is one against which the borrower (the debtor) has pledged certain collateral to the lender (the creditor) that the lender can call upon to recover any losses arising due to the borrower's failure to repay the principal or any interest (the debt). An unsecured loan is one against which no collateral is pledged. "Collateral," in this context, refers to anything against which the lender has recourse to satisfy the debt and includes personal property, real property, and guarantees.

When loaning money to a small business, lenders typically try to secure their loans, as a secured loan has more chance of being repaid. The law is such that as a secured creditor, a lender will, with few exceptions, rank in priority ahead of any unsecured creditors on the distribution of the assets of the business if the business becomes insolvent or goes bankrupt. This priority can help ensure that any money and property remaining in the business upon bankruptcy or insolvency will first be used to satisfy the debt owing to the secured creditors.

There are several ways for a lender to secure a loan, each dependent on the type of security the lender wishes to take. In turn, the type of security a lender may wish to take depends on —

🍁 the lender's confidence in your ability to repay the loan,

🍁 the type of loan involved and the amount you are borrowing,

🍁 the purpose for which the loan is being used,

🍁 the kinds of assets you can put up as collateral (i.e., offer a security interest in), and

🍁 any security interest you may have already granted to other lenders.

Once a lender has considered these issues, it can then choose from among a variety of different types of security to secure its loan.

(a) Security over Personal Property

Personal property refers to all your business property other than land or an interest in land (such as may be granted to you under a lease). A lender can take security over your personal property in a number of different ways.

(i) General security agreement

A general security agreement grants the lender a security interest in all personal property of the borrower. Moreover, it applies both to the borrower's personal property existing at the time the loan is made and to any personal property acquired afterward, up until the debt created by the loan is repaid. Collateral typically covered by a general security agreement includes all the borrower's accounts receivable (unpaid debts owed to the borrower), inventory, equipment, intangibles (e.g., intellectual property), money, cheques, securities (e.g., shares in other companies, options, rights), and proceeds from the sale of any of these.

A general security agreement provides that the borrower grants the lender a security interest in all collateral, subjects the borrower to a variety of restrictions regarding what it can and cannot do with the collateral in the absence of the lender's consent, and sets out the lender's remedies if the borrower defaults (i.e., if the borrower is unable to pay his or her debt to the lender or otherwise breaches the terms of any loan document). Those remedies usually include the right to sell, lease, or use any of the collateral to recoup the borrower's debt. Because it is virtually all encompassing, a general security agreement is nearly always required by lenders.

(ii) Debenture

A debenture is in many ways similar to a general security agreement, with the exceptions that it secures both the personal and real property of the borrower and that it also evidences the debt of the borrower by containing a promise to pay. A debenture may contain a fixed charge or floating charge over the collateral. A fixed charge creates a security interest in specific property of the borrower. By contrast, a floating charge is one that covers all the borrower's real and personal property, both at the time the loan is made and thereafter. Under a floating charge, the property of the business is not subject to the security interest until default, when the charge "crystallizes" and becomes fixed.

Because of their complexity, debentures are used primarily to secure very large loans and, even then, almost always in conjunction with a general security agreement.

(iii) Assignment of accounts receivable

A lender will sometimes require the borrower to assign the borrower's accounts receivable to the lender. That effectively gives the lender the right to collect those debts and retain the amounts owing to satisfy any unpaid portion of the borrower's debt. An assignment of accounts receivable can apply to all debts owing to the borrower as of the date the loan is made or specify certain specific receivables, such as rents due to a borrower who is a building developer.

(iv) Bank Act security over inventory

Under the federal Bank Act, Canadian chartered banks can take security over the present and future inventory of manufacturers, retailers, wholesalers, and those involved in the production of agricultural, fish, forestry, and mining products. By completing (and registering with the Bank of Canada) a specific set of documents, including an assignment by the borrower of the inventory to be charged, a bank acquires the right to sell that inventory to satisfy any unpaid debt.

(v) Conditional sales contracts

Conditional sales contracts are sometimes used when your business purchases goods it has not paid for in full. The supplier may, when delivering the goods to you, issue an invoice stating that the supplier retains title to the goods until payment in full. The invoice will also state that if the invoice is not paid according to the purchase terms, the supplier has the right to repossess the goods and keep as damages any amount already paid.

(vi) Pledge of shares

A lender will sometimes oblige a borrower to pledge to the lender any shares the borrower might hold in another company. If the borrower defaults, the pledge gives the lender the right to those shares and the rights they embody. Therefore, if the shares are entitled to a dividend, the right to that dividend will (on default) belong to the lender. Alternatively, the lender can simply sell the shares to a third party on default.

(b) Security over Real Property

Real property refers to land or an interest in land (such as would be granted under a lease). There are three types of security a lender can take in real property: mortgage of land, assignment of lease, and debenture.

(i) Mortgage of land

Most borrowers either own or lease the premises out of which they operate. If the borrower owns the premises, a lender will often require a mortgage against those premises. A mortgage is a written legal document creating a security interest in real property. It grants the lender the right, if there is a default, to seize or foreclose on the premises and sell them to recoup its losses.

Obtaining a mortgage requires filling out the necessary forms, having them signed by the borrower (the mortgagor) and filed by the lender (the mortgagee) in the appropriate land registry/ titles offices. If the borrower is merely leasing premises, a lender can take a mortgage against that lease, giving the lender the right to assume the lease on default of the loan. A mortgage is sometimes simply referred to as a charge.

(ii) Assignment of lease

A lender may, rather than take a mortgage of the borrower's lease, request an assignment of lease. That effectively transfers the right to use the leased property from the borrower (the assignor) to the lender (the assignee) if the borrower defaults on the loan. In the event of an assignment, the borrower remains liable under the lease unless released by the landlord. Most leases require the person leasing the premises (the lessor or tenant — in this case, the borrower) to obtain the prior written consent of the landlord to any assignment. A lender will, therefore, often require you to obtain that consent. The lender may also seek a non-disturbance agreement from the landlord (or require the borrower to obtain one) to ensure that the lease will continue on the same terms if the borrower assigns the lease to the lender.

(iii) Debenture

As noted, a debenture is capable of creating a security interest in land. Provided it is in registerable form, a debenture can, like a mortgage, be registered against title to that land, thereby providing notice to the public of the lender's interest in it. However, because they are so similar, a debenture is often not used if the use of a mortgage is available (and no personal property is being secured). Yet, unlike a mortgage, a debenture is both capable of applying to land in various jurisdictions (e.g., different provinces) and to land acquired by the borrower after the debenture is made. Where those circumstances arise, a lender will typically choose to secure its interest both by way of debenture and mortgage.

(c) Security from Third Parties

In the context of a loan, a third party is anyone not directly bound to repay the loan to the lender. For example, if your company receives an operating loan from a bank, your company will be directly bound (usually by the terms of a loan agreement) to pay that loan back. A shareholder in the company (yourself included) or one of its officers or directors will not be bound to pay back that loan. The shareholders, officers, directors, and any other person or company not bound to pay back the loan are third parties to the loan.

Unfortunately, this will rarely allow them to escape any obligations to the lender. To ensure the repayment of their loans, lenders will often require certain types of third parties, such as shareholders, to provide some sort of security, including perhaps the two most common: guarantees and letters of credit.

(i) Guarantee

A guarantee is precisely that: an assurance made to a lender by a person (the guarantor) that he or she will pay the debts or satisfy the obligations of the borrower if the borrower fails to do so itself. Most lenders insist on some sort of personal guarantee from small business owners for loans made to their business. Not only does this add another layer of security but it encourages an owner to take a genuine interest in ensuring that his or her business is able to repay its debts, since a personal guarantee gives a lender recourse to the guarantor's personal assets to satisfy any unrecovered amount. Moreover, a guarantee provides that in the event of default, the lender does not have to pursue the borrower for repayment before it acts on the guarantee.

A guarantee made by two or more people is usually "joint and several," meaning that each of the guarantors alone — as well as both together — is responsible to pay the whole of the debt. It is not uncommon for a lender to ask that the spouse of an owner of a small business sign a personal guarantee. Spouses will usually be required to obtain legal advice to ensure that they know what they are letting themselves in for. Only if the spouse has a direct interest in the business or will directly benefit from it will a lender likely waive the requirement of independent legal advice.

Because they cover personal assets (your yacht, Mercedes, and Rembrandt), guarantees are often complicated documents drafted to ensure that the guarantor can be relieved of these items with as little interference by the courts as possible. But the law also recognizes that the relationship created by a personal guarantee is open to abuse by an unscrupulous lender. Lenders must exercise their rights under guarantee with great caution and with a view to doing what is "reasonable" in any given set of circumstances. Alberta is the only jurisdiction in Canada with legislation designed specifically to help ensure that potential guarantors are fully apprised of their rights and obligations when entering into a personal guarantee.

When requesting a corporate guarantee — a guarantee from a corporation holding shares in your corporation — an issue may arise under corporate legislation regarding the ability of the guaranteeing corporation to meet its own debts. In most circumstances, a corporation cannot guarantee a debt (or provide any other type of financial assistance for that matter) when to do so would render it unable to pay its debts when they become due. This matter should be discussed with your lawyer should it ever arise.

Finally, any person or company providing a guarantee may be asked to provide security to back up that guarantee. For example, a shareholder in a company that has received a loan may be required by the lender not only to provide a guarantee of that loan but to pledge his or her shares in the company to the lender as security for the loan.

(ii) Letter of credit

A letter of credit is a letter, usually from a bank, containing a promise to pay a specified amount to a third party on the terms set out in the letter. It may be used, for example, when a business wishes to purchase certain goods from another business. To secure payment for those goods, the seller may request a letter of credit from the purchaser's bank. By issuing the letter of credit, the bank promises to pay for those goods (usually on delivery of the letter to the bank).

Before a bank will issue such a letter, it will first obtain its own security directly from the purchaser in an amount to at least cover the amount payable under the letter of credit. In addition, it will charge the purchaser a service fee.

An irrevocable letter of credit is one that the bank has no right to refuse to pay if its terms are met. That, in effect, assures the seller of payment, and so irrevocability is typically sought by a seller when requesting a letter of credit as security.

(d) Miscellaneous Security

There are various other kinds of security available to lenders.

(i) Insurance

Some lenders require a borrower to have its property and liability insurance endorsed to name the lender as loss payee. Any proceeds resulting from any claim under the insurance policy would then be payable directly to the lender. A key-person life insurance policy on key people involved with the business may also be required by a lender, with the lender being named as beneficiary. (See Chapter 7, Insurance.)

(ii) Control of your business

It is not uncommon for a lender of large amounts of money to demand the right to have a say in your business affairs. Among other things, lenders may wish to have a say in who runs the business and under what circumstances, if any, the business can incur any other major debt.

(iii) Intercreditor agreement

An intercreditor agreement is sometimes made between two or more creditors of a company to provide for their rights and obligations toward each other. For instance, a shareholder of a company may be owed a debt by the company for a past loan. As well, a small financing company might have lent some money to the company and taken security in its assets under a general security agreement. A lender proposing to make a substantially larger or more important loan may insist that both the shareholder and the financing company (i.e., the other creditors) postpone or subordinate their prior claims over the company's assets to the subsequent claims of the lender. That is the purpose of an intercreditor agreement or, as it is sometimes called, a postponement agreement, priority agreement, or subordination agreement.

(iv) Purchase money security interest

A purchase money security interest (PMSI) is a special type of security interest created under the various provincial personal property security acts that allows a lender to obtain a special priority with certain types of collateral.

Suppose a borrower has received a substantial loan from a bank. As part of its security, the bank has taken a general security interest in all assets of the borrower, including any assets acquired after the date the loan was made. Now suppose further that while the loan to the bank is still outstanding, the borrower wishes to buy a large piece of equipment; for example, a lathe. The seller, in selling the lathe to the borrower, may agree to deliver the equipment now but allow the borrower to pay for it over a period of two years. In effect, then, the seller is also lending money to the borrower (the unpaid portion of the purchase price). Now suppose, finally, that the borrower cannot pay its debt to the bank.

Should the bank have the right to seize the lathe as part of the collateral covered by its general security interest? The law says no, not if the person who sold the lathe to the borrower has a valid PMSI. The reason is simple: when the bank originally made its decision to provide a loan to the borrower, it did not do so on the basis that it would someday have recourse to the lathe as part of the security for that loan. To grant it that recourse would not only be unfair to the seller of the lathe but would effectively prevent the borrower from obtaining any future credit from other financiers such as the seller. PMSIs exist to allow people providing equipment or inventory on credit to obtain a special security interest in that equipment or inventory and any proceeds arising from its sale. Obtaining a valid PMSI requires compliance with the applicable provisions of the personal property security legislation of your province. These should be discussed with your lawyer, especially if you think your business might be in the position of the seller.

(e) Registration of Security Interests
(i) Personal property

Each province except for Newfoundland, Prince Edward Island, and Quebec has a *Personal Property Security Act* (PPSA) and an accompanying personal property registry system. In each case, the PPSA provides the basic legal framework for the registration of security interests in personal property. Personal property includes accounts, equipment, inventory, consumer goods, money, and shares. Anyone obtaining a security interest in such property can register that interest in the personal property security registry, thereby not only notifying other creditors and potential creditors that there are security interests outstanding on all or certain of the assets of the business, but also taking advantage of the priority granted by registration if competing security interests are at issue.

The PPSA usually sets up a scheme of priority based on the rule, First in time, first in line:

if there are competing security interests, priority will go to the first creditor to have registered its interest under the PPSA. However, things aren't as simple as all that, for several reasons:

* The rule applies only if the security interests have been "perfected" by registration (as opposed to by some other means). As with so many terms used in the PPSA, "perfection" is difficult to define. It is enough to know that it is used to define the rights of a secured party in relation to other secured parties. Perfection occurs when the borrower has signed a security agreement containing a description of the collateral sufficient to define it and has either filed a financing statement under the PPSA or taken possession of the collateral. Again, most registered security interests are perfected and so the rule applies.

* An intercreditor agreement can be used to reconfigure the priorities of the various creditors, despite the order in which they were registered;

* A PMSI, when properly registered, can grant a creditor a special priority over a prior secured interest.

* The law provides that certain unsecured creditors have a "super priority" ahead of anyone else. This status is usually granted to government agencies and ministries, such as the Ministry of National Revenue, for unpaid taxes.

The PPSA is a complicated item of legislation, to say the least. As a small-business owner, you need not know all that it does and does not do. It is enough for you to know that it exists and that you should discuss its implications with your lawyer every time you or your business borrows or lends money. Your lawyer can guide you through the relevant provisions of the PPSA and how it applies to you.

(ii) Real property

Each province has a system (and in some cases, systems) for registering interests in real property. Registration serves several purposes, including providing a publicly available record of interests held in land. To take security in real property, a lender will register its mortgage, debenture, or other security document against title to the land. In so doing, the lender can take advantage of the rights associated with registration under the applicable legislation.

4. Summary

Financing your small business through loans has its advantages. For one thing, you don't lose any of the equity in your business. As a consequence, lenders can't share in the future success of your business. Your only obligation is to pay back the loan and any interest. Nonetheless, by taking a loan you are putting your business in debt. Among other things, that means paying interest, likely subjecting your business assets to a security interest (which could be used to offset any losses created by the failure of your business to repay the loan), and putting your personal assets at risk if you need to provide a guarantee.

d. Government

Government can be a source of both debt and equity financing. At both the federal and provincial levels, there are a number of assistance programs designed to meet the needs of small businesses through loans, loan guarantees, subsidies, and grants. However, one must qualify for this assistance, which is not always easy as many of the programs are designed to assist specific sectors of industry or society.

The Business Development Bank of Canada (BDC) provides various financing services to small businesses, including term loans and venture capital. It also offers both financial and management counselling services. To find out if you qualify to receive any of its services, contact your local BDC branch.

To find out what is available from your provincial government, contact your local ministry of consumer and commercial affairs or similar government agency.

e. What Kind of Financing Is Right for Me?

When it comes to financing, there are no easy answers. The type of financing that is best suited to your particular needs depends on a number of factors:

* What those needs are. Do you need a quick injection of capital to take advantage of a special opportunity or are you looking for long-term operating funds?

* The type of business arrangement you want. Are you looking for someone to buy into your business or do you just need a loan?

* What is available to you. Is your business likely to qualify for a loan or is it already too deep in debt? Would others be interested in investing in your business or are loans your only option?

These questions must be considered alongside the advantages and disadvantages of debt versus equity financing discussed in this chapter. Then, with the assistance of your accountant and lawyer, you can try to determine the type of financing that is right for you.

7
Insurance

No business is immune to the possibility that something might go terribly wrong. The ability to recover from a mishap often depends on whether you were insured against it. This chapter will examine the different types of insurance available to you and assist you in determining which is most appropriate for your small business.

a. What Types of Insurance Will You Need?

Assessing your insurance needs involves knowing both the risks to which your business may be exposed and the losses your business could face if something goes wrong.

In large part, potential risks and losses will depend on the type of business you operate. For example, do you store items in a warehouse? If so, you may be concerned about destruction due to fire. Are there hazardous wastes associated with your business? If so, coverage for damage to the environment may be a concern. Would your business suffer a serious setback through the loss of certain key persons? If so, you should be insured against the loss of those persons. Questions such as these must be explored to determine what losses you might suffer in the event of a mishap.

Of course, the time to ask those questions is before it's too late, preferably before you open for business. If you are expanding your business into different types of commercial activity — for example, your service station will be selling donuts and coffee — you should make certain your insurance coverage accounts for the risks and potential losses associated with that move.

b. What Types of Insurance Are Available?

Once you have identified the potential risks and losses associated with operating your small business, you are in a position to determine the kinds of insurance you will need. The types of insurance available today are virtually limitless. The following is an overview of some of the main types of insurance available to you and your small business.

1. Property Insurance

Property insurance protects your business against loss or damage to specific items of business property. That property can include buildings, equipment, furniture, machines, tools, and inventory. It can also include property belonging to others.

The types of loss- or damage-causing events that are covered can range from the very specific — for example, fire — to "all risks," which can include loss or damage caused by explosions, vandalism, and theft.

As you might expect, the cost of your coverage increases with the amount and value of property insured and the types of perils against which you insure it. You should carefully consider exactly what property you must protect and what you must protect it against. For example, if you run a consulting business, you will probably not need to protect any expensive equipment except, perhaps, your computer. The opposite is likely to hold true if you own a manufacturing company.

If you regularly take your property off your business premises — for example, if you photograph weddings and therefore use your camera equipment off site — be sure to check that your insurance coverage will continue to apply.

2. Business Interruption Insurance

Business interruption insurance protects your business against any indirect losses or damages it may suffer through events that temporarily prevent you from carrying on business as usual. Specifically, business interruption insurance is designed to address the financial setback a mishap might cause, and can also extend to cover payments to suppliers and employees during the period of interruption.

Suppose a major piece of equipment is destroyed by fire. The cost of replacing that equipment will probably be covered by your property insurance. However, the losses incurred by not being able to carry on business will not be covered unless you have business interruption insurance.

3. General Liability Insurance

Regardless of what type of business you operate, general liability insurance is a must. It will cover you for any legal liability you may have to others if something goes wrong. Accordingly, it usually extends to financial losses, bodily injury, and property damage, and covers all aspects of the operation of your business.

To understand the importance of this type of insurance, consider some of the situations for which you may be liable. For example, by failing to shovel your walk, you may accidentally injure someone who visits your business premises. You may fail to honour a contract with a supplier. You may neglect to perform certain emission tests, thereby releasing hazardous waste into the environment. You may wrongly accuse an employee of theft and be subject to a legal claim for injury to that employee's reputation. The list of potential threats to your business is limitless; protecting yourself against them is essential.

4. Key-Person Insurance

The death or disability of a person who brings a special skill or talent to your business can seriously affect your profitability. It can even mean the end of your business. Consider whether your small business employs anyone (including yourself) who cannot be replaced and without whom your business would otherwise fail. If so, you should obtain key-person insurance for him or her, which will compensate you for the loss of anyone who is indispensable to your business.

5. Directors and Officers Liability Insurance

Directors and officers liability insurance is purchased to protect the people serving in those positions. The great number of statutes in Canada that hold directors and officers personally liable for the actions of their companies has resulted, in recent years, in the introduction of insurance policies designed to protect against losses associated with such liability. Directors and officers often make such insurance a condition of their service in those positions.

6. Product Liability Insurance

Product liability insurance will cover you if your products or services cause harm or loss to anyone purchasing them. This insurance is particularly important for small manufacturing businesses. (See Chapter 10, Dealing with Consumers.)

7. Automobile Liability Insurance

Automobile liability insurance should be obtained for any vehicles that either belong to your business or are used in your business, even if only occasionally. For example, if you operate a garage, your tow truck should be insured because it belongs to the business and will (presumably) be used exclusively for purposes of the business. However, if you occasionally use your own car to run errands for your business, then that car, too, should be insured for business as well as personal use. The insurance you obtained for personal use of your car may not cover you for loss or damage resulting from your use of that car for business purposes. Note also that your insurance policy should cover loss or damage not only to the other vehicle, its occupants, and their property, but should also cover your vehicle and its occupants (including employees).

8. Environmental Liability Insurance

Environmental liability insurance is particularly relevant to businesses producing, storing, or other-wise dealing in hazardous wastes. It is designed to protect against damage or injury resulting from the accidental discharge of that waste. It will not protect you if you deliberately discharge such materials, unless you were not aware of the danger at the time of the discharge. Be sure to discuss these details with your insurance provider if this insurance is relevant to your small business.

9. Credit Insurance

Credit insurance will cover you if a major creditor — for example, someone to whom you have supplied goods or services — does not pay his or her account.

Many insurers have standard policies, but you should know that not everything presented to you is written in stone. Be sure to negotiate the coverage that is best suited to the particular needs of your business.

10. Cybersecurity Risk Insurance

It is no longer unusual to hear of major data breaches or losses caused by, among other things, third-party hacking, viruses, malware, employee theft, and other forms of data misappropriation. Acccordingly, those who do business online or deal with customer information, personal information, or financial information (e.g., credit card or banking data) will want to consider obtaining cybersecurity risk insurance.

In general, cybersecurity risk insurance can protect your business in two ways. First-party coverage can cover you for events such as the costs of replacing damaged hardware and software, notifying affected persons of data breach (e.g., your customers), and compliance with government investigations. Third-party coverage can come to your aid in connection with liability for inadvertently transmitting a virus or malware, and failing to comply with applicable legislation.

c. How Do You Obtain the Insurance You Need?

The insurance you need will most often be available either through an insurance agency or a broker.

An insurance agency sells insurance on behalf of one or more insurers. As agencies usually are paid on a commission basis, they have an interest in getting you to obtain insurance from the insurers they represent — a point worth remembering when shopping for coverage.

Unlike agencies, brokers are not tied to any particular insurer(s), and so you may think that a broker is in a better position to provide you with the coverage most suited to your specific needs. Remember, though, that brokers also work on a commission basis. Regardless of how you obtain insurance, it is in your interest to understand your own needs and be informed regarding what coverage is available.

Certain professional and other associations also offer insurance to their members and should be canvassed for relevance to your business.

Self-insurance may also be an option for your business. Simply put, self-insurance involves setting aside a fund to meet business losses. Self-insurance is often used to cover losses that exceed or are not covered by other types of insurance. Obviously, only businesses with significant excess funds on hand are able to self-insure.

The insurance industry is highly competitive, and so it is to your advantage to shop around for quotes to see which insurer can offer you the best coverage at the lowest price.

d. What Can Nullify My Insurance Coverage?

Circumstances may arise that can result in your insurance coverage being nullified, depriving you of coverage and rendering your policy invalid. To make certain this doesn't happen to you, you should know — and avoid — the circumstances that commonly lead to nullification. The two most common of these are —

(a) *Misrepresentation*. When applying for coverage, it is important not to misrepresent any of the material facts with which you persuade the insurance company to provide coverage. A material fact is one that if known to the insurer could reasonably have affected its decision to insure you. Your coverage can also be nullified if you "forgot" to disclose a material fact.

(b) *Dishonesty*. Faking a claim or otherwise doing something that fraudulently gives rise to a claim (e.g., deliberately setting fire to your business premises) are grounds for nullification. It could also lead to criminal charges being brought against you.

Be sure, as well, that you read your policy carefully to ensure that there are no mistakes regarding your coverage that could nullify it or otherwise affect its value to you. For example, if a specific item of machinery is protected, make certain that it is accurately described in the policy in terms of things like its serial number and location. Doing so can avoid disputes about exactly what was insured should the issue ever arise.

e. Statutory Insurance

Some types of business insurance are required by law. In some instances, the insurance is administered by a government agency or authority. Most provinces have some form of worker's health and safety insurance coverage. Be sure to check whether or not any types of insurance are mandatory for your business.

f. Summary

Insuring yourself against the risks and potential losses associated with owning and operating your small business is a must. When searching out insurance coverage, remember to assess your potential losses, cover your risks, comparison shop, and negotiate the terms of your policy.

D i s c o v e r y

Loss Prevention and Risk Reduction

Although you may have obtained the insurance you think you need to carry on your small business, you must not become complacent about loss prevention or risk reduction. Always ensure that you conduct yourself and your business in a manner designed to minimize any loss or risks, both to others and to your business. There are good business reasons for taking this approach (after all, nobody wants to work or do business in a dangerous environment), but there are strong legal ones as well. For one thing, your insurance may not adequately cover the losses suffered as a result of your behaviour. For another, those losses could be exempt from coverage under the terms of the insurance policy. More important, you could be faced with a legal action in which you are held personally responsible for your misconduct, leaving you subject to, among other things, a fine or, in cases of gross misconduct (e.g., in which you deliberately neglect the health and safety of your employees), imprisonment. It's important to be certain that you operate your small business always with a view to preventing losses or injury to yourself, your business, and others.

D i s c o v e r y

Workers' Compensation Insurance

Depending on the type of business you operate and the number of people you employ, you may be required under the relevant workers' compensation legislation to obtain workers' compensation insurance for your employees. That legislation generally works by requiring employers to contribute to an accident fund maintained by the relevant government board or agency. In exchange, the employer is not liable individually to pay compensation or health care benefits to any of its employees who may be injured while on the job; rather, that money comes out of the fund. Of course, if you fail to make your contributions, your business will not be covered, and so your business will be liable to compensate its workers for any injuries suffered on the job. Contact the workers' compensation board or agency in your province to determine what you need to do to ensure that your business is covered.

Part III
Ongoing Operations

Your small business is now up and running. However, your legal concerns as a small-business owner don't end there. Your business affairs will bring you into contact with the law on a daily basis — whether that involves drafting a supply contract, hiring an employee, or dealing with a dissatisfied customer. In the next chapters, we look at the legal issues facing small-business owners in their day-to-day operations. Your ability to recognize and deal with these issues as they arise can play an important part in your ongoing success.

8
Intellectual Property

Your business assets may include items of intellectual property, such as trademarks, patents, and copyrights. This chapter identifies the main types of intellectual property and considers the following business concerns:

* What do I need to know to protect my intellectual property rights?

* What do I need to know to prevent myself from infringing the intellectual property rights of others?

a. Copyright

Because it applies to so many of your business assets, copyright is the intellectual property right you will most often encounter in your business operations, and one about which it is important to be informed. By claiming a copyright in work you produce for your business, such as instruction manuals, books, pictures, diagrams, and musical jingles, your exclusive right to those works is legally preserved.

1. What Is a Copyright?

Copyright extends to any original literary, dramatic, musical, or artistic work and gives you, as the owner of the copyright, the exclusive right to produce, reproduce, or publish that work (or any part of it) in any material form.

In general, the person who creates the work (i.e., the author) owns its copyright. There are, however, exceptions, as in the case of employees (see section e. later in this chapter).

In Canada, copyright is governed by the federal *Copyright Act*.

2. What Requirements Must You Meet to Claim Copyright in a Work?

To claim a copyright in a work, you must meet the following requirements:

* *The work must be an original production.* This does not mean that it has to be creative or exciting, like a good novel, but it does have to come about as the result of your efforts as the author. So even a company policy manual or videotape of the annual staff picnic, no matter how mundane, can be copyrighted works if you created them.

* *The work must be expressed in a material form.* It must, for example, be written down on paper or recorded on videotape.

It is not enough simply to give your staff a motivational speech; to claim a copyright in it, you must have committed it to some tangible form.

❦ *You, as the author, must meet the residence requirements of the* Copyright Act. If those requirements can't be met, you will have to pursue your rights in Canada by way of the laws of your country of residence.

You do not need to take any special action to claim a copyright in a work. It is enough if you meet the above requirements. For this reason, copyright in a work is sometimes said to be automatic.

3. What Kind of Works Can You Claim a Copyright In?

In theory, you can claim a copyright in almost every tangible expression of your ideas or information. Take the notion of an "artistic work." The *Copyright Act* defines this as including "paintings, drawings, maps, charts, plans, photographs, engravings, sculptures, works of artistic craftsmanship, architectural works, and compilations of artistic works." If you operate a photography studio or have your own architectural firm, you'll want to bear this definition in mind.

If you operate a small theatre company or film-production company, you should know that the *Copyright Act* protects "dramatic work," which is defined to include "any piece for recitation, choreographic work or mime, the scenic arrangement or acting form of which is fixed in writing or otherwise; and, any cinematographic work."

Most small businesses, however, encounter copyright issues primarily in the context of what the *Copyright Act* calls "literary works." Be assured that artistic merit is not the issue here. The term "literary" simply refers to things that are recorded in written form and includes charts, computer programs, business forms (such as invoices or delivery slips), manuals, pamphlets, lectures, illustrations, compilations (as in the form of an encyclopaedia), and mortgage tables. Of course, it also includes books, novels, plays, and poetry.

4. What Can You Not Claim a Copyright In?

You cannot claim a copyright in the following:

❦ *Information or ideas*. Copyright protects the expression of information or ideas, not the information or ideas themselves. For example, no one can copyright the plot to Romeo and Juliet (indeed, Shakespeare himself "borrowed" it). Nor can anyone copyright the information in a telephone book. But you can claim a copyright in a particular compilation of information — for example, information in the form of a flow chart — provided that the compilation meets the requirements set out above.

❦ *Common expressions of ideas and information*. After all, how many ways are there to say "Happy New Year" or "Spain is in Europe"?

❦ *A single word, name, or title*. Trademark law protects your rights in these (see section b. below).

5. How Long Does Copyright in a Work Last?

In Canada, copyright in most works lasts for the life of the author plus 50 years from the end of the year in which the author died. If you created a copyrighted work in June 1999 and died in February 2031, your copyright in that work would last until the end of December 2081.

6. Must You Register Your Copyright?

You do not need to register your copyright. Copyright, as noted earlier, is automatic. However, you may, if you wish, register your copyright with the federal Copyright Office. To do so, you will have to fill out the required application and pay a fee.

The purpose of registration is merely to create the legal presumption that you own the copyright in a particular work, and you will obtain a certificate to that effect from the Copyright Office. It will, however, always be open to others to challenge whether you are in fact the true owner of the copyright in a work or whether you were merely the person to register a copyright in it, perhaps after having copied the work from someone else. From a business perspective, there is little real benefit in registering a copyright in a work, especially if it does not have some unique, artistic value.

7. Can You Transfer Your Copyright in a Work to Someone Else?

Provided you own the copyright, you can transfer it. To transfer the whole of the copyright so that you retain nothing, you must assign the copyright. If you just want to transfer a right or interest in your copyright — for example, the right to publish the work — you can do so by way of a license. Under a license, you retain ownership of the copyright.

An assignment of a copyright is valid only if it is in writing and signed by the assignor (the person transferring the copyright). Simply licensing the use of the work or of a part of it does not have to be done in writing to be effective.

8. What Does It Mean to Infringe a Copyright?

Copyright infringement means doing something with a work that only the owner of the copyright in that work has the right to do, such as copying or publishing it (or a part of it).

Where copying is concerned, there must be substantial similarities between your work and the one you are alleged to have copied. A photocopy will create such substantial similarities. In fact, every time you photocopy someone else's work, you are infringing that person's copyright. (Of course, the difficulty to the copyright holder is being able to prove you did so.)

You should also know that selling or renting work — for example, a movie video — may expose you to liability if you know that the person to whom you are renting or selling it is going to copy it.

Remedies that may be sought by a person whose copyright has been infringed include an injunction to force you to stop the infringing behaviour, damages (i.e., an award of money), and delivery to the copyright owner of the infringing material (e.g., pirated videotape copies).

Finally, not all copying of copyrighted works necessarily amounts to infringement. The *Copyright Act* lists various exemptions to infringing behaviour, including using the work for "research or private study, criticism or review, or news reporting." In each case, however, I strongly recommend that you reference the source of your information.

Discovery

Internet Domain Names

Today, many small businesses do business on the Internet, and this has created a whole new set of legal issues for lawyers and businesspeople alike to contend with, not the least of which is how to legally protect a business's interest in its Internet address; that is, its "domain name." At present, domain names are not controlled by government; rather, they are controlled, registered, and granted by a private company located in the United States, which has established its own rules regarding protection of domain names. According to those rules, to protect your domain name, you must register it as a trademark. Once this is done, it cannot be taken over by someone else. Before choosing to register a domain name, you should, however, both check the Internet and do a trademark search to ensure that you are not violating anyone else's rights. As you can imagine, the law is rapidly changing in this area. Be sure to contact a qualified intellectual property lawyer to discuss the steps you need to take to protect your domain name.

9. Is There Anything Else You Should Know about Copyright?

The *Copyright Act* gives authors the moral right to the integrity of their work. In practical terms, this means that the author has the right to, among other things, be associated with the work as its author. It also prevents anyone else, regardless of whether or not they own the work, from destroying it or dealing with it in a way that detracts from its integrity.

Moral rights cannot be transferred; they can only be waived. This is important to understand in instances where a businessperson acquires a copyrighted work such as a song to be used in commercial or a picture to be used in an advertising campaign. Moreover, moral rights must be explicitly waived; merely assigning a copyright is not enough to waive an author's moral rights. (Sample 4, at the end of this chapter, shows an assignment of copyright and waiver. Be sure to have anyone who transfers a copyrighted work to you sign one.)

Failure to respect an author's moral rights can lead to legal repercussions, including being sued for damages and a return of the work.

b. Trademarks

If you are planning to distinguish the goods and services offered by your small business from similar goods and services offered by others, some knowledge of trademarks law will be of use to you.

1. What Is a Trademark?

A trademark is a mark used to both identify your goods or services to the general public and distinguish your goods or services from similar goods and services offered by others.

A trademark can be a word, a series of initials or numbers, a slogan, a logo, a name, a shape, or any combination of these. Almost anything is acceptable.

Trademarks law exists both at the federal and provincial level. Federally, the *Trademarks Act* is the governing legislation.

2. What Requirements Must You Meet to Claim a Valid Trademark?

As noted, almost anything can be used as a trademark. The key criterion is that it be distinctive. In Canada, the test for determining a mark's distinctiveness is whether it is distinctive to the average Canadian.

You must meet special requirements to use your trademark in Quebec. Among other things, your trademark should be translated into French, if only to avoid complications arising from Quebec's language laws.

3. What Can You Not Use as a Trademark?

You will likely not be able to claim any of the following as a trademark:

* *A person's name or surname.* This is not to say that you can't do business under your name, just that you can't hold a monopoly on the right to do so.

* *Anything merely descriptive.* For example, you probably won't be able to register the trademark "Leather Shoes," as to do so would effectively deprive others of the right to identify their shoes as made of leather. You may, however, be allowed to register a descriptive trademark if you disclaim any right to the descriptive portion. You might be able to register the trademark "Softwear Leather Shoes," provided you disclaim any trademark right in the words "leather shoes."

* *Anything deceptively misdescriptive of your goods and services.* For instance, you cannot use the trademark "Ontario Maple Syrup" if your maple syrup comes from Vermont.

* *Anything that is merely ornamental.* Your trademark must identify your goods and services, not just decorate them.

* *A mark that is confusingly similar to a registered trademark.* You must search the records of the Canadian Trademarks Office before using a new trademark or trying to register it.

4. Must You Register Your Trademark?

You can register your trademark under the *Trademarks Act*. However, you do not have to do so to acquire rights in it or to prevent others from using the same or a confusingly similar trademark. Registration exists primarily to create a legal presumption that your trademark is valid and is yours.

Registration also gives you the right to —

* use your trademark throughout Canada,

* prevent anyone else in Canada from using a confusingly similar trademark, and

* register the mark in certain foreign jurisdictions, including most industrialized countries.

Once registered, the registry system will keep a record of the trademark, the goods and services to which the trademark relates, and the owner of the trademark.

5. How Do You Register Your Trademark?

To register a trademark you must file an application and submit the applicable fee to the Trademarks Office. Your application will then be examined and searched against other trademarks. It will also be advertised in the trademarks journal, which the office publishes to allow others to raise objections to registration. If there are no objections or if the objections are without merit, your trademark will be registered. The entire process usually takes a little more than a year.

6. How Long Does Your Trademark Last?

Your trademark lasts as long as you use it to distinguish your goods and wares. Registration of a trademark takes effect on the date of registration and lasts for 15 years, unless renewed, expunged, or cancelled.

D i s c o v e r y

Although you are not required to do so by law, you may wish to use a trademark notice to indicate to the public that you are claiming rights in a particular trademark. Here are some guidelines to follow:

(a) If your trademark has been registered with the Trademarks Office, use the symbol ©, placed at the upper right-hand corner of your trademark.

(b) If your trademark is unregistered, use the letters TM, placed in the upper right-hand corner next to your trademark. You may also use this symbol for a registered trademark instead of the ©.

7. Can You Lose the Right to Your Trademark's Registration?

A registered trademark may either be expunged or cancelled. Either will deprive you of registration.

A trademark may be expunged if it is found to be confusingly similar to a trademark already registered or if you had no right to the trademark in the first place. Expungement usually occurs because of a successful legal challenge.

Grounds for cancelling a trademark include not using the trademark in connection with your goods or services. Cancellation allows the Trademarks Office to clear old trademarks from the registry system. To keep your trademark, make sure you use it by ensuring that it appears on your goods at the time they are sold. If your business provides services rather than goods, your trademark should be conspicuously displayed when performing or advertising those services.

8. Can You Transfer Your Trademarks to Someone Else?

You can transfer your trademark either by way of assignment or license.

An assignment transfers the trademark itself. If the trademark is registered, the assignment can be registered as well, though the assignment will not be invalid simply because it is not registered.

A license transfers only the right to use the trademark to the licensee. However, to maintain the distinctiveness of the trademark, you should ensure that you, as the owner, have direct authority and control over the character and quality of the goods or services sold in connection with your trademark. To protect your control, have a qualified lawyer draft a license agreement on your behalf.

9. What Does It Mean to Infringe Trademark?

The rights of a trademark owner are infringed when someone uses the trademark without the owner's consent. This includes selling, distributing, or advertising goods or services under the trademark. Infringing a trademark owner's rights in this way could result in the offender being sued for "passing off" his or her goods or services as those of another.

In either case, the court can grant an injunction or award damages. It also has the power to order the destruction of the infringing goods.

10. Is There Anything Else You Should Know about Trademarks?

Two concepts are closely related to trademarks: a "trade guise" (or "trade dress") and a "certification mark." The terms trade guise or trade dress refer to a distinguishing shape of goods or their containers. The familiar shape of the Coca-Cola bottle is one example. A trade guise can be registered under the *Trademarks Act*.

A certification mark is a trademark used to distinguish goods or services that have met a certain defined standard, such as a standard of quality, safety, or performance. For example, toys or sporting equipment are often certified to meet a certain standard, as shown by the use of a certification mark. A certification mark can be registered under the *Trademarks Act* but cannot be licensed.

c. Patents

An invention can sometimes form the very cornerstone of a successful small business. An understanding of patent law is crucial to protecting your rights in that invention.

1. What Is a Patent?

A patent is a right to make, use, and sell an invention in Canada. The right is granted by the federal *Patent Act* and belongs exclusively to the owner of the patent, known as the patentee. By obtaining a patent, you acquire a monopoly over your invention.

2. What Requirements Must You Meet to Patent Your Invention?

Your invention, to be patentable, must be —

* *New*. It can't be something for which a patent already exists. It is important to know that in Canada patents are issued on a first-to-file system rather than a first-to-invent system. "New" in the context of patent law means that the first person to file a particular patent application will be the first to obtain the patent, regardless of whether he or she was the originator of the invention;

* *Useful*. Your invention must serve a practical purpose. It must perform a function. Something such as an abstract theory about the nature of time cannot be patented. But a time-travel machine can be.

* *Not obvious*. There has to have been some inventiveness or creativity involved in bringing about your invention. A good test of inventiveness is to ask yourself whether anyone ordinarily skilled in your trade or industry could have easily invented the same thing.

The cautious approach is always to assume that your invention is patentable.

Discovery

Your lawyer is legally competent (though not necessarily qualified) to attend to patent-related matters on your behalf, with the exception that he or she cannot bring a patent application before the Canadian Patent Office. Only a patent agent can do that. Many lawyers who specialize in intellectual property matters are also patent agents. Be aware of this difference when searching out legal advice.

3. How Do You Obtain a Patent for Your Invention?

To obtain a patent for your invention, you must file an application with the Canadian Patent Office. The application must describe the invention and how to use it. It must also define the limits of the rights you are claiming. (For instance, your new flea collar may work only on certain types of fleas.) An examiner at the Patent Office will then review the application to ensure that it complies with the legal requirements of a patent. (Occasionally, an application must be amended.) If a patent is granted by the Patent Office, you will receive a notice of allowance and your patent will "issue," or take effect.

It can take up to three years for a patent to issue. During that time your invention is not protected under the law. If you wish to do any work with the invention in the interim and that work involves disclosing some or all of the information about the invention to others, you should be sure, at a minimum, that those persons are subject to a secrecy agreement. (See Section d. below).

You should also note that obtaining a patent can be an expensive process and can easily run into the thousands of dollars.

4. How Long Will Your Patent Last?

At present, any patent application filed after September 30, 1989, lasts for 20 years from the date on which the application is filed. After that time, anyone has the right to copy, produce, and sell your invention. The term cannot be extended or renewed.

Discovery

Patent protection lasts only 20 years, but a trade secret can remain secret forever. With this in mind, some business owners choose not to protect their invention by patent if they believe the value in the invention extends beyond the 20-year period. For example, the recipe for Coca-Cola has been a closely guarded trade secret for more than 100 years. Be sure to speak with a qualified patent lawyer about how best to protect your invention.

5. What Does It Mean to Infringe a Patent?

Infringement is any behaviour that interferes with a patentee's rights to make, use, construct, and sell an invention in Canada during the term of the patent. Copying an invention would constitute infringement. So too would selling someone else's invention, unless you were licensed to do so.

To help protect yourself against a possible infringement claim, you can conduct searches of the Patent Office's records to determine if there are any patents or potential patents that might be infringed by your proposed manufacture, sale, or use of a product.

A person who infringes a patent can be liable to the patentee for damages, among other things. In addition, a court may, and likely will, order that the infringement stop.

6. Can You Transfer Your Patent?

You can transfer your patent by assigning it. Assignment gives the person to whom you are assigning the patent — the assignee — all your rights of ownership over the patent, including the right to make or use the invention the patent covers. If a patent has not yet issued for your invention (or you don't intend to patent it), you can simply sell the invention itself to another person. The buyer then has the option of deciding whether or not it wishes to pursue a patent for the invention it has purchased from you. As a final option, you can license all or certain of your rights in the invention.

A license grants another person the right to exploit some aspect of your invention — perhaps the right to manufacture it — for a fee, often in the form of a royalty. By licensing your rights, you do not transfer them, and so ownership remains with the patentee.

Deciding what to do with your invention is always a question of knowing whether you have the inclination and resources to exploit its profit-making potential.

d. Other Intellectual Property

Various other types of intellectual property are protected by the law.

1. Industrial Designs

Under the federal *Industrial Design Act*, you can register and claim an exclusive right to certain ornamental designs, shapes, configurations, or patterns. The key criterion is that the design be original. The shape of a chair, mannequin, or knife handle, if original, are registerable industrial designs. Rights last ten years from the date of registration.

2. Integrated Circuit Topographies

Under the federal Integrated *Circuit Topography Act*, you can register and claim an exclusive right over the topography relating to the design of an integrated circuit. This will be of particular interest to those in high-tech industries. Rights last ten years from the date of registration.

3. New Varieties of Plants

If you operate a nursery or work in a related industry, you should know your rights under the federal *Plant Breeder's Rights Act*, which protects your legal right to exclusive ownership of new varieties of plants that you breed. If you are doing business in this area, be sure to speak with your lawyer about protecting your rights.

4. Trade Secrets

Confidential business information — or trade secrets, as such information is sometimes called — are those items of business information that you take steps to keep secret and which because of their secrecy have a commercial value to you.

Regardless of what type of business you operate, it is likely that you own some item of confidential business information. Perhaps it is a secret marketing strategy or plans for a car of the future. Many a successful restaurant has been built on a "secret recipe."

But not everything you call secret is protected by the law as a trade secret. To ensure that the law is on your side, you must prove that you have taken all steps necessary to protect your trade secrets from others. After all, a secret isn't a secret if everyone knows about it. In fact, to successfully sue someone for obtaining unauthorized access to your trade secrets or for making an unauthorized use of them, you will have to show the court that you did the following:

* *You took reasonable steps to ensure the confidentiality of the information.* For example, you could show that the book in which you kept the recipe for your special sauce was marked confidential on the cover and locked in a safe.

* *If you disclosed your confidential information to others, you did so in circumstances in which an obligation of confidence arose.* For example, you could show that the employees who had been given access to your secret recipe had signed a secrecy agreement.

* *Your confidential information was used to your detriment.* For example, you would have to show that the restaurant across the street is now attracting your former customers with your secret recipe.

At the end of this chapter, you will find a sample secrecy agreement that you can use, with the necessary modification, in your small business (Sample 5).

The key to protecting your trade secrets is vigilance. Make sure your secrets are just that — secret. Loose lips can sink more than just ships.

e. Other Issues
1. Employees and Your Intellectual Property

A person employed by you under a contract of service — an employee — does not hold the right to any item of intellectual property he or she produces as part of the employment. That belongs to the employer (i.e., your business).

An independent contractor — that is, someone working for you under a contract for services — on the other hand, retains ownership over any item of intellectual property he or she produces unless the two of you agree otherwise. Accordingly, if you wish to obtain the right of ownership over that property, you should be sure that the independent contractor agreement provides that all rights to any intellectual property, including ownership, belong to you.

2. Protecting Your Intellectual Property Abroad

Canada subscribes to several international treaties and reciprocal agreements that provide for the protection of your intellectual property abroad. Most industrialized countries adhere to these treaties and agreements. It is, however, important to speak with your lawyer about protection outside Canada if you are planning to make any item of your intellectual property available abroad.

f. Summary

Intellectual property is often one of your most valuable business assets. Think of McDonald's golden arches, Lego blocks, or KFC's "secret recipe of herbs and spices." All these are immediately recognizable by consumers. Be sure that you seek and obtain qualified legal advice in trying to protect your intellectual property.

Ownership of Intellectual Property

To help ensure that you maintain the ownership right over any intellectual property a contractor may create in the course of performing services for you, you should include the following provision in the service contract:

Intellectual Property

The parties agree that all intellectual property ("Intellectual Property"), including, without limitation, all inventions (whether patentable or unpatentable), discoveries, ideas, trade secrets, know-how [list other applicable items of intellectual property, e.g., data compilations, soundtracks], *and works subject to copyright protection, used or developed by* [name of consultant] *in the course of providing its services under this Agreement shall be at all times, both during and after the expiry date or termination of this Agreement, the exclusive property of Yourco and that* [name of consultant] *shall have no rights in the Intellectual Property. The provisions of this Section shall survive termination or expiry of this Agreement.*

Sample 4
Assignment of Copyright and Waiver

TO: Kai's Music Limited

FOR VALUE RECEIVED, the undersigned, _____,

being the author and the owner of the copyright in the work titled _____

_____, (the "Work") hereby assigns to Kai's Music

Limited all copyright in the Work and, in his capacity as the author, hereby waives all moral right

in and to the Work in favour of Kai's Music Limited.

DATED this 5th day of May, 20--.

_____   _____
Witness   Name

Secrecy Agreement

THIS AGREEMENT, made ___September 1, 20--___ , between:

YOUR COMPANY
123 Fourth Street, Somewhere, ON M1M 1M1
("Yourco")

-and-

OTHER COMPANY
11 Green Lane, Anywhere, ON L3T 1M2
("the Recipient")

RECITES THAT:

a.   On and subject to the terms and conditions of this Agreement, Yourco intends to disclose certain Confidential Information to the Recipient for purposes of the Activity (as those terms are defined in this Agreement);

THEREFORE, in return for the promises and mutual agreements contained in this Agreement and other good and valuable consideration (the receipt and sufficiency of which is acknowledged by each of the Parties), the Parties agree as follows:

1.   **DEFINITIONS.** In this Agreement, unless the context otherwise requires:

"Activity" means ___the preparation of a market report for Yourco by the Recipient;___

"Agreement" means this secrecy agreement and any document signed by the Parties amending this secrecy agreement;

"Confidential Information" means any and all information disclosed or otherwise made available to the Recipient by Yourco in connection with the Activity, whether oral, written, or otherwise, and includes, without limitation —

(i)   ___a report entitled "New Paint Additives"___ ;

(ii)   any information ascertainable by the inspection or analysis of such information; and

(iii)   any information resulting from or arising out of the performance of the Activity.

"Parties" means, collectively, Yourco and the Recipient, and "Party" means either of the Parties;

"Representatives" means any one or more of the directors, officers, employees, associates, contractors, agents, advisors, and representatives of a Party.

2. USE AND DISCLOSURE RESTRICTIONS. The Recipient acknowledges and confirms that the Confidential Information is confidential and is being disclosed to the Recipient for purposes of the Activity only. Accordingly, under the terms of this Agreement, the Recipient agrees —

    (i) to maintain the Confidential Information in confidence at all times;

    (ii) to use the Confidential Information for purposes of the Activity only;

    (iii) to handle the Confidential Information with at least the same degree of care normally used to protect its own confidential information, provided that such care must always and at a minimum be reasonable;

    (iv) not to use the Confidential Information for its own benefit or the benefit of third parties;

    (v) not to make any copies of the Confidential Information except as necessary to carry out the Activity; and

    (vi) not to disclose the Confidential Information, in whole or in part, in its original form or by way of summary or analysis, to anyone except as explicitly provided in this Agreement or otherwise directed by Yourco in writing.

3. EXCEPTIONS TO USE AND DISCLOSURE RESTRICTIONS. The restrictions on use and disclosure set out in this Agreement do not apply to any part of the Confidential Information that —

    (i) is or comes into the public domain other than through a breach of this Agreement;

    (ii) the Recipient knew about before disclosure by Yourco (and not acquired by the Recipient directly or indirectly from Yourco on a confidential basis), as shown by documentary evidence sufficient to establish such knowledge;

    (iii) is lawfully received by the Recipient from a third party, as shown by documentary evidence; or

    (iv) is required by law to be disclosed, provided that the Recipient gives Yourco immediate notice of such requirement so that Yourco may seek a protective order or take other appropriate action.

4. DISCLOSURE TO REPRESENTATIVES. The Recipient may disclose some or all of the Confidential Information to its Representatives who require access to it for purposes of the Activity, provided that —

    (i) each Representative is advised by the Recipient of and agrees to comply with the terms of this Agreement, and

    (ii) the Recipient agrees to be liable for any failure on the part of its Representatives to comply with the terms of this Agreement.

5. RETURN OF CONFIDENTIAL INFORMATION. At any time and for any reason if Yourco requests, or on completion of the Activity, the Recipient must immediately —

    (i) cease any and all use of the Confidential Information; and

(ii)   return to Yourco all the Confidential Information in its possession or control, including, without limitation, any and all copies, reproductions, summaries, memos, analyses, interpretations, evaluations, and compilations of the Confidential Information.

6.   BEGINNING AND EXPIRY OF RECIPIENT'S OBLIGATIONS. The Recipient's obligations under this Agreement take effect as of the date of this Agreement and survive until _twenty (20)_ years from that date, the completion of the Activity, or Yourco's request for a return of the Confidential Information, whichever comes last.

7.   INDEMNITY. The Recipient indemnifies and holds Yourco harmless from and against any and all loss, liability, damage, claim, cost, and expense (including legal fees) however arising, out of any breach or non-performance by the Recipient or its Representatives of any of the Recipient's obligations under this Agreement including, without limitation, the Recipient's obligations regarding the use of the Confidential Information.

8.   INJUNCTION. The Recipient acknowledges that a breach by it or any of its Representatives of any of the Recipient's obligations under this Agreement may cause irreparable harm to Yourco which may be difficult or impossible to ascertain, and that an award of damages will not be a sufficient remedy for such breach. Accordingly, Yourco will be entitled to specific performance of this Agreement and an injunction to prevent any breach or threatened breach of this Agreement. No remedy referred to in this section is exclusive but each is cumulative and in addition to any other remedy otherwise available at law or in equity, including damages.

9.   GENERAL.

9.1   Nothing in this Agreement is to be interpreted to —

    (i)   obligate Yourco to disclose the Confidential Information or any part of it to the Recipient;

    (ii)   obligate Yourco to enter into any further agreement with the Recipient; or

    (iii)   grant to the Recipient any right, title, or interest in the Confidential Information or in Yourco's business, products, or operations.

9.2   Yourco makes no representation or warranty, explicit or implicit, regarding the Confidential Information or its fitness for a particular use or purpose.

9.3   Any communication under this Agreement is deemed to have been properly made when, in the ordinary course of delivery or transmission, it is sent to a Party at its address above or other address as a Party advises, in writing.

9.4   Notwithstanding any dispute arising between the Parties, the Recipient must proceed diligently with the performance of this Agreement.

9.5   No delay or failure of a Party to exercise any of its rights under this Agreement operates as a waiver of such right or affects any other of that Party's rights or the exercise of those rights.

9.6   This Agreement benefits and is binding on the Parties and their respective heirs, executors, administrators, successors, and permitted assigns, as the case may be.

9.7 This Agreement is governed by and must be construed in accordance with the laws of the province of ___Ontario___ and the laws of Canada as applicable in that province, and the Parties irrevocably submit to the non-exclusive jurisdiction of the courts of ___Ontario___ for the interpretation and enforcement of this Agreement.

9.8 If any term of this Agreement is held to be invalid, illegal, or unenforceable, it will not affect the validity of any other terms of this Agreement and this Agreement will be read as though the invalid term does not exist.

9.9 The Recipient agrees not to assign this Agreement or any of its rights, obligations, or interests under this Agreement without the prior written consent of Yourco. Notwithstanding such consent, no assignment relieves the Recipient of any of its obligations under this Agreement.

9.1 This Agreement expresses the final Agreement between the Parties as to the subject matter of this Agreement. Accordingly, the Parties agree not to amend this Agreement except by and in accordance with a document signed by the Parties.

EACH OF THE PARTIES have executed this Agreement and in so doing confirm their authority and intention to bind the Party they represent.

YOUR COMPANY

By: _____

Name: _____

Title: _____

OTHER COMPANY

By: _____

Name: _____

Title: _____

9
Contracts

There is perhaps no legal subject as important — and intimidating — to a small-business owner as contract law. Yet, if you own a small business, you likely enter into dozens of contracts each day. It happens every time you sell an item, buy an item, hire an employee, write a cheque, pay a bill, accept a credit card, tell someone a business secret, watch a video, lease equipment, take a loan, make a loan, use someone's services, provide someone with your services, order in lunch, purchase an airline ticket, lease some property, sublease some property, fill the company truck with gasoline, or take a client to a hockey game.

Of course, there is a difference between entering into a contract and knowing what it means — from a legal perspective — to do so. A basic understanding of contract law can help you in that regard. However, rather than focus primarily on legal principles, this chapter will provide you with practical insight into the legal aspects of contractual relationships so that you will be able to read and write contracts with the critical eye of a commercial lawyer.

But first, the basics.

a. What Is a Contract?

A contract is, quite simply, a legally enforceable agreement. To be legally enforceable, a contract requires three elements: an offer, acceptance, and consideration.

1. The Offer

Every contract begins with an offer. That offer can take a limitless variety of forms. It may be an offer to buy some goods. It may also be an offer to sell some goods. It may be an offer to wash a car, purchase shares in a company, or buy some land. The sky is the limit.

It is not important at law whether the offer is made verbally, in writing, or otherwise for it to be legally effective. As long as the person making the offer (the offeror) communicates the offer to the person to whom it is being made (the offeree), the offer is capable of giving rise to a contract.

But not everything that looks like an offer is an offer. You might, for example, tell someone about how your delivery van would be ideally suited to that person's business needs. That does not necessarily translate into an offer to sell your van to that person.

2. Acceptance

Once an offeror makes an offer, the offeree has the choice either to accept or reject the offer.

To accept an offer, the offeree must communicate acceptance to the offeror. Again, the way in which that acceptance is communicated does not matter unless the offer itself requires a specific type of communication. If an offeror says, "I offer to sell you my goods. If you agree to accept my offer, you must communicate your acceptance to me in writing," then a verbal acceptance will not be enough.

Of course, an offeree must meet any other conditions that the offeror requires for acceptance of the offer. For example, an offeror might say, "I offer to sell you my goods. If you agree to accept my offer, you must communicate your acceptance to me in writing no later than March 22, 2018." In those circumstances, an offeree could not accept the offer on March 23, 2018 (or thereafter), even if he or she tried to do so in writing.

Some conditions are implied in an offer by operation of the law. Most important among these is the condition that any offer that is not subject to a specific time limit for acceptance is open for a reasonable time. You cannot, therefore, accept an offer made to you several years ago if it would be unreasonable to conclude that the offer was still open for acceptance.

Once an offer has been accepted, the offeror cannot withdraw, or revoke, the offer. Similarly, once an offeree has communicated its acceptance of the offer to the offeror, the offeree cannot revoke his or her acceptance. The offer and acceptance stand unless the offeror and the offeree agree otherwise.

If the offeree decides to reject the offer, the offeree may do so either by communicating rejection to the offeror or remaining silent. Note, however, that taking actions that indicate your acceptance may amount to acceptance regardless of what you do (or do not) say. If someone offers to sell you goods and delivers them to your business, you will be deemed at law to have accepted those goods (on the terms on which they were offered to you) if you, for example, in turn sell those goods to your customers — even if you do not tell the offeror that you are accepting those goods or even if you simply remain silent.

Also bear in mind that if you, as an offeree, change the terms of an offer (e.g., through negotiation) and present them to the offeror, you then become the offeror and the original offeror becomes the offeree. It is important, therefore, that whenever you negotiate changes to an offer, your counteroffer sets out the terms on which you require acceptance (e.g., in writing).

As soon as you make a counteroffer, the original offer made to you is deemed at law no longer to be open for acceptance by you. That is, you can't both make a counteroffer and, if not accepted, accept the original offer.

Finally, just as an offer must be clearly communicated to the offeree, so too must acceptance of the offer be clearly communicated to the offeror. Thus, not everything that looks like an acceptance is an acceptance. For example, the response "I'll think about it" is not an acceptance. Nor is it acceptance if someone verbally agrees to accept an offer but the offeror requires acceptance to be made in writing as a condition of the offer. In that case, the offeror would be well advised to obtain a written acceptance of the offer before he or she acts on it.

3. Consideration

The third element necessary to bind people to an agreement is consideration. Consideration means that to get something, you have to give something. A simple offer to do something — for instance to sell certain goods — will not be enforceable against the person making that offer unless the offeree gives something of value in return, such as money. This is called "giving consideration," and it entails that some benefit or right is bestowed on the person agreeing to obligate himself or herself.

In most contractual arrangements, both the offeror and the offeree obligate themselves to do certain things. For example, the offeror might obligate himself or herself to sell certain goods to the offeree, and the offeree might obligate himself or herself to pay the offeror for those goods. Consideration must, therefore, flow both ways, and the offeror and offeree must each receive something in return for what they are obligating themselves to do. This is why the law — in requiring consideration as part of any contractual arrangement — is often said to enforce only bargains or exchanges and not simply agreements or gratuitous promises.

That said, it will always be a question of fact whether or not an exchange truly took place. Courts have had to deal with a variety of legal issues that have arisen from the practical application of the doctrine of consideration. Perhaps most important among these are the problems of adequacy and sufficiency of consideration.

Adequacy of consideration refers to whether, from the point of view of the consideration actually given, the exchange was a fair one. The general principle in Canadian law is that courts will not inquire into the adequacy of consideration; that is left to the parties to determine. If you choose to sell your antique sports car for one dollar, that is up to you. Courts will not question your business judgment. The court is likely to interfere and overturn a contract only in instances in which it is clear that there was fraud or that a party was incapable of looking after his or her own interests.

In matters of "sufficiency of consideration," courts take the position that regardless of the value of the things exchanged relative to each other, those things must have at least some value in the eyes of the law. In short: consideration must be real to be sufficient and it must be sufficient for a contract to be binding.

It is worth noting that consideration is generally thought to be sufficient if, in exchange for a benefit, the person receiving the benefit merely suffers some sort of detriment, as opposed to giving a benefit in return. For example, my promising to paint your house in exchange for your agreeing to take down your satellite dish would be deemed sufficient consideration.

However, it is not sufficient consideration for a person who has been promised something simply to do something in reliance on that promise. For example, Makiko plans to open a flower store, and Robert, her friend, promises to take pictures of the opening-day events. Makiko is not giving sufficient consideration to Robert for his promise simply by having her hair done on that day in reliance on Robert's promise. She cannot, therefore, legally bind him to that promise on the basis of that reliance (nor can she seek to be reimbursed by him for the cost of her new hairdo).

Nor is simple fulfilment of a condition sufficient consideration (for example, if A promises to give B $100 if B jumps off a bridge, and B jumps off the bridge) unless, of course, meeting that condition (e.g., jumping off the bridge) in some way benefits the person making that promise.

For these reasons, one almost always finds a contract prefaced with words similar to —

> *In consideration of two dollars and other good and valuable consideration (the receipt and sufficiency of which is acknowledged by each of the parties), the parties agree as follows:*

Such wording establishes written evidence of consideration, thereby indicating the parties' mutual intention to be legally bound by what they each have agreed to do. Another way of expressing the same intention (and one that is gaining favour among lawyers) is simply to write —

> *For value received, the parties agree as follows:*

Regardless of which wording you prefer, I recommend that written evidence of consideration be recorded somewhere in every contract you write.

b. What Does a Contract Do?

A contract does three important things in the eyes of the law. First, it determines your rights and obligations; second, it allocates risk; and third, it provides a legal basis for restitution.

1. Determines Your Rights and Obligations

A contract determines the rights and obligation of the persons it binds. Moreover, a contract is capable of changing or completely revoking the rights and obligations that a person might otherwise have under the common law or statute. For this reason, no contract should ever be taken lightly. Read your contracts to ensure that they do not take anything from you which you do not want to give and that they give you everything you have asked for.

2. Allocates Risk

A contract is, in practical terms, about allocating risk. If you agree that a nail supplier will supply you with 1,000 boxes of wood nails so that you can build a deck for Mrs. Hannessen, who should bear the risk if the nails aren't delivered? What if they are delivered, but three months after you needed them? What if the nails are of such poor quality that they can't hold the wood together?

It is the purpose of any contract you enter into — either with your supplier or with Mrs. Hannessen — to try to anticipate these possibilities and address them in advance. In part, that involves knowing what can go wrong and how to fix it, and knowing who is responsible if something does go wrong.

3. Provides a Legal Basis for Restitution

A contract, as noted previously, is a legally enforceable agreement. Every contract has the weight of the law behind it. If someone fails to abide by a contractual obligation — that is, if he or she breaches an obligation — that breach can give rise to a legal claim for restitution. Specifically, it can require the person in breach to put the non-breaching person in the same position as he or she would have been in had the contract been carried out.

c. Who May Enter into a Contract?

A contract may be entered into by any individual or entity having the legal capacity to do so. Such a person is referred to as a "party" to the contract.

1. An Individual

Almost any individual can be a party to a contract. The most important exception is a person who is a minor.

The age at which a person is considered to be a minor varies between provinces but usually refers to people of less than 18 to 21 years of age. Such persons are incapable of binding themselves to a contract unless it is a contract for necessities. A 14-year-old boy who buys a hockey card from your collectibles shop is entitled to return that card for a refund simply because he is a minor. That 14 year old would not, however, be allowed to return groceries simply by virtue of the fact that he purchased them as a minor.

In a written contract, the full name of each person who is a party to the contract should be set out in the agreement. This is usually done at the beginning of the agreement, where all parties are listed. It should always be done at the end of the agreement — on a signature line — to evidence each person's consent to be bound by the contract's terms. That is accomplished by having the person sign his or her name on the signature line (see Section d. below).

To ensure that you are dealing with the person with whom you think you are dealing, ask him or her to provide you with evidence of his or her name, such as a driver's license or birth certificate.

2. A Business Entity

Any type of business entity — sole proprietorship, partnership, or corporation — can be a party to a contract. In each case, the name of the business entity should be set out at the beginning of the agreement and above a signature line.

A sole proprietor should sign the agreement on the signature line. In effect, a sole proprietor is binding himself or herself to the terms of the agreement since a sole proprietor is not separate at law from his or her business.

Any partner may sign on behalf of his or her partnership unless there is something in the partnership agreement that states otherwise. The signature of a partner then binds the partnership to comply with the obligations of the agreement. If you can, have each partner sign on behalf of the partnership to pre-empt any question about whether or not a partner is acting without the authority of the other partners.

The person authorized to sign on behalf of a corporation is set out in that corporation's by-laws. The by-laws will also set out whether the company seal is required to validly execute an agreement.

No matter what business entity you enter into an agreement with, always obtain some evidence from it as to its precise legal name and who is authorized to sign on its behalf. In the case of sole proprietorships and partnerships, obtain a copy of the business name registration from the relevant government authority. In the case of a company, obtain a copy of its articles (or other incorporating document) and by-laws.

In some situations it may not be clear to you who is authorized to sign on behalf of a specific entity. Talk to your lawyer about how you can determine whether the person purporting to contractually bind that entity actually has the authority to do so.

d. Whom Does a Contract Bind?

A contract binds the parties to it. No one else. Anyone who is not a party to a contract is considered a third party and cannot be obligated to do anything the contract requires. In contract law, this is know as the doctrine of privity.

For example, Inge may agree with Gerda that Klaus is going to deliver certain goods to Gerda at a certain date and time, but unless Klaus is a party to that agreement — that is, unless he agrees to that arrangement — he is not obligated to either Inge or Gerda to carry out that obligation. Therefore, if you are imposing an obligation on someone to do something, that person should be added as a party to the agreement and his or her signature obtained to evidence consent.

e. When Are You Exempt from Your Contractural Obligations?

Every contract to which you are a party requires you to comply with your obligations as set forth in the contract. In legal terms, you must "discharge" or "perform" your obligations. Similarly, every other party to the contract must also perform their respective obligations.

If you or any of the other parties fail to perform your respective obligations, you will have breached the contract, and any party to the contract who has suffered a loss as a result of your breach is allowed to bring a legal claim against you for restitution. However, the law recognizes circumstances in which a party will not be required to perform its obligations under a legally binding contract.

1. Frustration

A contract is frustrated when circumstances make it impossible for the contract to be performed. If you contract with someone to deliver and install an oven in your new restaurant, and your restaurant burns down before delivery, the contract will have been frustrated. Other instances of frustration can arise when a party to a contract dies, an ice storm shuts down a city, or an event that should have occurred doesn't occur. (An example of this last type of frustration would be if you have agreed to provide your city council with catering services for the Queen's planned visit to your home town, and she cancels. The contract between you and the city council will be frustrated.)

In determining whether a contract has been frustrated, a court will always look to what is reasonable in the circumstances and then make its decision based on whether or not performance of the contract by the party claiming frustration would lead to a radical change in its obligations. In other words, would requiring performance fundamentally change the agreement? Using a previous example, to require you to follow through on your obligation to have an oven delivered and installed in your restaurant would require you to rebuild your restaurant. Clearly, that was not something you obligated yourself to do when contracting for the delivery and installation of the oven.

When a contract is frustrated, it ends at the time of frustration. From that point on, the parties are released from further performing the contract. Of course, any rights or obligations that have accrued up to the time of frustration still remain in place. For example, any payment obligations for delivered goods would still have to be made, even if delivery of further goods became impossible as a result of some frustrating circumstance.

2. Agreement/Termination

Parties may agree not to perform their obligations (or certain obligations) under a contract in several ways.

A party may agree to release another party from performing its obligations under a contract. By releasing another party, you (the releasor) are stating that you do not require the party you are releasing (the releasee) to perform certain or all of its obligations under the contract.

A party might also agree to allow an obligation to be satisfied in a way that was not provided for in the contract. For example, a party might agree that another party make payment by way of certified cheque rather than by cash.

In addition, both parties might agree to alter their respective obligations under the contract by amending or modifying the contract's terms. For example, the parties might agree to alter a delivery date, thereby agreeing to adjust their obligations of delivery and (presumably) acceptance of the goods being delivered.

Finally, both parties may agree to terminate their obligations under a contract.

I strongly recommend that an agreement be amended or terminated in writing (for the same reason that the contract itself should be in writing). Sample 6 shows an amending agreement, while Sample 7 shows a termination agreement.

3. As a Result of a Breach

A party will not be required to perform its obligations under a contract if another party has breached an essential term of the contract. There are two ways this might occur.

First, a party might breach an obligation before actually being obligated to perform it. Imagine that a supplier who has agreed to deliver a quantity of goods to you tells you that he has sold those goods to someone else and will not be obtaining any replacements. He will have breached a contractual obligation to you. Consequently, you — as the injured party — will not be required to perform your obligations under the contract, and, in addition, may sue the other party for damages. (See Section f. below.)

Second, a party might breach an obligation at the time it is to be performed. This occurs, for example, when someone who has agreed to pay you on a certain date does not do so. You — as the injured party — may sue for damages. Furthermore, you will not be required to perform your obligations under the contract, provided, however, that you remain ready, willing, and able to do so, to avoid being considered in breach yourself.

However, not every breach of a contract by another party will allow you simply to treat the contract as at an end. The breach must be of an essential term and must go to the very heart of the contract. It is not enough to treat a contract as at an end if a party delivers only 99 of the 100 pairs of scissors that party promised to deliver to you; both you and the other party would be required to continue to perform your obligations under the contract. However, you would have the right to sue the other party for any loss caused by the failure to deliver all 100 pairs of scissors. You would also have to pay that party for the 99 pairs of scissors only and not for all 100.

Note, finally, that a breach may occur by an act or expression. A party may act in a manner that does not comply with its obligations under a contract or may simply communicate to you that it is not going to comply with those obligations. In either case, such behaviour is considered a breach.

f. What Remedies Are Available to You If Another Party Breaches Your Contract?

A contract is breached when a party to it fails to comply with its obligations under that contract. This chapter has already examined whether or not a breach may allow you to consider your obligations under the contract as at an end, and has stated that a breach gives you the right to sue. But what can suing get you?

1. Damages

Every breach of a contract entitles the injured party to an award of damages — that is, money — for any losses that party has suffered as a result of the breach.

The court's purpose in granting an award of damages is to compensate the innocent party for those losses. In practical terms, that means that the amount of damages the innocent party will be awarded will be such as to place that party, as much as possible, in the position it would have been in had the contract been performed (i.e., had it not been breached).

Of course, the exact amount or "quantum" of damages may not be easy to determine. If someone fails to deliver and install an oven in your restaurant, your restaurant will presumably have lost the profits that the oven could have earned for it. But how do you determine how much that is?

Loss of profits isn't the only ground for obtaining damages. Other grounds include reliance and the cost of replacement. What if you had hired an electrician to hook up the oven to your fuse box on the day it was delivered? You would have suffered a loss (what you paid the electrician) in reliance on the assumption that the oven was going to be delivered.

Suppose also that you replaced that oven with a similar oven but could do so only at a higher cost. Again, you would have suffered a loss (the higher cost of the new oven) due to the original failure to deliver.

Of course, you will not always be able to recover all such losses when suing for damages. Much depends on the particular facts of the case and what you can actually prove to be a loss. Moreover, there is an obligation at law to mitigate your damages: you must take any reasonable step available to you to reduce the extent of the damage caused by the other party's breach. In the case of the undelivered oven, you would be responsible for obtaining a replacement oven as soon as possible. You could not simply leave your restaurant without an oven indefinitely, continuing to incur a loss in profits for which you might then sue the other party. The law will compensate you only for a loss due to the breach, not for your failure to behave reasonably after the breach has occurred.

In addition to an obligation to mitigate, the onus is on the innocent party to show that any losses it suffers are attributable to the breach and not to something else. For example, the loss of profits you claim as a result of the failure to have your oven delivered must be attributable to that failure and not to the fact that your cook was at home with a cold.

Nor can your damages be too "remote." To claim damages for losses, those losses must have been in the reasonable contemplation of the parties at the time they entered into the contract. For instance, the parties would have reasonably contemplated that your restaurant would have suffered a loss of customers (and hence profits) if the oven was not delivered on time. It is likely, however, that the parties did not reasonably contemplate that the failure to deliver the oven would have caused you to drive home in a rage and slam your Ferrari into a tree. Accordingly, you could not recover from the breaching party the losses caused by that accident.

Damages are not intended to punish the breaching party. Although punitive damages exist, an award of that type is reserved for circumstances in which a party has behaved in a truly reprehensible manner; for example, if someone has deliberately breached a contract with a specific view to substantially injuring the other party. Even then, punitive damages are rarely awarded in Canada.

2. Specific Performance

As an alternative to damages, a party may sue a breaching party for "specific performance" of a contract. An award of specific performance means that the breaching party will be ordered to do what the contract says that party is obligated to do. In the case of the undelivered oven, an award of specific performance would require the party responsible to deliver and install an oven in your restaurant.

Because of the problems associated with an order of specific performance, courts will make such an order only if an award of damages would not provide adequate restitution.

Consider the issues that would arise if the court ordered the breaching party in the example above to deliver an oven to your restaurant. When should that party be required to do so? The date on which the oven should have been delivered has already passed, and the damage has been done: you have already suffered a loss of profits. Moreover, you may no longer wish to deal with this person. Should you be forced to? And what if the oven is out of stock, obsolete, or you no longer require it because you obtained a replacement? All these issues and more must be addressed in an award of specific performance, whereas an award of damages could settle matters once and for all.

Now consider what might have happened if instead of an oven, someone was obligated to deliver to you a painting by a famous artist. As a work of art, it is by definition original, unique, and irreplaceable. Determining its monetary value is difficult; determining its value to you is almost impossible. The work stands alone as an object among objects. There is no substitute for it in the way that one oven can be substituted for another. Clearly, money will not be enough to settle the losses you would suffer as a result of a failure to deliver that painting. Indeed, all the money in the world (so to speak) could not recompense your loss. Only actually receiving the painting itself would put you in the position you would have been in had the contract not been breached. A court would, in all likelihood, make an order to that effect in these circumstances. Thus, to obtain an order for specific performance for a breach of contract, what you are seeking must in some way be unique and priceless.

g. In What Circumstances Might You Not Be Able to Obtain a Remedy for a Breach of Contract?

Not every breach of a contract will automatically lead to an award of damages or specific performance. Circumstances can arise in which a court decides that a contract (or a term of it) is invalidated — that is, of no legal effect — and will, accordingly, refuse to enforce it.

1. Misrepresentation

Contractual misrepresentation is a difficult area of the law to summarize because of the many different types of misrepresentation possible.

First, there is *pre-contractual misrepresentation*. This might arise during negotiations leading to a contract. For example, someone might guarantee that the oven he's selling you is self-cleaning. You agree to buy the oven on that basis. When the oven arrives, you discover that it is not self-cleaning.

Then there is *negligent misrepresentation*. This might arise if a party selling you an oven tells you it is self-cleaning without having actually looked into the matter.

There is also *fraudulent misrepresentation*. This would arise if the person selling you the oven intentionally misled you regarding the oven. For example, he might have known that the oven was not self-cleaning but told you otherwise.

Finally, there is *innocent misrepresentation*. Simply put, this is a misrepresentation in which neither fraud or negligence are present.

Depending on the circumstances of the case and the type of misrepresentation involved, a party that misrepresents a matter in a contract or in negotiations leading to a contract may be sued for damages, or the contract may be invalidated. In the above example, that would mean either that you could recover any losses resulting from the fact that the oven is not self-cleaning or would not have to buy the oven.

Finally, you should remember that not every misstatement in a contract constitutes a misrepresentation. To be considered a misrepresentation, a statement must be false, concern a matter of fact (not opinion), be addressed to the party that was misled by the statement, and actually have induced the party to whom it was addressed to enter the contract. If you did not rely on a statement in entering a contract (e.g., if you would have bought the oven whether it was self-cleaning or not), you cannot sue for misrepresentation if the statement turns out to be false.

2. Mistake

A contract may be invalidated because of a mistake. As with contractual misrepresentation, there are a variety of mistakes that may occur in a contractual setting.

A mistake may occur due to a failure to accurately set out in a contract the intentions of the parties. Imagine we agree that you are to deliver an oven to my restaurant on September 31, 2018. Of course, no such date exists, and the question thus becomes, "When must the oven be delivered?"

Another kind of mistake occurs if we agree that I will pay you $1,000 for the delivery and installation of an oven, but through some oversight, the cheque I give you is for $10,000. At law, the general rule is that the person who receives the cheque is not entitled to the overpayment. The one exception — not often encountered — is in situations in which it would be unfair to require that person to refund the overpayment.

There are other kinds of mistakes, to be sure. For example, when I said I was going to sell you my "wheels," you might have thought I was referring to a car, when in fact I meant my bicycle. Or you and I agree that you will sell me a certain type of food additive, without either of us knowing that it was recently banned. Still another kind of mistake may arise when I sell you what I think is a self-cleaning oven, but turns out not to be one.

Obviously, any number of mistakes can arise in a contractual setting, and so arguing that there has been a mistake in relation to a contract is often the last refuge for someone who cannot find any other reason to have a contract set aside. Accordingly, for a court to set aside an agreement on a basis of mistake, the mistake must affect a fundamental term of that agreement.

3. Unconscionability

A court will sometimes refuse to enforce a contract on the ground that it would be unfair or unconscionable to so, as in situations where a stronger party exercises its bargaining power in a unscrupulous manner to take advantage of a weaker party.

A good example is the standard form contract, which often reflects a "take it or leave it" approach to doing business. Such contracts also tend to favour the interests of the stronger party and completely ignore those of the weaker party.

In these circumstances — that is, those in which enforcing a contract (or a particular provision) would clearly be unfair — a court will not hesitate to refuse to enforce it. The test of unfairness, however, is whether or not it would be reasonable to enforce the contract in light of standard commercial practices, with a view to what parties bargaining freely on equal terms might have done.

It should be noted, though, that inequality of bargaining power is a fact of business. Not every deal sees both sides negotiating from a position of strength. Moreover, a court might enforce what you consider to be an unfair contract. Your safest

approach is to try avoid entering into a contract that is unfair to you in the first place.

However, if you find you have little choice in the matter, there are certain steps you can take to mitigate the differences in bargaining power:

* *Convince the stronger party that there is something to be gained from taking your interests into account*. This is not a simple task. It involves selling the stronger party on what you have to offer, even if that doesn't seem like much. No business, no matter how strong, wants to be involved with someone who is going to be unhappy, particularly if there is to be an ongoing relationship. Use that to your advantage by convincing the stronger party that your proposed amendments will be mutually beneficial.

* *Once you have the stronger party's ear, focus on what really matters to you*. Don't nit-pick. For example, if you are negotiating to be an independent sales representative for the stronger party, it is probably not that important that you be reimbursed by the stronger party for your travel expenses on a weekly basis, in accordance with your accounting practices, instead of biweekly, in accordance with the stronger party's. It is, however, likely to be of some importance to you whether or not your right to act as the stronger party's sales representative will be exclusive. Concentrate your energies on that.

* *Understand the motivations behind the stronger party's demands, then work around them to come to a mutually acceptable arrangement*. For example, if the stronger party demands the right to immediately terminate your agreement if you default in observing any of its terms, it is likely that the stronger party fears it will not be able to extricate itself quickly from what

might turn out to be a bad business relationship. You can address both that fear and your own needs by trying to negotiate a five-day grace period in which you are given the right to correct any default. In that way, the stronger party still has a quick out, and you have the opportunity to deal with the inevitable oversight.

* *Reflect on the practical realities.* Sure the contract has a dozen standard terms regarding your obligations to safely store and handle hazardous waste products, but what is the likelihood that those terms will ever actually apply to you? If the likelihood is small, using up your bargaining chips to negotiate around those types of obligations is probably not worth the effort. Perhaps more important, if you will be dealing with hazardous waste products on a regular basis, then regardless of how much you want to negotiate, the stronger party is still not likely to grant you any concessions. Stronger parties tend to be overinclusive in what they demand from a weaker party (simply because they can be). The real issue for the weaker party is if and to what extent those demands will have any actual bearing on the relationship.

* *Leave yourself an out.* For example, negotiate the right to terminate your arrangement with the other party — for any reason — on giving notice. Then, even if you have accepted all the stronger party's other demands, you still have the option of simply walking away if the situation becomes untenable.

Of course, there is no guarantee that a stronger party will grant any of your requests. Still, it never hurts to try. Moreover, it gives you a better idea of what you are letting yourself in for.

h. What Do You Need to Know about Reading a Contract?

Somebody has asked you to sign a contract they have prepared. What do you do?

First, read it. Read all of it. Every word. Don't skip the fine print. Don't ignore the back. Don't skim it. Read it. Under the law, every word counts.

As you are reading the contract, consider these questions:

* Does this contract accurately express your agreement? Does it say what you agreed would be the arrangement between you and the other party about the subject of the contract?

* What are your obligations under the contract? What are the other party's obligations? Is the other party responsible for delivery and installation of an oven, or just for delivering it? Are you responsible for paying the other party, and if so, when and how much? Will you have the money to pay the other party when payment is due?

* To what risks does this contract expose you? To what risks is the other party exposed? Who is responsible if the oven is damaged during delivery? Who is responsible if it becomes damaged through normal use within one year of delivery?

* Does this contract cover everything it is supposed to cover? Does it clearly state who is doing what, when they are to do it, where, and how? Is anything not said in the contract that should be said?

* What is the big picture? What transaction does the contract describe? When does it come into effect? Immediately? Sometime in the future? When does it end? When the oven is delivered? A year after the oven is delivered?

As you consider these matters, you should make notations on the contract itself. These should form the basis of any changes you wish to propose to the other party. Only after those changes have been made and the contract says what you want it to say should you sign it.

i. What Do You Need to Know about Writing a Contract?

If you can write well, you can write, or draft, contracts well. A written contract does nothing more than express the intentions of the parties to it. Provided those intentions are clear — and clearly expressed in the contract — your contract should serve you well.

Your contract can be in either standard contract form or letter form. (Sample 7, the Termination Agreement, shows a contract in letter form, while Sample 8, the Contract, shows a contract in standard form.) Although they appear to be different, their legal effect is the same: both represent a legally enforceable agreement.

As you examine the samples, you will notice that they contain certain key elements in common, all of which should be present in any contract you write.

1. Date

The date of the contract should appear at the top of the agreement. Adding a date to a contract is important because it establishes when the contract was entered into by the parties. Moreover, unless there is something in the agreement to the contrary, the date recorded at the head of the contract establishes when the obligations set out in the agreement take effect.

2. Parties

Every contract must also contain the names of all of the parties to it. This is important both for the sake of clarity and for purposes of privity.

In the standard form agreement, Sample 8, the names of the parties are listed after the date, at the head of the agreement.

By contrast, in a letter agreement, Sample 8, the party writing the letter puts its name and address at the top of the first page and in the centre. Alternatively, it can simply print out (or write or type) the letter on its letterhead. The other parties to the agreement are then listed as addressees on the first page of the letter, below the date, and on the far left-hand side of the page.

3. Background

Every agreement typically begins with a few brief statements about the background to the agreement; that is, how it arose. This establishes a context within which to read the agreement.

In the standard form of agreement, the background information is sometimes referred to as the recitals, and appears immediately after the names of the parties. In the letter form of agreement, the background is usually set out in the first paragraph.

In either case, the background information is of no legal effect; its purpose is purely to inform. The parties are not bound by anything contained in the background information, so that is not the place to set out any of the parties' obligations.

4. Terms

The terms, or provisions, of the agreement are its guts. They set out the rights and obligations of the parties to the agreement and explain what the agreement is about. Therefore, the terms are often considered to be the most important part of the agreement.

The terms should be organized in a logical sequence. In a commercial context, that usually means setting out the following:

* What the first party is going to do (e.g., deliver and install an oven)

- What the second party is going to do (e.g., accept delivery and installation of the oven and pay the first party)

- Terms of payment (e.g., payment to be made within three days after delivery and installation, in the amount of $1,000, by certified cheque or cash)

- Matters relating to termination of the agreement (e.g., the agreement may be terminated before delivery of the oven if the second party's restaurant does not open for business)

- Warranties of the parties. A warranty is a collateral promise made by one party to another that, if false, will allow the other party to sue for damages for any losses it suffers (e.g., the party delivering the oven might warrant that the oven will remain in good working order for one year after installation)

- Conditions precedent to the agreement. A condition precedent is an event that must occur before the party in whose favour the condition precedent was drafted must fulfil its obligations under the agreement (e.g., the first party may be obligated to deliver the oven only if it is satisfied with its credit check of the second party)

- Indemnities. An indemnity is a collateral guarantee. A party will sometimes add an indemnity to an agreement to protect it from unforeseeable contingencies (e.g., the party accepting the oven might be asked to be indemnified by the party delivering it against any damage that the first party causes to the restaurant as a result of delivering and installing the oven)

- General matters relating to the rights and obligations of the parties or to the contract in general. This is often referred to as the boilerplate.

The samples of both the standard and letter forms of the agreement provide examples of some of the above. You will notice that the terms are set out in the same way in both, with the exception that the letter form of agreement appears less formal.

Because the terms can be extensive, it is good practice to number them and provide them with headings. Numbered terms are usually referred to in an agreement as "sections," "articles," or "paragraphs."

Discovery

By inserting a notwithstanding clause in an agreement, you can except a specific item or matter from the agreement that the agreement might otherwise be interpreted to cover. For example, you could write, "Notwithstanding anything contained in this agreement, the Buyer is not obligated to accept any damaged goods from the Seller."

5. Signature Lines

Each party should sign the agreement to indicate that it agrees to be bound by the agreement's terms. That should be done at the end of the agreement, after all terms have been set out.

If an individual party rather than a representative of a business is signing the agreement, the individual's name should be written out under a solid horizontal line. The individual should then sign on that line. Further, a line should be placed directly opposite the line bearing the individual's signature so that a witness's signature can be added. The witness should then sign on that line after the individual has signed.

If any business entity other than an individual is signing the agreement, the business entity's name should be set out above a blank line on which the entity's representative would then sign his or her name. No witness signature is required. However, if the entity is a corporation, it is recommended that the corporation also apply its seal next to the representative's signature.

A sole proprietor should sign the agreement on behalf of his or her sole proprietorship.

The sample agreements show different ways of having a document signed.

Note, finally, that if the letter form is used, it is enough for the party sending the letter to sign it in closing. The other parties should then simply acknowledge their agreement with its terms (see Sample 6).

At the end of this chapter you will find Checklist 2, Ten Guidelines for Drafting the Perfect Contract. When writing your contract, refer to this checklist, to the section on drafting the boilerplate, and to the list of commonly used definitions (below). Finally, when drafting a contract, you should apply the guidelines relating to how to read a contract, as they are also relevant.

j. Summary

It is always in your best interest to have a lawyer review a contract before you sign it. That is true whether you drafted the contract or someone else did. After all, no one but a lawyer is qualified to advise you regarding the law.

However, by drafting your own contracts or being able to read contracts presented to you with a basic understanding of what is important, you are in a better position to help your lawyer focus on what is important to you. In turn, you can take better charge of your business affairs.

The Boilerplate

The term "boilerplate" refers to contractual provisions which, because they apply to almost every contractual arrangement, appear in almost every written contract. Usually, you will find the boilerplate located at the end of a contract, under the heading "General."

That does not mean that the boilerplate is insignificant and can safely be overlooked. On the contrary, a boilerplate provision is at least as important as any other provision in the contract. You should, therefore, both know what the boilerplate means and insert any applicable boilerplate provision in your own contracts. The following is a brief list of boilerplate provisions.

1. **Headings** — *The inclusion of headings in this Agreement is for convenience of reference only and shall not affect the construction or interpretation of this Agreement.*

   Explanation: This provision informs the reader that any headings used in your agreement are there simply to enable particular provisions to be located with ease. For example, you may choose to head a provision "Warranty" so that it is easily found when scanning the agreement. However, the other party may wish to rely on your use of that heading to argue that to be considered a warranty, any provision of your agreement must appear under that heading. This could lead to difficulties if you wish to argue that another provision of the agreement also constitutes a warranty. Insert the above boilerplate provision into your agreement to avoid this problem.

2. **Gender and Number** — *In this Agreement, unless the context otherwise requires, the singular includes the plural and the plural includes the singular. Further, words importing gender include all genders.*

   Explanation: You are allowed to use either masculine or feminine pronouns in your agreement with the understanding that by using one you include the other. You can, therefore, avoid having to constantly write "he/she" in your agreements. The provision also extends the meaning of words to include both the plural and the singular. You can, therefore, simply fill in the blank on an order form where the number of widgets being purchased is indicated.

3. **Currency** — *Except where otherwise provided, references to currency amounts in this Agreement are to the lawful currency of [Canada].*

   Explanation: This provision is particularly important where payment terms are identified in dollars, pounds, or other types of shared currency references. After all, it is presumably of some importance to you whether you are paid your 200 dollars in US, Canadian, or Hong Kong currency.

4. **Entire Agreement** — *This Agreement constitutes the entire agreement between the Parties pertaining to the subject matter of this Agreement and supersedes all prior agreements, understandings, negotiations, and discussions, whether oral or written, of or between the parties to this Agreement.*

   Explanation: This provision ensures that the signed and written agreement of the parties in which it appears is understood by the parties to express the one and only agreement between them regarding the subject matter of the agreement (and not just part of it). Of course, it is important in that regard to ensure that the agreement does, in fact, set out everything comprising the agreement between the parties.

5. **Time of Essence** — *Time is of the essence of this Agreement and every provision of this Agreement.*

Explanation: In the simplest terms, this provision is meant to ensure that the parties under- stand that they are required to perform their obligations under the agreement at the time set out for performance — not later. Be sure to include this provision also in any document granting an extension (for example, an extension in the date by which someone must pay you for work you have done) so that it is clear, once again, that the new time (i.e., the extended time) you stipulated for performance is understood to go to the very heart of the agreement.

6. **Severability** — *The invalidity of any provision of this Agreement shall not affect the validity of any other provision of this Agreement, but this Agreement shall be interpreted as if the invalid provision had been omitted.*

   Explanation: If a provision of the agreement is found by a court of law to be invalid, the rest of the agreement is not declared invalid on that ground. Thus, a promissory note will not be declared invalid (and the debt it evidences no longer payable) if it turns out that the interest rate provided for in the note exceeds the maximum allowable by law.

7. **Assignment** — *Neither this Agreement nor any of the rights, benefits, or obligations of a party under this Agreement are assignable either in whole or in part by that party without the prior written consent of the other party.*

   Explanation: Unless the parties otherwise agree, they alone will: (i) be responsible for the performance of their respective obligations under the agreement; and (ii) be solely entitled to exercise their respective rights or receive their respective benefits under the agreement. This becomes important if, for example, you hire company A to fix your roof, and company A unilaterally decides that it will assign that obligation to the much less reputable company B.

8. **Successors and Assigns** — *This Agreement enures to the benefit of and binds the parties to this Agreement and their respective heirs, executors, administrators, personal representatives, successors, and permitted assigns.*

   Explanation: Anyone who steps into the shoes of a party is bound to assume the obligations (and is able to obtain the benefits) of that party. This can happen in situations where a party to an agreement dies and his or her heirs want to continue receiving the benefits under it, or, in another case, if you agree to allow the other party to assign the agreement.

9. **Amendments** — *No amendment of this Agreement shall be valid or binding unless it is in writing and signed by each party to this Agreement.*

   Explanation: This clause is self-explanatory. Its primary purpose is to ensure that a party does not unilaterally purport to change (or be able to change) the terms of an agreement.

10. **Waiver** — *Failure by a party to exercise any of its rights, powers, or remedies under this Agreement or a party's delaying to do so shall not constitute a waiver of those rights, powers, or remedies or of any other of that party's rights, powers, or remedies contained in this Agreement. The partial exercise of a right, power, or remedy by a party shall not prevent its subsequent exercise or the exercise of any other right, power, or remedy.*

    Explanation: This clause ensures that you are not prevented from exercising any of your rights, powers, or remedies simply because you may not have insisted on doing so when the right first arose. For example, just because you refuse to sue the other party for late payment at the moment your right to do so arises should not mean that you are prevented from doing so at some later time.

11. **Governing Law** — *This Agreement shall be governed by and construed in accordance with the laws of the Province of [Ontario] and the laws of Canada applicable therein.*

    Explanation: Entire books have been written on the law surrounding the choice of governing law for the resolution of disputes. For purposes of this book, suffice it to say that you would in all likelihood wish any dispute to be settled according to the laws of the jurisdiction in which you carry on business. Accordingly, you may wish to add the above provision to your agree- ments with the appropriate change in province (or territory).

12. **Schedules** — *Schedule A forms part of this Agreement and is incorporated into this Agreement by this reference.*

    Explanation: Once again, this provision is self-explanatory. The intent is to ensure that the parties understand that any schedule forms part of the agreement and as such is subject to its terms. The important thing for you to remember is to mark any schedule as a schedule (e.g., "Schedule A") and staple it to the back of the agreement.

13. **Notice** — *Any notice, direction, or other instrument required or permitted to be given by any Party under this Agreement shall be in writing and shall be sufficiently given if delivered personally, sent by prepaid first class mail or transmitted by facsimile:*

    (1) In the case of a notice to _____, at:
        [679 Windermere Avenue
        Toronto, Ontario G6T 3N8]
        Attention: _____
        Facsimile: _____

    (2) In the case of a notice to _____, at:
        [39 Salome Street
        Toronto, Ontario L6F 2N9]
        Attention: _____
        Facsimile: _____

    or at such other address as a party may provide notice of to all other parties in accordance with this section.

    Any such notice, direction, or other instrument, if delivered personally, shall be deemed to have been given and received on the date on which it was received at such address, or, if sent by mail, shall be deemed to have been given and received on the date which is five days after which it was mailed, provided that if such day is not a business day, then the notice shall be deemed to have been given in receipt on the business day next following such day. Any notice transmitted by facsimile shall be deemed to have been given and received on the date of its transmission provided that if such day is not a business day or if it is received after the end of normal business hours on the date of its transmission at the place of receipt, then it shall be deemed to have been given and received at the opening of business in the office of the recipient on the first business day next following the transmission thereof.

    Explanation: By setting out in advance where any notice is to be delivered to another party, you avoid the argument that a notice was incorrectly delivered or that it was never even received. This is particularly important where notice of termination or breach are concerned.

Commonly Used Definitions

Here are some commonly used definitions you may wish to employ in your agreements:

"Agreement" means this agreement and all schedules attached to this agreement, in each case as they may be amended or supplemented from time to time, and the expressions **"hereof," "herein," "hereto," "hereunder," "hereby,"** and similar expressions refer to this agreement. Further, unless otherwise indicated, references to an **"Article" or "Section"** are, respectively, to an article or section of this agreement.

"Business Day" means any day other than a Saturday or a Sunday on which banks generally are open for business in [*province*].

"Closing Date" means [*month, day, and year*] or such other time as the Parties may in writing agree; and "Closing" means the completion of the transactions contemplated in this Agreement. (*This definition can also be used for other dates such as "Delivery Date" and "Installation Date."*)

"Goods" has the meaning set forth in Section [x.x]. (*Section x.x might then read something like: "The Seller agrees to sell to the Buyer, 14 RBO Low Radiation Computer Screens [the "Goods"].*)

"Parties" means, collectively, [*the buyer*] and [*the seller*]; and "Party" means either of them.

"Prime Rate" means the rate of interest per annum charged by [*the seller's*] bank to its customers in [*city, province*] for loans of Canadian dollars, as the same is adjusted from time to time.

For ease of reference, your definitions should always be arranged in alphabetical order at the outset of your agreement. I also recommend that you capitalize the first initial of each defined term wherever it appears in the agreement to indicate to the reader that it is a defined term.

Sample 6
Amending Agreement

YOUR COMPANY
123 Fourth Street
Somewhere, ON M1M 1M1

May 12, 20--   Via courier

Other Company
11 Green Lane
Anywhere, ON L3T 1M2
Attention: Mr. G. Businessperson

Dear George:

Re: Secrecy Agreement between Your Company and Other Company, May 1, 20-- (the "Agreement").

It was a pleasure meeting with you and Ms. Wilde to discuss Otherco's interest in acquiring some of my secret recipes. During our meeting, you mentioned that you wish to review my secret recipe for "pumpkin soup." As we already have a secrecy agreement in place for certain of my other secret recipes, I have prepared this Amending Agreement to amend the Agreement according to your new request and certain other matters to which we have agreed.

You will recall that the Agreement provides that it may be amended by written agreement of the parties. Therefore, for good and valuable consideration (the receipt and sufficiency of which is acknowledged by each of the parties), we agree as follows:

1.   Unless otherwise indicated in this Amending Agreement, all capitalized terms used in this Amending Agreement have the meaning ascribed to them in the Agreement.

2.   The Agreement is amended by adding the words, "Yourco's secret recipe for pumpkin soup" to section 1 of the Agreement as part of subsection (i) of the definition of "Confidential Information."

3.   The Agreement is amended by deleting the word "immediate" from subsection 3(iv) of the Agreement.

4.   The Agreement is amended by deleting section 5 of the Agreement and adding the following in its place,

     DESTRUCTION OF CONFIDENTIAL INFORMATION. Within three (3) days of the completion of the Activity or at any time within three (3) days of Yourco's request, the Recipient must —

     (i)   cease any and all use of the Confidential Information;

(ii) destroy all the Confidential Information in its possession or control, including, without limitation, any and all copies, reproductions, summaries, memos, analyses, interpretations, evaluations, and compilations of the Confidential Information, except that the Recipient may retain one (1) copy of the Confidential Information for its records, provided always that copy remains subject to the use and disclosure restrictions set out in the Agreement; and

(iii) confirm to Yourco, in writing, that it has destroyed the Confidential Information in accordance with this section 5.

5. The amendments set out in this Amending Agreement take effect as of [*the date of the secrecy agreement; the date of this amending agreement; or some other date*] and are incorporated into the Agreement and treated in all respects as forming a part of the Agreement.

6. All other provisions of the Agreement remain unamended and in effect.

Please confirm your agreement with the terms of this Amending Agreement by signing the enclosed duplicate of this Amending Agreement and returning it to my attention. Kindly retain this copy for your files.

Yours truly,

Per: _____

Other Company agrees with the terms of this amending agreement.

Dated this _____ day of _____, 20--,

OTHER COMPANY

Per: _____

Name: _____

Title: _____

I have authority to bind the company.

Sample 7
Termination Agreement in Letter Form

[YOURCO LETTERHEAD]

[*Insert date of letter*]

Delivered by Hand

[*Insert Name
and Address of Recipient*]

Dear [*Insert Name of Representative of Recipient*]:

Re: Supply Agreement between Yourco and [Recipient] dated the 14th day of January, 20-- (the "Supply Agreement").

The Supply Agreement provides in section 5 that the parties may, "... terminate the Supply Agreement at any time upon mutual written agreement of the parties." Accordingly, this letter will confirm our recent discussions in which we agreed to terminate the Supply Agreement pursuant to section 5 and on the following terms:

1.   **Termination**

Upon and subject to the terms and conditions of this Agreement and effective as of the date hereof, the parties hereby terminate the Supply Agreement and all the rights and obligations of the parties under the Supply Agreement such that neither of the parties shall have any past, present, or future rights, obligations or liabilities under the Supply Agreement.

2.   **Release**

Except as expressly set forth in this Agreement, each of the parties hereby releases the other party and its respective directors, officers, and employees from any and all actions, causes of action, claims, possible claims, or other liabilities or obligations of any nature whatsoever under, in respect of or arising out of the Supply Agreement and the actions of the parties under the Supply Agreement.

3.   **Successors and Assigns**

This Agreement shall be binding upon and enure to the benefit of the parties and their respective successors and assigns.

4.   **Governing Law**

This Agreement shall be interpreted and construed in accordance with the laws of the province of British Columbia and the laws of Canada applicable therein and shall be treated in all respects as a British Columbia contract.

5. Further Assurances

Each of the parties shall, at all times and from time to time hereafter and upon every reasonable written request from the other party to do so, execute, deliver, or cause to be made, done, executed, and delivered all such further acts, deeds, assurances, and things as may be required for more effectually implementing and carrying out the true intent and meaning of this Agreement.

6. Confidentiality

No disclosure by way of publication or otherwise of the Supply Agreement or this Agreement or any part thereof or hereof or the subject matter thereof or hereof shall take place by any of the parties save for such disclosure as is authorized by the parties in writing; may be necessary to implement the obligations of the parties under this Agreement; or, as may be necessitated by law.

7. Authority

Each of the parties has full power and authority to enter into and perform this Agreement, and the persons signing this Agreement on behalf of each have been properly authorized and empowered to enter into this Agreement.

Would you please indicate your agreement with the terms and conditions set forth in this Agreement by signing and dating the duplicate copy of this letter in the space provided below and returning it to Yourco, whereupon this Agreement shall constitute a valid and binding obligation of each of the parties to this Agreement.

Yours truly

[*Insert name and signature of Yourco's signing officer*]

I confirm my agreement with and acceptance of the terms of this Agreement.

Dated this _____day of _____, 20--.

[*Name of recipient*]

By: _____

Name: _____

Title: _____

Contract

THIS AGREEMENT, made the _____ day of _____, 20--, between **Two Suns In The Bay Marine Ltd.** (the **"Lessor"**) and _____, an individual residing at _____ (the **"Lessee"**).

WITNESSES THAT, for good and valuable consideration (the receipt and sufficiency of which is hereby acknowledged by the parties), the Lessor and the Lessee agree as follows:

1. **Lease of Boat** — Subject to the terms of this Agreement, the Lessor hereby leases to the Lessee the boat and ancillary equipment (collectively, the **"Boat"**) described in Schedule A to this Agreement for the term (the **"Term"**) set forth in Schedule A.

2. **Title to Boat** — The only right to the Boat granted to the Lessee under this Agreement is the right to retain and use the Boat during the Term, on the terms of this Agreement. The Lessee acknowledges and confirms that title to and ownership of the Boat will remain with the Lessor at all times throughout the Term.

3. **Rent** — The rent (the **"Rent"**) payable for the Boat by the Lessee under this Agreement is as set forth in Schedule A. The Rent is payable in full and in advance together with all applicable sales, use, goods and services, and other taxes properly payable under applicable law. The Lessee is also responsible for the payment of all gas and oil used in the operation of the Boat during the Term.

4. **Use of Boat** — The Lessee will —

    (a) keep and use the Boat only for the purposes for which it was manufactured and intended;

    (b) not alter the Boat in any manner;

    (c) take reasonable care to protect the Boat from damage, theft, loss, fire, and unreasonable wear and tear;

    (d) operate the Boat according to applicable laws, by-laws, rules, regulations, and codes or other enactments of competent authorities;

    (e) store and service the Boat according to any operating or other instructions supplied with the Boat or as directed by the Lessor; and

    (f) operate the boat in a safe manner exercising due care and skill.

5. **Return of Boat** — The Lessee will return the Boat to the Lessor prior to the expiry of the Term and in the same condition as it was in at the time of delivery to the Lessee under this Agreement (reasonable wear and tear excepted). The Lessee will return the Boat with not less than the amount of gas in the engine(s) as was present at the commencement of the Term.

6. **Overholding Rent** — If the Lessee fails to return the Boat to the Lessor prior to the time of expiry of the Term, then, in addition to any other damages the Lessor may suffer as a result, the Lessee agrees to pay to the Lessor, for each 24-hour period (or part thereof) after expiry of the Term and prior to the return of the Boat to the Lessor, overholding rent ("Overholding Rent") at the same rate as the Rent. The Lessee agrees that it will pay any Overholding Rent on demand together with all applicable taxes and charges.

7. **Risk** — The Lessee acknowledges and confirms that —

    (a)   it is using and operating the Boat at its own risk; and

    (b)   the Lessor will not be liable to the Lessee or any third party for any loss, damage, injury, or death caused by the Boat or use of the Boat at any time after its delivery to the Lessee and prior to acceptance of its return by the Lessor.

8. **Indemnity** — The Lessee hereby indemnifies and saves the Lessor harmless from and against any and all claims, demands, liabilities, losses, costs, fines, penalties, damages, and expenses which may be suffered or incurred by the Lessor arising out of any damage to or loss of property, or injury to or death of any person, or arising from the use, operation, storage, or transportation of the Boat at any time after its delivery to the Lessee and prior to acceptance of its return by the Lessor.

9. **Licenses, Permits, etc.** — The Lessee represents and warrants to the Lessor (and acknowledges that the Lessor is relying on such representation and warranty in agreeing to lease the Boat to the Lessee) that the Lessee —

    (a)   is and will remain throughout the Term duly qualified to use and operate the Boat; and

    (b)   holds all necessary licenses, approvals, certificates, and permits to allow and enable it to lease the Boat from the Lessor on the terms of this Agreement.

10. **Disclaimer** — The Lessor does not make any warranty, representation, or condition in favour of the Lessee with respect to this Agreement, the Lessor, or the Boat, whether express or implied, collateral, statutory, or otherwise, including any with respect to the fitness or condition of the Boat (including fitness for any particular purpose). The Lessee acknowledges that it has inspected the Boat prior to signing this Agreement and that the Boat is in good order, appearance, and condition and is satisfactory for the Lessee's intended purpose.

11. **Termination** — In the event that the Lessee breaches any term of this Agreement, the Lessor may at any time after the breach terminate this Agreement, with or without notice to Lessee. Regardless of whether the Lessor has terminated this Agreement, it may, in the event of default by the Lessee, demand immediate return of the Boat and will be entitled to repossess the Boat by any method permitted by law. In so doing, the Lessor, its employees, and its agents may use reasonable force to gain entry to any premises of the Lessee where the Boat may be located without liability for damage caused or for trespass or any other liability whatsoever. Termination of this Agreement as a result of the Lessee's default will not relieve the Lessee from any of its obligations to Lessor, including its obligation to pay Rent, nor will the Lessor's election to terminate this Agreement or to repossess the Boat preclude the Lessor from exercising any other remedies available to it at law, including its right to claim and recover damages for breach of contract.

12. **General** — This Agreement constitutes the entire agreement between the Lessor and the Lessee with respect to the rental of the Boat. Schedule A forms part of this Agreement and is incorporated into this Agreement by this reference. No amendment of any term of this Agreement is binding on the Lessor unless first approved by the Lessor in writing and signed by a duly authorized employee or representative of the Lessor. Neither this Agreement nor any of the Lessee's rights, obligations, or benefits under this Agreement may be assigned by the Lessee without the prior written consent of the Lessor. This Agreement is governed by the laws of the Province of Ontario and the laws of Canada applicable therein.

IN WITNESS WHEREOF, the parties have executed this Agreement as of the date first written above,

TWO SUNS IN THE BAY MARINE LTD.

by: _____
Authorized Officer

_____
Signature of Witness

_____
Signature of Lessee

_____
Name of Witness (Please Print)

_____
Name of Lessee (Please Print)

SCHEDULE A

Description of Boat: [*Insert detailed description of Boat, including serial number, make and model, engine, and related equipment.*]

_____

_____

_____

_____

_____

_____

_____

_____

Term: From and including   , 20--, to

3:00 p.m. on   , 20--.

Rent: $_____, plus applicable taxes.

Ten Guidelines for Drafting the Perfect Contract

1. **STRUCTURE YOUR CONTRACT ACCORDING TO A LOGICAL SEQUENCE OF EVENTS**

   By structuring your contract according to a logical sequence of events, you make it easy to read and easy to understand. In many ways, a good contract should read like a good book. Start by setting out the background information: the date, the parties to the contract, the events leading up to the contract, and definitions of key terms. Then, state what the parties are going to do. Finally, elaborate on the where, when, why, who, what, and how of what the parties are going to do. The result is an organized and informative document that should serve you well in the resolution of any disputes.

   Example:

   Do not write: "On September 2, 20--, goods will be delivered to the buyer, a company incorporated under the laws of Ontario as 7654321 Ontario Ltd. The goods will be delivered to the buyer by the seller, a company incorporated in British Columbia as 1234567 B.C. Inc. The buyer agrees to buy the goods from the seller and the seller agrees to sell the goods to the buyer. In this agreement, the term "goods" means 14 RBO Low Radiation Computer Screens."

   Rather, write: "The buyer is a company incorporated in Ontario as 7654321 Ontario Ltd. The seller is a company incorporated in British Columbia as 1234567 B.C. Inc. In this agreement, the term "goods" means 14 RBO Low Radiation Computer Screens. The buyer agrees to buy the goods from the seller and the seller agrees to sell the goods to the buyer. The seller will deliver the goods to the buyer on September 2, 20--."

2. **WRITE IN THE ACTIVE VOICE**

   By writing in the active voice, there is never any question as to who is performing what action. This is particularly important in a contractual setting because the parties should always know exactly which party is being obligated to do something in any given instance.

   Example:

   Do not write: "The goods will be delivered to the buyer on September 2, 20--."

   Rather, write: "The seller will deliver the goods to the buyer on September 2, 20--."

3. **DEFINE KEY TERMS**

   Defining key terms allows you to save space and avoid unnecessarily repeating yourself.

   Example:

   Do not write: "1234567 B.C. Inc. will deliver to 754321 Ontario Ltd. 14 RBO Low Radiation Computer Screens on September 2, 20--. If 754321 Ontario Ltd. decides, within three days of September 2, 20--, that it does not want the 14 RBO Low Radiation Computer Screens, then 754321 Ontario Ltd. may return the 14 RBO Low Radiation Computer Screens to 1234567 B.C. Inc. within seven days of September 2, 20--."

Rather, write: "1234567 B.C. Inc. (the "Seller") will deliver to 754321 Ontario Ltd. (the "Buyer") 14 RBO Low Radiation Computer Screens (the "Goods") on September 2, 20-- (the "Delivery Date"). If the Buyer decides, within three days of the Delivery Date that it does not want the Goods, then the Buyer may return the Goods to the Seller within seven days of the Delivery Date."

Alternatively, you should define your terms at the outset of the contract so that it reads:

In this Agreement, unless otherwise indicated,

"Buyer" means 7654321 Ontario Ltd;

"Delivery Date" means September 2, 20--;

"Goods" means 14 RBO Low Radiation Computer Screens; and

"Seller" means 1234567 B.C. Inc.

Then you can simply write:

"The Seller will deliver to the Buyer the Goods on the Delivery Date. If the Buyer decides within three days of the Delivery Date that it does not want the Goods, then the Buyer may return the Goods to the Seller within seven days of the Delivery Date."

4. FOLLOW THE RULE OF ONE IDEA FOR ONE SENTENCE

By simplifying your sentences, you reduce the likelihood of creating ambiguities. You also make the contract easier to read.

Example:

Do not write: "The Seller will deliver the Goods to the Buyer on September 2, 20--, at which time the Buyer will open the packages containing the Goods, inspect the Goods, and advise the Seller if the Goods are acceptable to the Buyer or will return them to the Seller for a refund if the goods are not acceptable."

Rather, write: "The Seller will deliver the Goods to the Buyer on September 2, 20--. On receipt of the Goods, the Buyer will inspect the Goods. The Buyer will then advise the Seller if the Goods are acceptable to the Buyer. If the goods are not acceptable to the Buyer, the Buyer will return the Goods to the Seller for a refund."

5. AVOID UNDEFINED ADJECTIVES AND ADVERBS

Adjectives and adverbs are often open to interpretation of their precise meaning. Who, after all, can say with any certainty what constitutes "prompt" service or distinguishes "bad" weather from "good"?

Example:

Do not write: "The Seller will promptly deliver the Goods to the Buyer."

Rather, write: "The Seller will deliver the Goods to the Buyer on September 2, 20--."

6. **USE PLAIN LANGUAGE**

   It should not be your intention to impress your reader but rather to inform him or her. The best way to do so is to use plain language in a precise manner.

   Example:

   Do not write: "The parties mutually agree with one another that, in the event that the Buyer is unable to utilize the Goods prior to the 11th day of June 20--, then the Buyer may return same or any part thereof to the Seller forthwith, at that point in time."

   Rather, write: "The parties agree that if the Buyer cannot use the Goods before June 11, 20--, the Buyer may return the Goods or any part of them to the Seller at that time."

7. **BE CONSISTENT IN YOUR USE OF TERMS**

   By being consistent in your use of terms, you avoid confusing your reader.

   Example:

   Do not write: "The Seller will be responsible to replace any Goods that are lost or broken. However, the Seller is not required to replace any Goods that the Buyer has damaged."

   Rather, write: "The Seller will be responsible to replace any Goods that are lost or damaged. However, the Seller is not responsible to replace any Goods that the Buyer has damaged.

8. **AVOID AMBIGUITY, EVEN AT THE COST OF SOUNDING REDUNDANT**

   An ambiguity in a contract is generally always resolved against the person who drafted it. Even if you didn't draft the contract, trying to resolve an ambiguity can mean incurring legal costs and, ultimately, going to court to determine what was meant.

   Example:

   Do not write: "The Seller will transfer the Goods to the Buyer at its premises."

   Rather, write: "The Seller will transfer the Goods to the Buyer at the Buyer's premises."

9. **SAY ONLY WHAT YOU HAVE TO SAY, NO MORE**

   The saying, "Give 'em enough rope..." applies in the contractual setting as much as anywhere else. In addition, saying more than you have to can merely crowd your agreement with inessential information.

   Example:

   Do not write: "The Seller will deliver the Goods to the Buyer on September 2, 20--. The Buyer has a loading dock at which it can receive delivery of the Goods. If that loading dock is unavailable at the time of delivery, delivery may not take place at the loading dock but will have to take place somewhere else."

   Rather, write: "The Seller will deliver the Goods to the Buyer on September 2, 20--."

10. **AVOID LEGALESE**

The term "legalese" refers to the archaic language sometimes used by lawyers. By avoiding its use, you avoid falling into the trap of using impressive sounding words whose meaning you (and anyone else reading your agreement) may not understand.

Example:

Do not write: "Until such time as the parties may agree otherwise, the herein quoted prices shall include, inter alia, the cost of delivery."

Rather, write: "Unless the parties otherwise agree, the prices quoted in this agreement include the cost of delivery."

10
Dealing with Consumers

Everyone has heard the saying, "The customer is always right." But what does the law say?

In this chapter, we examine the legal rights of consumers and how those rights affect your small business. The purpose is to make you aware of what the law expects from you in dealing with consumers and remind you of your legal rights when faced with unreasonable consumer demands.

a. What Is a Consumer?

A consumer is the ultimate end-user of the products or services your business develops, manufactures, or sells. Consumers usually can be split into two categories: "customers," those who use or "consume" your goods; and "clients," those who "consume" your services.

Your legal involvement with consumers is a cradle-to-grave affair. It begins with the design and manufacture of your products and the legal liability a defective product can impose on you. Once the product is manufactured, it (or any services you provide) is subject to packaging, labelling, and advertising laws. Sale of goods legislation also requires you to meet certain legal standards as a seller. Ultimately, everything your business does is subject to the laws governing acceptable business practices.

b. Product Liability

If you manufacture goods, you should be aware that the law imposes two important duties on you concerning how those goods are designed and manufactured. These are —

(a) to take reasonable care in the design and manufacture of your goods, and

(b) to warn consumers about any reasonably foreseeable dangers associated with the use of your goods.

Anyone who suffers personal injury as a result of your failure to meet either of these duties can sue you for negligence. To avoid that possibility, it is worth examining these duties more closely.

1. The Duty to Take Reasonable Care

Every manufacturer of goods has a legal duty to ensure that the goods his or her business designs or manufactures do not create an unreasonable risk of harm for anyone who uses them.

Suppose you are in the business of designing and manufacturing hand-held hair dryers. Competition is fierce, and you are under pressure to create a product that will better meet the needs of consumers. To gain a competitive edge, you design and manufacture a new type of hair dryer that is both lighter and more energy-efficient than any other on the market. However, you had to use a special type of plastic that when heated for an extended period can produce toxic fumes. In this case, the hair dryer clearly creates an unreasonable risk of harm for, simply by using the hair dryer as it is intended to be used, a consumer puts himself or herself at risk of injury. For that reason, anyone who is injured by that defect has a legal claim against you, the manufacturer.

But the law does not stop there. A manufacturer is also responsible to ensure that its products do not present a risk to consumers who put those goods to an unintended yet reasonably foreseeable use. For example, hair dryers are not intended for any use other than to dry hair. However, it is reasonably foreseeable that one be used for some other purpose; possibly for drying clothes. Therefore, anyone who designs a hair dryer that if used to dry clothes presents a danger of injury (e.g., shorting out wires and causing a fire) is potentially liable. Of course, a manufacturer is less likely to be liable if the hair dryer caused injury through some wholly unforeseeable use by a consumer, such as using it as a hammer.

The best way for a manufacturer to avoid the possibility of liability is to ensure that its goods are designed and manufactured with safety as the main priority. As already mentioned, this applies not only to how the goods are intended to be used but also to any unintended but reasonably foreseeable uses as well.

2. The Duty to Warn about Dangers

In addition to the obligation to take reasonable care in the design and manufacture of its goods, a manufacturer is also obligated to warn consumers about any dangers associated with the use of those goods. A failure to do so creates a basis for liability. Moreover, the duty to warn also applies to intended and reasonably foreseeable unintended uses of your goods. A manufacturer of stepladders, then, has a legal duty to warn consumers that standing on the top step could cause the ladder to tip over. Similarly, the manufacturer would have to warn consumers that using the ladder as a base for a scaffold (or some other unintended but reasonably foreseeable use) poses a danger of injury.

There is, however, no duty to warn of obvious dangers. For example, no one needs to be told that a knife can cut the person handling it.

Discovery

To ensure that it meets its duty to warn, a manufacturer should always place its warnings in a conspicuous place on both the goods themselves and the packaging. Furthermore, the warning should always be clear and easy to understand.

3. Summary: The Basis of Liability

In Canada, anyone who suffers personal injury as a result of a design or manufacturing flaw in a product has a negligence claim against the manufacturer. To successfully defend against such a claim, a manufacturer would have to prove that it took all reasonable care in the design and manufacture of its products to ensure that those products did not pose a risk of injury to consumers. However, the facts will often speak for themselves.

Successful plaintiffs are usually awarded compensation for their injuries, including loss of income and any costs of future care.

c. Packaging and Labelling

Packaging and labelling legislation exists at both the federal and provincial levels. Its primary purpose is to help ensure that consumers know what they are buying.

Packaging and labelling legislation applies to all prepackaged products sold in Canada. A prepackaged product is one that is packaged in the container in which it is ordinarily sold to a consumer.

Federally, the two most important items of legislation are the *Consumer Packaging and Labelling Act* (CPLA) and the *Food and Drugs Act* (FDA). These are broad-reaching acts that cover almost every type of prepackaged product sold in Canada. Provincial legislation tends to be less general in scope and is often oriented toward specific types of products or product packaging and labelling issues, such as bilingual labelling.

1. Federal Packaging and Labelling Requirements

Both the CPLA and FDA contain very complex and specific requirements. Much of what you need to know about how to label and package your products (or have them labelled and packaged for use) depends on the kinds of products you produce.

For instance, the CPLA covers most types of prepackaged products — everything from toasters to train sets. Some prepackaged products it does not cover include foods, drugs and medical devices, artists' materials, and products to be used strictly for commercial or industrial purposes and not to be sold to the public. The FDA covers all types of prepackaged food and drugs.

Regardless of the type of prepackaged product involved, nearly all must comply with the following statutory and regulatory requirements regarding labelling:

(a) The label of the prepackaged product must be applied to the container in which the product is displayed for sale to the consumer.

(b) The label must be applied to the main display surface of the product's container.

(c) The container must bear the label at the time it is sold to the consumer.

(d) The label cannot contain a false or misleading representation. (See Section d. below.)

(e) All labels must clearly display the following information, in both French and English:

(i) The generic or common name of the product (e.g., toaster oven, juice, rubber mallet), so that the product can be readily identified. This information must be included on the main display panel of the package.

(ii) The net quantity of the product (e.g., two hockey sticks and a puck). This information must also be included on the main display panel of the package.

(iii) The manufacturer's or dealer's name (e.g., "Manufactured by Hatco International Appliances, Inc."). This information can be shown in either French or English.

(iv) The manufacturer's principal business address. This information can also be shown in either French or English.

(v) Any other information required by law.

In addition to these, there are often requirements relating to the size of the print used (i.e., the height of letters) to display the information on the label, the need for boldface type in certain circumstances, and the appearance of foreign words or phrases.

For prepackaged food and drugs, the FDA raises literally dozens of matters that must be considered when labelling those products. They include issues relating to —

- nutrition information,

- dietary foods and the use of descriptions such as "sugar free" or "calorie reduced,"

- ingredient lists,

- packaging and durable-life dates, and

- the use of descriptive or comparative terms such as "organic," "creamy," "fresh," and "homemade."

As well, the FDA sets out specific labelling requirements for a large variety of foods and drugs, including mixed nuts, cheese, chocolate, artificial sweeteners, cereal, non-prescription drugs, cosmetics, and infant formula. For all these reasons, it is important that you obtain sound legal advice when planning to label your products.

The same can be said about packaging those products. Both the CPLA and FDA contain specific provisions regarding the appearance, construction, and size of the containers in which products can legally be packaged. Some of these include the obligations —

- not to mislead consumers about the size or quality of a product through the use of your packaging. For example, you can't put a pair of regular glasses in a tinted container and sell them as sunglasses; and

- not to package food in a container that can injure the health of anyone eating the food. This might occur if the container is made of a material that leaks toxic dyes onto the food.

2. Provincial Packaging and Labelling Requirements

As noted, provincial packaging and labelling legislation is aimed at specific types of products. As a result, provincial packaging and labelling law covers packaging and labelling of everything from meat and margarine to beer and mattresses. The key is for you to determine whether any of the legislation applies to your business and ensure that you adhere to the provisions of that legislation.

You will also need to comply with the packaging and labelling laws of every province in which you intend to manufacture or sell your products. This raises special issues regarding the use of the French language if you plan to manufacture or sell your products in Quebec.

Under federal law, all mandatory information on a label must appear in both English and French. This usually means nothing more than that the identity of the product and its net quantity must be displayed in French, as there is often little else that is mandatory under the law.

If, however, that product is sold in Quebec, the Charter of the French Language requires that everything inscribed on a product, its container, and anything supplied with it (such as a warranty card) must appear in French. An English version of the same information can also appear, but it must not be more prominent than the French version.

3. Summary

You are liable to a variety of fines if you fail to comply with the provisions of packaging and labelling legislation. Nonetheless, these would likely prove insignificant next to the cost of having to redo your packages and labels. Accordingly, it is imperative that you obtain the advice of someone knowledgeable in this area of the law when labelling or packaging your products.

d. Advertising

Perhaps the best way to promote the use and sale of your goods or services is to advertise them. To do so legally, you must comply with the numerous items of federal and provincial legislation governing advertising in Canada. You should also comply with the ethical and professional codes and standards established by various industry organizations and associations.

Advertising legislation is often aimed at specific types of goods and services. There are statutes covering everything from textiles to tobacco, from cosmetics to non-prescription medicines. Depending on the products you plan to advertise, the provisions of those statutes may apply to you.

Legislation has also been passed to deal with advertising issues generally. There is the federal *Competition Act*, for instance, which because of its general applicability has become the primary legislative source in Canada for determining what you can or cannot legally do to advertise your goods or services.

The *Competition Act's* provisions regarding false or misleading advertising are particularly important to small-business owners.

1. False or Misleading Advertising

Many statutes — both federal and provincial — contain prohibitions on false or misleading advertising. The *Competition Act* is, however, the broadest in scope. It applies to all types of advertising in every medium and covers all of Canada.

The *Competition Act* has various provisions regarding false or misleading advertising done (either directly or indirectly) to promote the sale or use of a product or service.

(a) False or Misleading Representation

Making a representation to the public that is false or misleading in a material respect is an offence under the *Competition Act*. Whether something is "misleading in a material respect" depends on the point of the view of the average consumer. The issue is whether that consumer would, as a result of the overall impression created by the advertisement, have been misled. Industry Canada has provided some guidelines as to what constitutes a misleading representation:

(a) The representation is partially true and partially false, or is capable of two meanings, one of which is false (e.g., "Receive a new dishwasher," if "new" means that your old one will merely be replaced by another dishwasher).

(b) The representation is literally true but misleading since it fails to reveal certain essential information (e.g., "Kids eat free," if the free meal only applies if specifically requested).

(c) The representation is literally or technically true but creates a false impression (e.g., you should not claim, "This air conditioner is quieter than any other available," if the difference is incapable of being detected by the human ear).

(d) The representation is literally true insofar as oral or written statements are concerned, but the accompanying visual part of the representation may create a false impression (e.g., you can't advertise the sale of a particular type of stereo system by quoting its price and then show in the print advertisement another type of stereo system).

The issue of whether a statement is misleading in a material respect is usually resolved by considering whether the false or misleading portion of an advertisement would — had it not been false or misleading — affect the consumer's decision to use or buy the advertised good or service.

(b) Representation without Proper Testing

Making a representation about the performance, efficacy, or length of life of a product that is not based on an adequate and proper test is also an offence under the act. This provision essentially prohibits you, as an advertiser, from misrepresenting the things your products can do (especially in relation to other products) when you have not taken the adequate and proper tests to ensure what you say is true. You shouldn't, for example, advertise that the vacuum cleaner you manufacture has "twice the pick-up power" of other vacuum cleaners unless you've conducted scientifically valid tests that have lead to this conclusion. The onus is on the person making the claims to perform the relevant tests, and the tests must have actually been performed before the claim is made.

(c) Misleading Warranty or Guarantee

The *Competition Act* prohibits you from making a representation regarding a warranty or guarantee of a product (or promise to repair or replace a product) if the form of the purported warranty, guarantee, or promise is materially misleading or unlikely to be carried out. Note, again, that the test of whether a representation is materially misleading depends on the general impression created in the mind of the average consumer.

(d) Misleading Price Representation

Making a misleading representation regarding the price at which a product is, was, or will be ordinarily sold is an offence under the act. If you never sold a particular product at a certain price, you cannot then use that price in comparison with a lower price for which the product is actually being sold. In addition to prohibiting this type of price-related misleading advertising, the *Competition Act* also —

(a) requires that wherever two or more prices are clearly shown on a product, that product must be sold at the lower price;

(b) prohibits you from advertising a product at a bargain price if you are unable to supply the product in reasonable quantities for that product's market, the nature and size of the business carried on by the advertiser, and the nature of the advertisement (though in most cases you can protect yourself if it appears you are contravening this provision of the act by giving out rain checks); and

(c) prohibits selling (or renting) a product at a price higher than the price advertised.

These provisions apply to any way of making a representation, whether orally, in writing, through visual images, or by some other method. Anyone who fails to comply with these provisions is subject to a fine and possible imprisonment (though the latter is reserved for extreme cases). Moreover, you can be sued by anyone who has suffered damages as a result of your false or misleading representations.

2. Promotional Contests

To advertise their goods or services, small businesses sometimes hold promotional contests. Yet regardless of whether you're giving away a blender or a trip to Banff, you must comply with the relevant provisions of the *Competition Act* and the Criminal Code to avoid running afoul of the law. Major provisions are discussed below.

(a) No Purchase Necessary

Contestants must be allowed to enter the contest on a no-purchase-necessary basis. To avoid the application of the illegal-lottery provisions of the Criminal Code, a contest holder cannot require a purchase as a pre-condition of entering the contest. It is illegal, for example, to require someone to buy a pair of skates in order to become eligible to win tickets to a hockey game. Eligibility must always be on a no-purchase-necessary basis.

(b) Element of Skill

The contest must involve a genuine element of skill. Even if no purchase is required, a contest will constitute an illegal lottery under the Criminal Code if a prize is awarded by any game of chance.

The Supreme Court of Canada has decided that a game of chance is one in which there is no element of skill. Recent case law has narrowed this approach by requiring a genuine element of skill to make a contest legal. Accordingly, a simple mathematical question is not enough to avoid legal repercussions. However, a test in the following form has been upheld by the courts as sufficient to avoid the element of chance in a contest:

Step 1: Multiply 25 times 4

Step 2: Add 10,824 to the answer from Step 1

Step 3: Divide the answer from step 2 by 3

Step 4: Subtract 112 from the answer to Step 3

(c) Disclosure of Key Facts

The contest holder must disclose certain key facts relating to the contest. The *Competition Act* requires a contest holder to give fair and adequate disclosure of —

(a) the number and approximate regular market value of the prizes to be awarded,

(b) the areas to which the prizes relate, and

(c) any fact within the knowledge of the contest holder that materially affects the chances of winning.

In practical terms, this means that a contest holder must, at a minimum, disclose the following information — in a reasonably conspicuous manner — to avoid violating the *Competition Act*:

(a) The contest rules

(b) The regional allocation of prizes (e.g., one toaster to be awarded per province), if applicable

(c) That no purchase is required to enter the contest

(d) The chances of winning (sometimes dependent on the number of entries received)

(e) The requirement to correctly answer a skill-testing question

(f) The date on which the contest closes

(g) Where the entry form must be delivered

(h) The date the contest will take place

(d) Contest Information Readily Available

The contestant must not be inconvenienced in obtaining information about the contest. The Marketing Practices Branch of Consumer and Corporate Affairs Canada has published an advisory opinion stating that the contest information must be provided to the participant before he or she is inconvenienced in some way or committed to the contest holder's product or to the contest itself. In other words, a contestant should not be required to listen to your time-share in Windsor pitch before he or she is allowed to enter your contest for a week's stay in Toronto.

Therefore, if you, as a manufacturer, advertise a contest on a product's package, you should not keep the required information inside the package, where it is not accessible at a glance. At a minimum, a short list of the contest rules should appear on the outside of the package. A short list of the rules should also appear in any advertisement of the contest in a newspaper, magazine, or other print media. If the contest is advertised in non-print media (e.g., television or radio), the prospective entrant should be told how to obtain the rules.

The *Competition Act* also requires that the distribution of the prizes is not unreasonably delayed (within 60 days of the draw is usually appropriate) and that the selection of the participants is random (except for the element of skill). In practical terms, this means not granting the right to enter the contest to only a select group of individuals.

Because a variety of federal, provincial, and local laws govern the holding of promotional contests, it is important that every contest you propose to hold first be reviewed by a lawyer. Failing to do so could lead to fines and other penalties.

3. Advertising Codes

In addition to the legal requirements you must meet when promoting your goods or services, there are industry-approved codes of advertising standards. These have been developed by various industry organizations and associations and are intended to supplement federal, provincial, and municipal laws affecting advertising.

Which code applies to you usually depends on the type of business you do. To determine which, if any, apply to you, you can contact Industry Canada, consult trade publications, or simply ask others involved in your industry.

Advertising codes that are not industry specific but which may still apply to you include the Canadian Code of Advertising Standards and the Broadcast Code for Advertising to Children.

The Canadian Code of Advertising Standards applies to all advertising messages in all media anywhere in Canada. It deals with several important issues relating to the promotion of your goods or services, including avoiding deceptive price claims, ensuring the accuracy and clarity of your advertisements, and avoiding the commercial exploitation of human misery or fears. You

can obtain a copy of this code by contacting the Advertising Standards Council.

Discovery

Advertising Standards Canada
175 Bloor Street East
South Tower, Suite 1801
Toronto, ON M4W 3R8
Fax: (416) 961-7904
Website: www.adstandards.com

Canadian Association of Broadcasters
350 Sparks Street
Suite 306
P.O. Box 627, Station B
Ottawa, ON K1P 5S2
Phone: (613) 233-4035
Fax: (613) 233-6961
Website: www.cab-acr.ca

The Broadcast Code for Advertising to Children was developed by the Canadian Association of Broadcasters to deal with issues relating to the broadcast of children's advertising. Among other things, it prohibits placing undue pressure on children through advertising and sets guidelines for scheduling of commercial messages. Compliance with this code is a condition of licensing with the Canadian Radio and Television and Telecommunications Commission (CRTC). You can obtain a copy of this code by contacting the Canadian Association of Broadcasters.

Generally, a consumer does not have the right to sue you if you violate the provisions of an advertising code. Nor, in most cases, can you be fined or imprisoned. An angry consumer (or competitor, for that matter) can, however, complain to the relevant association or organization. The complaint will be reviewed, and if found to be valid, you will be requested to amend or withdraw your advertisement. Not to comply with that request is to risk losing your good name among both consumers and others in your industry.

4. Summary

To avoid running afoul of the law when advertising your goods or services, be sure —

* to fairly and accurately represent your goods and services to consumers;

* to fairly and accurately represent the price of your goods or services to consumers;

* that any comparison you make to a consumer between your products and anyone else's is fair, accurate, and based on tests; and

* to immediately correct any mistakes in your advertising so that consumers become aware of the mistake before they are inconvenienced. For example, a consumer who reads in a newspaper that you are selling a certain brand of shoe at a discounted price should not have to come into your store to find out that the advertisement was wrong. Instead, you should have the newspaper reprint the false portion of the advertisement with the correct information. In addition, you should place a correction notice in your store window.

e. Sale of Goods

Each province and territory in Canada has what is known as sale of goods legislation. This legislation codifies the law governing sales contracts.

1. What Is a Sales Contract?

As its name suggests, a sales contract is one in which a seller agrees to transfer ownership of goods to a buyer in exchange for money. It's the kind of contract your business enters into whenever it sells goods to or buys goods from someone. In this context, "goods" covers everything from pins to tractors but does not include interests in real estate, money, or shares in a company.

Under sale of goods legislation, a contract for services is not a sales contract unless it also involves a sale of material and the buyer is paying primarily for the materials rather than for the labour.

A lease is also not a sales contract unless, on the expiry of the lease, the lessee exercises an option to buy the leased goods.

A contract for a conditional sale of goods is a sales contract under the legislation. A conditional sale is typically one in which the buyer takes possession of the goods (and takes them home, for example) but the title or ownership of the goods remains with the seller until the buyer meets some sort of pre-determined condition, such as paying the full purchase price. A typical conditional sale is the "buy now, pay later" deals some furniture or appliance stores offer.

A contract for the sale of goods is subject to all rules that apply at law to contracts (see Chapter 9, Contracts). This means, among other things, that the contract does not have to be in writing. It also means that a sales contract is completed if there has been an offer (either to buy or sell), an acceptance of that offer by the other party, and the giving of consideration.

Because it applies to every sales contract into which your business enters (whether as a buyer or a seller of goods), you should be aware of some of your rights and obligations under sale of goods legislation.

2. The Obligation to Carry Out the Terms of the Contract

Sale of goods legislation provides that unless a sales contract is frustrated, both the buyer and the seller are required to carry out their obligations under the contract and comply with the provisions of the legislation. (See Chapter 9, Contracts, for a discussion of the meaning of "frustrated.")

(a) What Are the Seller's Obligations?

Under sale of goods legislation, the primary obligation of the seller is to deliver the goods to the buyer (or to whomever the buyer says the goods should be delivered). To deliver the goods means to voluntarily transfer possession of the goods.

As a seller, you should be aware of the three features of sale of goods legislation regarding your obligation to deliver: what you must deliver, when you must deliver it, and to where you must deliver it.

First, you must deliver the quantity and quality of goods that the buyer purchased. The buyer may reject all the goods and return them to you if the quantity is either less or more than the buyer agreed to buy or if the quality is different from the quality the buyer agreed to buy. A buyer may also reject any quantity of goods that is more than the quantity he or she agreed to buy and keep the rest, provided the buyer pays for those goods at the agreed-on price. The buyer may also keep all the goods delivered, provided again that he or she agrees to purchase them at the agreed price.

A buyer does not have to accept delivery of the goods in installments — that is, in a series of smaller deliveries made over a period — unless you and the buyer agree to delivery in that manner.

Second, unless you and the buyer agree otherwise, you must be ready, willing, and able to deliver the goods to the buyer within a reasonable time after the buyer pays for them. What is reasonable depends on the circumstances. For example, a buyer should receive, at the time he or she pays for them, pre-packaged goods that he or she has removed from your store shelf and brought to your checkout counter. There is no reason for you not to deliver those goods to the buyer at that time. On the other hand, it is reasonable that if someone buys lumber stored off site in a warehouse, the lumber be delivered as soon as it can be accessed and transferred to the buyer.

In most commercial contexts, it is obvious that delivery and payment should be coincidental (i.e., happen at the same time), as in the case of a purchase made at a retail store. Otherwise, a written contract will usually provide for a specific time of delivery, as in the example of the person who bought the lumber. Usually, and unless the parties agree otherwise, goods remain at the risk of the seller until they are delivered to the buyer.

Finally, unless you and the buyer agree otherwise, you must deliver the goods to the buyer at your business premises. You can, however, agree to deliver the goods to the buyer's business premises or anywhere else.

If the goods are located somewhere other than your business premises and the buyer is made aware of this, then that place must be the place of delivery (again, unless you and the buyer agree otherwise).

If you sell goods, be sure that you and the buyer have agreed on each of the above issues. Set out your agreement in writing — whether in a contract, on an invoice, or the back of a napkin — and have the buyer sign that document to evidence his or her agreement.

(b) What Are the Buyer's Obligations?

The primary obligation of the buyer under sale of goods legislation is to accept the goods and pay for them at the agreed price.

As a buyer, you should be aware of three features of sale of goods legislation regarding your obligation to accept and pay for the goods sold to you: what you must accept, when you must accept it, and what you must pay for it.

First, you must accept the quantity and quality of goods that you agreed to buy. If you do not, the seller can sue you for your refusal to take delivery. Of course, you do not have to accept goods of a quantity or quality that you did not agree to buy: you can reject these.

You do not need to tell the seller that you are "accepting" the goods. For example, acceptance may be implied from your behaviour if you keep the goods and don't, within a reasonable time after delivery, tell the seller that you do not want them, or if you use the goods in a way that suggests you have taken possession of them. You can't, in other words, order lumber and build a shed with it, only to say then that you never agreed to buy it and therefore will not pay for it.

Second, unless you and the seller otherwise agree, you must accept the goods within a reasonable time after the seller is ready, willing, and able to deliver them to you. Again, what is reasonable depends on the circumstances.

Finally, you must pay the agreed-to purchase price in exchange for the delivery of the goods. If no price was agreed to, you must pay what is reasonable.

It is particularly important to be aware of your rights as a buyer when dealing with suppliers of your business. As much as possible, strive to set out in writing all details of the quantity and quality of the goods you are buying, the time of delivery of those goods, and what you must pay for them.

3. Implied Conditions

Sale of goods legislation contains several important implied conditions. The conditions are said to be implied because, unless they are specifically and explicitly waived by the parties, they form part of every sales contract. In other words, you don't need to explicitly provide for these conditions in a sales contract — whether as a seller or a buyer — to have them apply. They apply automatically.

(a) The Seller Has a Right to Sell the Goods

The seller must be in a legal position to deliver the goods (transfer ownership of them) to the buyer. If it turns out that the seller was not able to deliver the goods — for example, because they really belonged to the seller's brother-in-law's company — the buyer may rescind the contract and sue the seller for damages.

(b) The Goods Are of a Merchantable Quality

This condition applies in situations in which a buyer buys goods that are not necessarily available for inspection and are bought based on a description; for example, when the goods are contained in a package. Under sale of goods legislation, if the goods are not of a merchantable quality, the buyer may rescind the contract and sue for damages.

It is not clear at law what is meant by "merchantable quality." However, it appears to imply that any goods sold must — based on their description — meet the reasonable expectations of the buyer. Therefore, a circular saw sold as one capable of meeting "all your construction needs" will not be of merchantable quality if the toughest thing it can cut through is a loaf of bread.

If the buyer inspects the goods (as opposed to just the packaging), the implied condition of merchantable quality may not apply. However, this is the case only in circumstances in which inspection would have revealed the deficiency. For instance, if the buyer of the circular saw took it out of its box and saw nothing obviously indicating its lack of strength, the buyer's inspection of the saw would not negate the implied condition. Simply put, you aren't expected to know what is not available for you to know.

(c) The Goods Are Fit for a Particular Purpose

The condition that goods be fit for a particular purpose is in many ways like the merchantable-quality condition, only much narrower in scope. The implied condition of fitness for a particular purpose provides that if a buyer lets a seller know that he or she needs a particular type of good for a particular purpose and further suggests — either by words or actions — that he or she is relying (at least partly) on the seller's skill in informing him or her about those goods, then those goods must be able to fulfil the purpose for which they are being sold. If they do not, the buyer may rescind the contract and sue for damages.

A example of where this implied condition typically arises is where a buyer asks an employee of a paint store to assist him or her in picking out a paint for a particular purpose, such as for a garage door. The implied condition of fitness for a particular purpose will have been breached if the paint runs when it rains.

The buyer need not explicitly state the purpose for which he or she plans to use the goods; the purpose is sometimes obvious from the circumstances. For instance, the purpose of a bird feeder, car wax, or pair of ice skates should be obvious. They should, therefore, be fit to serve the purpose for which they were sold.

(d) The Goods Comply with Their Description

The condition that goods comply with their description also applies where a buyer purchases goods that are not necessarily available for inspection but are bought based on a description. For instance, you agree to buy a bakery good described — whether in words or in writing — as "a three-tier wedding cake with white icing," to be delivered next Friday. Come Friday, you are delivered a raspberry torte. That delivery would be in breach of the seller's implied condition to deliver goods complying with their description. Again, the remedy would be to rescind the contract and sue for damages. Of course, you could accept the raspberry torte (so that you have a cake at your wedding reception). However, if you do, your remedy would be limited to an award of damages.

(e) The Goods Sold by Sample Will Comply with Their Sample

This condition applies only in circumstances of a sale by sample. For example, it applies if a seller shows a buyer a swatch of cloth, and based on that sample, the buyer agrees to buy a quantity of that cloth. It is an implied condition under sale of goods legislation that the bulk will be of the same quality as the sample. The buyer must be given a reasonable time to compare the two after delivery. If the bulk differs in quality from the sample — that is, if the sample is made of cotton and the bulk of polyester — the buyer may rescind the contract and sue for damages.

One or more of these implied conditions may apply in any given situation. For example, a good sold by description may also have been sold for a particular purpose. So, a good described to a buyer as a rechargeable power drill and sold by a hardware store employee to the buyer for the specific purpose of drilling holes in cement will result in the seller's breach of two implied conditions if the drill is neither rechargeable nor capable of drilling into cement.

Because the implied conditions place a heavy onus on the seller, many sellers try to avoid their obligations by drafting exemption clauses or waivers exempting them from liability in case a condition is not met. However, even when exemption clauses are included in a contract, they are not always recognized as valid by the courts. This is particularly true when goods are sold to consumers. Otherwise, sellers could simply exempt everything they sell from the implied conditions under sale of goods legislation. To be effective, an exemption clause must be clear, specific, and not unconscionable in the eyes of a court. Needless to say, what is unconscionable will always be a question to be judged on the facts.

4. Breaching the Contract

Under sale of goods legislation, a seller who has not been paid according to the terms of a contract of sale has several remedies:

* *The right to sue for the price of the goods.* This arises when the buyer has accepted the goods but, for whatever reason, has refused to pay for them. A refusal to pay in-

Exemption Clause

An exemption clause is typically inserted into a contract by a seller of goods when the seller wishes to make it clear that the goods are being bought on an "as is, where is" basis — that is to say, without any promise on the part of the seller as to the quality, condition, or merchantability of the goods or their fitness for a particular purpose. The following is a sample of that type of clause:

The buyer acknowledges and agrees that the seller is selling the goods and the buyer is buying the goods on an "as is, where is" basis. Without limiting the generality of the foregoing, the seller expressly disclaims any and all warranties or representations of any kind (including, without limitation, any warranty existing at common law or under applicable legislation) as to the quality, merchantability, or condition of the goods or their fitness for a particular purpose. The buyer further acknowledges and agrees that it has inspected the goods and found them to be satisfactory for the buyer's purposes.

If you believe that the insertion of the entire clause might be something of a hard sell (i.e., it will scare the buyer off), it may suffice to simply insert the first sentence of the clause into the contract.

cludes a situation in which a buyer is paid by cheque and the cheque is dishonoured.

* ❦ *The right to sue for non-acceptance of the goods.* This arises when the buyer who has not accepted the goods has no legitimate reason not to accept them. In such a case, the seller must mitigate his or her damages (see Chapter 9, Contracts); that is, the seller must attempt to minimize, as much as reasonably possible, the negative effects that follow from the buyer's actions. Usually, the seller must try to resell the goods to another buyer. If the seller resells them at a price lower than the price the first buyer originally agreed to pay, the seller can sue the first buyer for the difference.

Sometimes a buyer does not immediately pay a seller for goods the buyer has purchased, and the seller, fearing that the buyer will not pay at all, treats the buyer as having not accepted the goods and tries to resell them (i.e., tries to mitigate his or her damages). The buyer may — in the spirit of "the best defence is a strong offence" — sue the seller for failure to deliver the goods. This is a tricky legal matter and must be approached with caution. You should seek out sound legal advice in any situation involving non-acceptance or non-payment by the buyer of your goods.

A buyer who has not received delivery of the goods purchased in accordance with the sales contract has recourse to the following remedies:

* ❦ *The right to rescind the contract and reject the goods.* This right arises when the buyer has not accepted the goods and a condition of the sales contract has been breached.

* ❦ *The right to sue for specific performance.* This would require the seller to deliver the goods to the buyer in the manner determined by the courts. (See Chapter 9, Contracts, for a further discussion of the meaning of "specific performance.")

* ❦ *The right to sue for damages for non-delivery.* This right arises when the seller refuses to deliver the goods in accordance with the terms of the sales contract. In these circumstances, a buyer must mitigate his or her damages by, for example, seeking to acquire similar goods from another seller. If the buyer must acquire them at a price higher than agreed to with the

original seller, the original seller may be sued for the difference.

A situation may occur in which a seller does not immediately deliver goods the buyer purchased. The buyer may decide to mitigate his or her damages by purchasing similar goods elsewhere and suing for non-delivery (assuming the buyer has already paid). The seller may — as part of his or her own "the best defence is a strong offence" approach to business relations — sue the buyer for non-acceptance, thereby effectively reversing the liability. Again, sound legal advice is needed to ensure that the buyer protects his or her rights.

5. Summary

Sale of goods legislation offers several types of legal protection to both seller and buyer under a sales contract. For consumers, it is a particularly useful tool for ensuring that they get the full benefit of their bargains. The implied conditions of merchantable quality, fitness for a particular purpose, and compliance with description are broad enough in scope to allow any consumer with a legitimate complaint about goods they purchased to demand a refund. Your options as a seller are to refuse the refund or cheerily comply. If the demand is unreasonable, if it clearly has no basis in the law, you can refuse. However, if the complaint seems legitimate, your best course of action — from both a business and a legal perspective — may be simply to refund the buyer his or her money or offer an exchange.

f. Business Practices

Your potential business liability extends beyond the sale of your goods and services. Indeed, most provinces have legislation of general application, designed to deal with issues relating to unfair business practices. The purpose of the legislation is to ensure that you conduct your business in an ethical manner, dealing fairly with consumers and others.

The following are among the types of unfair business practices prohibited by the legislation:

* Taking advantage of a consumer's physical infirmity, ignorance, illiteracy, or inability to understand the language

* Charging the consumer a price that grossly exceeds the price at which similar goods or services can be purchased

* Making a misleading statement of opinion on which the consumer is likely to rely to his or her detriment

* Selling something to a consumer that the consumer has no reasonable possibility of paying for in full

* Making false, misleading, or deceptive representations to the consumer

* Subjecting the consumer to undue pressure

A business engaging in any of these unfair practices is subject to a stiff penalty. Anyone who engages in such practices is subject to a fine or imprisonment. Moreover, the consumer can rescind the contract and sue for damages. Finally, unfair practices amounting to fraud can result in criminal charges being laid.

If this is not enough to convince anyone to conduct a small business in a fair and ethical manner, consider the potential losses associated with a bad reputation among consumers. Those losses can make a fine or penalty seem small in comparison.

g. Summary

As the market for goods and services becomes more complex and consumers become more educated about their rights, small businesses are under increased pressure to be both better aware of their obligations to consumers and more mindful of their own rights under the law.

In addition to the various types of consumer protection legislation noted above, there are literally dozens of smaller items of consumer protection legislation, dealing with everything from safety standards on hockey equipment to motor vehicle leasing, from health club membership to loan brokering, from farm equipment to household appliances.

The key is to know the demands of your industry, understand the needs of those who buy your goods or services, and deal with people in a fair and ethical manner.

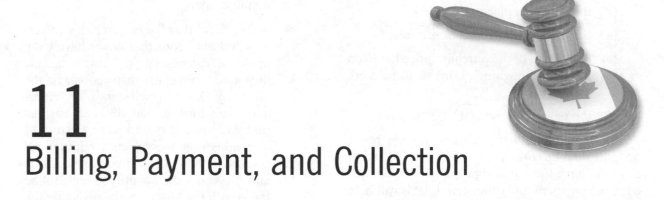

11
Billing, Payment, and Collection

Running a successful small business means providing consumers with high-quality goods and services. It also means being paid for those goods and services. After all, that's where your profits come from.

This chapter examines the legal issues associated with billing for the goods and services you provide and also looks at the legal issues affecting the different methods by which you can be paid — and what you can do to collect money owing to you.

a. Billing

The first step in ensuring your payment for your goods and services is, perhaps obviously, to ask for it.

Every sale, whether of a good or service, takes the form of a contract in which the buyer offers to purchase those goods or services and the seller accepts the offer. The seller then provides the goods or services in exchange for the buyer's payment of the purchase price.

Under sale of goods legislation, the buyer must pay for the goods it receives at the time it receives them, unless the parties otherwise agree. The common law requires the same where

you provide services. This arrangement places relatively few obligations on you when requesting payment: the requirement to pay is dictated by law. However, the following issues are nonetheless worth considering.

1. Communicating the Purchase Price

The price for which you are willing to sell your goods and services should be clearly communicated to the buyer. This is particularly important if the buyer is not required to pay the whole of the purchase price at or before the time he or she takes possession of the goods (or receives your services). Any dispute about the purchase price after that time will be difficult to resolve in the absence of some objective evidence that clearly indicates that the whole of the purchase price has not been paid and that further payments are required.

For that reason, you must issue a written bill or invoice with the sale of your goods or services. The bill should indicate, at a minimum —

(a) the date on which the goods or services were purchased,

(b) the nature of the goods or services (i.e., a description of what was bought),

(c) the buyer's name and your business name,

(d) the date and place of delivery,

(e) the price of the goods or services,

(f) how much of the purchase price has been paid and how much remains to be paid, and

(g) the payment terms (see below).

Your bill should be delivered to the buyer no later than the time the goods are delivered. If possible, have the buyer sign the bill to acknowledge the payment and other terms. This will help resolve any disputes about those matters in the future. (Sample 9 at the end of this chapter is a sample bill of sale that you, with a few modifications, can use in your own business.)

2. Setting the Payment Terms

When billing a client or customer, you must communicate the payment terms, including the following:

* A statement of the purchase price

* A statement of when the purchase price or portions of it are to be paid (e.g., "$200 on delivery plus monthly payments of $100 each, to be made on the first day of each calendar month, until the purchase price is paid in full")

* The methods of payment acceptable to you (e.g., cash or credit card)

* To whom payment is to be made (e.g., "All payments must be made by cash or certified cheque payable to the order of "Inge's Flags and Insignias, Inc."")

In addition, your bill should set out these and any other relevant terms relating to payment:

* Any refund allowances. For example, you might indicate on the bill, "All sales are final." Alternatively, you might write, "Any request for refunds must be accom-

panied by this invoice," or whatever else might apply.

* A statement that the bill excludes any errors and omissions that might have been made in calculating it. This is usually indicated by placing conspicuously on the bill "E. & O. E.," which stands for "errors and omissions excluded" and ensures that you are not bound to any errors or omissions that the bill may contain. Of course, if there is an error or omission and it favours the buyer, you will still be faced with the task of both correcting the error and convincing the buyer that the original bill was wrong.

* Any interest or service charges due on late payment.

3. Providing Estimates

It is a common practice — especially for those in service industries — to provide clients with an estimate of the cost of the goods or services to be provided. Doing so in a manner that will not unfairly prejudice your rights means you must fully consider what a particular job entails. Take into account the hours of work needed to complete it, labour requirements, the costs of any materials, and perhaps most important, any contingencies that may arise. Then provide the client with a written estimate for the job. The estimate should, at a minimum, set out —

* a description of the work to be carried out (e.g., "Sanding and refinishing hardwood floor in living room");

* any assumptions on which the work to be done is based (e.g., "The client has requested that an oil-based varnish be used");

* any work that will not be done by you but that might typically be done by someone doing the same or a similar job (e.g., "The client will remove all furniture from the

living room and replace it when the job is finished." This will preclude the client from arguing that you were to move furniture as part of the price of your services);

* the date on which the estimate is provided and the last date on which it will apply (e.g., you should state that the estimate is valid for ten days from the date of the estimate); and

* a statement that the estimate is an estimate only and, as such, subject to adjustment due to changes in circumstances or the nature of the services to be provided.

All this is crucial for two reasons. First, the estimate — whether written or not — will, in the absence of any final contract, compose the contract between the parties regarding the work to be provided. In other words, you will be legally bound to the terms of the estimate. Be sure you get them right.

Second, even if the estimate is not considered the final contract between the parties, it will probably serve as an important piece of evidence regarding the parties' intention. For instance, if you and the client disagree on the date that the job was to have been finished, a court might look to the estimate to see if it resolves the issue. A court can also resort to the estimate to resolve any issues about the purchase price. For that reason alone you should exercise special caution when providing estimates.

b. Payment

You have communicated the purchase price of your goods or services to the buyer, and the buyer has agreed to pay it. The question now is, by which method will the buyer pay?

1. Cash

From a legal perspective, cash is the best way to be paid. Apart from receiving counterfeit bills, there are relatively few legal issues associated with being paid in cash. The following points are, however, worth noting:

* You are not required to be paid in cash if you do not wish to be paid in cash.

* You are not required to accept the currency of any other country if offered to you or to exchange that currency for Canadian currency.

* You are not required to accept a torn bill if one is offered to you.

It is a crime for you to possess counterfeit money or to have been in possession of it. However, to convict you of that crime, it must be proven beyond a reasonable doubt that the money was counterfeit, that you had it in your possession, and that you knew it was counterfeit. If you suspect money that has been passed to you is counterfeit, advise the police.

2. Cheque

A cheque is defined in the federal *Bills of Exchange Act* (BEA) as "a bill drawn on a bank, payable on demand." Despite this definition's apparent simplicity, you must jump through several conceptual hoops to understand how a cheque works.

To begin, a cheque is a negotiable document: the person holding the cheque can demand delivery of cash on the terms set out in the cheque.

"Holding" a cheque means both physically having it in your possession and being either the person named on the cheque as the one to whom the funds are payable (the payee) or the person in whose favour the cheque has been endorsed (the endorsee).

An endorsed cheque is one that has been signed on the back by the payee, who thereby becomes the endorser. Nothing else is required at law to endorse a cheque. Anyone in physical possession of the endorsed cheque becomes its holder and is then entitled to negotiate it on its terms.

Estimate Contract Provision

Add the following provision to any estimate you may provide to a client for your goods or services. (You can modify it for use in your business.)

Prices quoted in this Estimate are for the goods and services only as set forth in this Estimate and are subject to change in the event of any change in those goods or services. This Estimate and the prices quoted herein expire on _____.

Discovery

Make certain the cheque is dated no later than the same day you receive it. One dated later than that — a post-dated cheque — is not negotiable until that later date. In the interim, plenty of things can happen to render the cheque incapable of being paid, such as a countermand by the drawer.

To negotiate a cheque — to be able to require payment — you must endorse and physically deliver the cheque to a person or entity willing to accept it. The person or entity who receives delivery of the endorsed cheque (the acceptor) then becomes the holder of the cheque in due course. For example, a bank becomes the holder in due course of any cheques you deposit with it. That bank then becomes obligated to pay you cash on the cheque's terms.

Now, if that bank is not the drawee of the cheque — that is, not the bank holding the funds of the person who made the original promise to pay (the person who signed the cheque or the drawer) — then that bank, in turn, must look to receive payment from the drawee bank under the rules established by the Canadian Payments Association or those of one of the several established international clearing systems. Those rules can affect your ability — as the person trying to negotiate the cheque — to receive payment on it.

(a) Pitfalls of Cheques

Before a bank will pay you cash for a cheque you deposit with it, it must be certain that the funds exist to satisfy its own attempts to negotiate that cheque. This is usually not a problem if you deposit a cheque with a drawee bank, because that bank maintains the account on which the cheque was drawn and it can easily determine whether or not there are funds in the account sufficient to satisfy payment of the cheque.

However, if you deposit a cheque with a bank that is not the drawee, that bank must first clear the cheque before it can pay you. That process ultimately entails sending the cheque through the drawee bank's cheque-processing centre and on to the drawee bank for payment. The drawee bank then determines whether or not it can make payment on the cheque and communicates its decision back to the bank submitting the cheque for payment.

If the cheque can be paid by the drawee bank, the funds are sent to the bank that submitted it for payment. That bank then credits your account for the amount of the cheque.

If the cheque cannot be paid by the drawee bank, it is returned to the bank that submitted it. That bank will then return the cheque to you and provide you with an explanation for why it could not be negotiated.

A cheque may be returned to you because, among other reasons —

* the cheque was not signed by the drawer; that is, it appears to have been signed by someone who is not entitled to draw a cheque on the account;

* the account on which the cheque was drawn does not have sufficient funds to pay the cheque; or

* the cheque has been countermanded; that is, a stop-payment order has been placed on it by the drawer.

(b) Certified Cheque: Protecting Yourself When Accepting a Cheque

Unless a cheque has been certified, there is no guarantee you will be able to negotiate it. A certified cheque is one that has been marked by the drawee bank to show that —

* the person purporting to draw the cheque on the drawee bank is, in fact, the person drawing the cheque (thereby eliminating any concerns about the cheque being returned because of the signature appearing on it);

* the cheque is drawn on an existing account with the drawee bank; and

* the account on which the cheque is drawn has sufficient funds to meet the payment required under the cheque.

Once certified, a cheque cannot be countermanded. The drawee bank is deemed to have accepted it and must make payment on it. It cannot, in the absence of fraud or error, refuse to do so. A certified cheque is the virtual equivalent of cash and is your best assurance of being paid when accepting payment by means of a cheque.

If you are not going to require that your customers or clients pay you with a certified cheque, you should observe the following guidelines when accepting uncertified cheques:

* Ask to see the drawer's identification (a credit card or driver's license) to assure yourself that the person named on the cheque as the holder of the account is also the person signing the cheque. Doing so will also allow you to compare signatures. Be sure to write the credit card or driver's license number on the back of the cheque, in case you want to track the drawer down at some later time.

* Make sure you recognize the name of the bank on which the cheque is drawn. In this way you can avoid accepting cheques drawn on non-existent banks. This is particularly important when receiving cheques drawn on foreign banks;

* Deposit the cheque as soon as possible after you receive it. Not only will that help to ensure that the cheque is not countermanded but it will also more quickly let you know whether or not the cheque can be negotiated.

* Hold back delivery of your goods and services (or part of them) until the cheque has cleared.

Discovery

If there is a discrepancy on a cheque between the amount shown in figures and in words, the amount in words is the amount payable. You should, therefore, always ensure that the amount written out in words on the cheque is correct.

3. Bank Draft and Money Order

A bank draft is a negotiable document addressed by a bank either to itself or to another bank. By comparison, a money order is a negotiable document that can be either drawn by a bank (or other financial institution), in which case it is a bank money order, or sold by a bank over the counter to the sender, in which case it is a personal money order.

Bank drafts and money orders are in many ways like a certified cheque because, by accepting one in payment for your goods or services, you are not relying on the buyer's credit. In other words, bank drafts and money orders provide assurance that payment will not be refused by the bank on which they were drawn because of a lack of funds in the buyer's account.

4. Traveller's Cheque

A traveller's cheque is not a cheque per se. The entity (usually a bank) issuing the traveller's cheque is, however, obligated to pay the amount specified on the cheque when it is presented for payment.

Bear in mind, however, that a traveller's cheque must be signed twice: first at the time it is purchased, and second at the time it is being cashed or used to purchase something. The two signatures must match. If they don't, your ability to negotiate the traveller's cheque may be affected.

5. Credit Card

Nearly every business accepts payment by credit card. Indeed, the use of credit cards has become as widespread as the use of cash. Yet the law in this area remains largely undeveloped, and wading through it is no simple task. To simplify matters, the discussion below focuses exclusively on the issues affecting you as the merchant accepting credit cards in payment for your goods and services.

(a) The Contractual Framework

A credit card arrangement takes the form of a contractual framework involving the card issuer (e.g., a bank), the cardholder, and the merchant (your small business). Each party is variously contractually obligated to the others.

The merchant is bound by separate contracts with the issuer and the cardholder, although the latter contract arises only when the cardholder uses the credit card to purchase something from the merchant.

(b) The Issuer-Merchant Relationship

If you, as a merchant, agree to accept a certain credit card at your establishment, you will be asked by the credit-card issuer (usually a bank or finance company) to enter into its standard form merchant contract.

As the term "standard form" implies, there is little to no room for negotiating the terms of that contract. Therefore, you must be aware of some of the obligations you are agreeing to assume. Merchant contracts usually state the following:

* You must allow the cardholder to use the credit card to pay for your goods and services at the named or ticketed price. You do not have the option of refusing to accept the credit card toward payment.

* You cannot charge a fee for the use of the credit card as a means of payment. In addition, you cannot charge a premium on the goods or services when they are bought with the credit card or require that a minimum amount of goods or services must be bought before the consumer may use the credit card.

* At the time of the purchase, you must invoice the cardholder by filling out a sales draft in the form supplied by the issuer. The invoice must also contain the information required by the issuer, including the date and purchase price. Your failure to use the proper slip or to fill it out as required may affect the issuer's payment.

* You must follow the issuer's instructions on how and where the sales slips are to be deposited with the issuer for reimbursement. Again, a failure to do so may affect the issuer's payment.

* You must compare the signature on the card with the one on the sales draft. Furthermore, you must obtain authorization for the use of the card for each transaction from the issuer's authorization centre.

* Regardless of whether or not you obtain authorization, the issuer can still refuse to credit you for the amount of a sales draft in any number of situations, including those in which the buyer's signature is forged, the cardholder returns the goods or claims the services were unsatisfactory, the sales draft is illegible, or you otherwise fail to comply with the merchant agreement.

In addition, the issuer generally requires that you pay a sign-up fee, rental fee (for things such as an imprinter), and a discount fee (the fee the merchant pays) for each transaction.

It is your responsibility to be aware of your obligations and make every reasonable effort to meet them so that there is no basis on which to claim you have breached the contract or to prevent you from recovering payment from the issuer.

(c) The Consumer-Merchant Relationship

Under the issuer's cardholder agreement, the cardholder is contractually bound to reimburse the issuer for any amounts the cardholder charges on the credit card. The issuer is then bound under its contract with the merchant to credit the merchant for that amount, provided that the merchant complies with the terms of the merchant agreement. In other words, the cardholder and merchant agreements do not create an obligation on the part of the cardholder to pay you — the merchant — for the goods and services the cardholder has purchased.

That is not to say that the obligation does not exist. The sale of the goods themselves creates a sales contract between the merchant and the cardholder. That may and should be evidenced by an invoice or written agreement other than the sales draft issued when accepting the credit card, which can then be used in a claim against the cardholder for the purchase price, if the issuer (for whatever reason) refuses to reimburse you for it.

Most merchant and cardholder agreements provide that the issuer is not responsible to the cardholder for any defect in the quantity or quality of goods the merchant provides to the cardholder. Moreover, the cardholder will typically be required under his or her agreement with the issuer to pay the issuer for the defective goods and services the cardholder purchased. As a result, the cardholder will look to you, the merchant, for a refund. Most merchant agreements provide that in such a situation, you must issue a credit voucher to the cardholder rather than provide a refund in cash. You must then deliver a copy of the voucher to the issuer, which will in turn credit it to the cardholder's account.

If you do not agree to provide a credit voucher but instead decide to repay the cardholder in cash, the issuer may not credit you for that repayment.

6. Debit Card

A debit card works by allowing the cardholder direct access to his or her bank account by using a specially designed electronic terminal located at your premises. The account is then debited for the amount the cardholder is paying you for your goods or services. The cardholder gains access to his or her account through the terminal by entering a personal identification number, or PIN. The PIN verifies the authenticity of the cardholder's instructions to debit the account and effectively serves as the customer's signature.

The use of debit cards to pay for goods and services is a relatively new phenomenon. Consequently, the law has little to say on the subject. Your rights and obligations as a merchant are determined by the issuer's contract.

Before you accept debit cards as a method of payment, be sure to carefully read the issuer's contract. It will likely contain many of the same risk-shifting clauses found in credit card agreements, especially for unauthorized use of the card.

7. Summary

It is up to you to choose which methods of payment you will accept. At law, you are not required to accept payment by any specific means unless you contractually bind yourself to do so. That may occur, for example, if you sign a credit card merchant agreement or deliver an invoice to a customer that requires "payment by certified cheque or bank draft." You cannot then refuse payment in that manner if it is offered to you.

Nonetheless, it may be in your interest to offer a variety of payment methods to consumers. That will help ensure that consumers do not avoid doing business with you because of the inconvenience of having to pay you in cash only, for example. It will also ensure that consumers are not caught off guard if they believe that a number of payment methods are available.

c. Collection

You have requested payment and specified the method acceptable to you. All that is left to do is collect.

In most cases, collecting payment will not be a problem. You simply follow the collection procedure for the method of payment selected. For example, if you are being paid by credit card, you must obtain the required authorization, make certain the customer signs the credit card sales slip, and so on.

When collecting payment, be sure to calculate and collect any applicable taxes, such as PST and GST. (See Chapter 14, Taxes.) Your business is legally responsible for doing so and will be held to account for any shortfall.

1. Receipts

Once payment has been collected, you should provide the person who paid you with a receipt. As its name suggests, a receipt is evidence that you have received payment for your goods and services. As such, you should not issue a receipt until you have, in fact, received payment. If you receive partial payment, you should give a receipt only for the amount you were paid.

Sample 10, at the end of this chapter, shows a sample receipt. The one you use in your business need not be as formal as the one illustrated. Instead, you may wish to simply print one from your cash register. Whatever the case, be aware that some jurisdictions require you to provide a receipt to a purchaser in certain circumstances. There are good reasons for providing your customers and clients with a receipt regardless of whether or not you are obligated to do so. A receipt can be used as evidence of, among other things, how much and when you were paid for an item. This is especially useful in collecting and remitting taxes, keeping business records, and settling disputes.

Accordingly, every receipt you issue should, at a minimum, contain the following information:

* What was purchased

* From whom it was purchased (i.e., your business)

* How much it was purchased for

* The date payment was made

* Any applicable taxes and other charges

Take note that you should only ever provide a purchaser with one original receipt for any purchase. If you are signing the receipt, sign only one original. Any copies of the receipt must be photocopies or be marked or otherwise clearly distinguishable as copies. The reason is simple: a receipt evidences payment. A person with two original receipts for the same purchase can claim to have paid you twice. After all, you are twice providing evidence of receipt of payment.

2. Collection Problems

Collecting payment may not always be easy, especially when dealing with an unscrupulous purchaser to whom you have already provided goods and services. Apart from taking legal action (see Chapter 13, Resolving Disputes), you may want to take the following steps should collection problems arise.

(a) Late Payment

Late payment occurs when a purchaser does not pay you for your goods or services at the agreed-on time. Rather, payment is made at some time thereafter.

The best way to avoid problems due to late payment is to ensure that you are paid on time by using the following strategies:

* *Make clear to the buyer when payment is due*. If payment is due after you provide your goods or services, be sure that you provide the buyer with some written indication of the payment due date. This can usually be set out in an estimate or invoice.

* *Don't provide your goods or services until you are paid*. Granted, that will not always be possible. For example, it is unlikely someone will pay you to fix his or her car before you have done so. In retail situations, however, the purchaser should not be allowed to leave the store with your goods until they are paid for in full. If it is part of your agreement with the purchaser that he or she may pay after taking delivery of your goods and services, be sure to have the purchaser sign an invoice or other document to that effect.

* *Don't accept postdated cheques*. Not only can they be countermanded or sent back by the bank because of insufficient funds, but they also don't allow you to be paid immediately.

* *Build incentives into being paid on time*. For example, offer a discount on the purchase price if payment is made earlier than the due date. You can also discourage late payment by charging interest on overdue payments.

If payment for your goods or services is overdue, consider taking the following steps:

* *Immediately let the purchaser know payment is overdue and request the amount owed*. This may be done in several ways, including by a simple telephone call. Document your collection attempts by sending the purchaser written notice, such as a demand letter requiring immediate payment. Sample 11 shows a demand letter.

* *Stop providing work to the purchaser until all payments are up-to-date*. Take this step with caution. For one thing, it may not be wise to do this if the customer is an important one who provides you with ongoing business. Just as important, the terms of any contract should be examined to ensure that they do not prevent you from taking this step.

* *Do not extend any credit or other indulgences to the purchaser until all payments are up-to-date*.

D i s c o v e r y

To prevent loan sharking and other unscrupulous practices, the Criminal Code prohibits interest being charged at a rate higher than 60 percent per year. Whether you are charging such a rate will be determined in accordance with generally accepted accounting principles. Under the federal *Interest Act*, wherever any interest is by the terms of a written agreement (e.g., an invoice) made payable at a rate or percentage per day, week, month, or other period less than a year, that agreement must state the annual rate of interest applicable or no rate higher than

5 percent may be charged. In other words, if your overdue account statement indicates that, "All overdue accounts will bear interest at 2 percent per month," it must also state the annual nominal rate of interest being charged (i.e., 24 percent, that is, 12 x 2 percent). Note that the annual nominal rate does not take monthly compounding into account, which when calculated would make the effective annual rate of interest (what will actually paid) equal to 26.8 percent.

If payment continues to be late despite these efforts, your only option may be to take legal action against the purchaser. (See Chapter 13, Resolving Disputes.)

(b) Partial Payment

Accepting partial payment for your goods and services when full payment is due can lead to problems. For example, the purchaser might assert that your acceptance of the partial payment actually represents payment in full.

To ensure that your legal rights are protected when accepting partial payment, indicate to the purchaser in writing and at the time of payment that what you are accepting on account of the purchase price is a partial payment only and not payment in full of the account.

For instance, if you accept $100 for a $400 item, you should mark the invoice, "$100 paid on account of the purchase price of $400, $300 remaining due and owing, dated July 20, 2002." In addition, have the purchaser acknowledge the amount outstanding by initialling your notation.

You should be vigilant about demanding payment of any outstanding amounts. Again, a demand letter should be used.

(c) No Payment

There are any number of reasons why you might not be paid for your goods or services. The purchaser may forget to pay you, may refuse to pay you (e.g., because he or she was not satisfied with your goods or services), or simply cannot pay you (e.g., he or she does not have the money).

To avoid these situations, you should follow the guidelines set out above for late or partial payment. If it is clear you are not going to be paid at all, you should still write and send a demand letter to the purchaser requiring payment by a certain date. You may, if you wish, state in your letter that if you do not receive payment in full by the specified date, you will take whatever legal action is necessary to enforce your rights. If payment is not made as demanded, you should consider beginning legal action against the buyer.

Discovery

Nearly every province has enacted legislation creating a lien — a right that allows you to retain possession (or some other claim) over property until the debt relating to that property is paid — in favour of a person who repairs or stores goods. In some jurisdictions, you are also entitled to sell the property to recover the amount owing on the debt. Be sure to raise the issue of a lien with your lawyer when dealing with a person who refuses to pay.

d. Summary

Payment, billing, and collection problems are among the most frustrating you will encounter in running your small business. There are few things worse than spending valuable time and energy trying to recover what is rightfully yours. The key, therefore, is to prevent problems from developing in the first place.

Sample 9
Bill of Sale

For good and valuable consideration (receipt of which is acknowledged), _____

_____ (the "Seller")

hereby sells and transfers possession of the following goods to _____

_____, (the "Buyer"):

The Seller warrants that he or she owns and has the right to sell the goods to the Buyer and that the goods are sold free and clear of all encumbrances.

Given under seal on _____, 20____.

Signed, sealed, and delivered to   )

the Buyer in the presence of   )

)

)

_____   )   _____

Witness   )   Seller

Receipt

TO: **Kimberley's Books & Philosophy, Inc.**

        Joanne's Coffees Ltd. acknowledges receipt of one thousand and seventy dollars ($1,070.00) as payment for one hundred units of coffee delivered under invoice number 141414, plus GST.

        DATED this 22nd day of March 20--.

JOANNE'S COFFEES LTD.

_____

Name:

_____

Title:

Sample 11
Demand Letter

THE WIDGET MAN

123 Fourth Street
Penticton, BC V2G H6H

April 1, 20--

Jan's Widget Shop
321 Tam Avenue
Penticton, BC V2G P0P

Attention: Ms. Jan Jones, President

Dear Sirs/Madames:

Re: Invoice No. 1414

Please be advised that the cheque enclosed with your letter of March 15, 20--, in payment of the referenced invoice has been returned to us marked "nonsufficient funds."

Accordingly, please take notice that if payment in the amount set forth in the invoice is not received in our offices by **5:00 p.m. April 15, 20--**, we will take whatever action necessary to enforce our rights, including possibly commencing legal proceedings against you without further notice.

Please take note that payment of the invoiced amount must be **made by way of cash or certified cheque.**

A copy of the invoice is enclosed for your ease of reference.

Yours truly,

James May

encl.

12
Employees

Many small businesses hire employees. As a small business person you should be aware of your legal rights and obligations when hiring or firing employees. This chapter examines your rights and considers what the law requires of you as an employer.

a. The Employer/Employee Relationship

1. What Is an Employee?

At law, an employee is someone who does work for you under a contract of service. A contract of service (often referred to simply as an employment contract or employment agreement) is an agreement by which an individual (the employee) consents to provide a business (the employer) with his or her service and by which the business consents to pay that individual for that service.

A contract of service is defined, in part, by —

* the employer's right to set the hours of work for the employee (subject to applicable legislation), including any vacation time;

* the employee's use of the tools, equipment, and premises of the employee;

* the employee's right to receive a salary or wage for his or her work, as opposed to a share in its profit; and

* the employee being subject to the employer's control in such matters as the duties that must be performed, the times at which they must be performed, and how they must be performed.

As you will see, these rights and obligations are in direct contrast to those found in a contract for services or, as it is commonly known, an independent contractor agreement. (See Section e. later in this chapter.)

The employer/employee relationship is primarily a contractual one and so is subject to all the principles of contract law, including those discussed in Chapter 9. Among other things, that means that an employment contract does not have to be in writing to be legally enforceable. A person simply agreeing to do certain work for a business and the business agreeing to pay the person for that work is enough to create a legally enforceable employment contract. Indeed, in a small business, most employment arrangements are made this way.

Other principles of contract law as it applies to the employer/employee relationship are examined later in this chapter. But first, consider the human dimensions of that relationship and how they affect the law.

2. Employment Standards and Human Rights Legislation

The employer/employee relationship is a unique one in law, because although the relationship is a contractual one, lawmakers have consistently shaped the law around its human dimensions. Employment, after all, involves more than a simple commercial transaction; it represents a person's livelihood.

That fact has led to a large body of law being developed to ensure that certain minimum standards exist to protect the interests of employees and potential employees. Employers are usually thought by lawmakers to hold the power in the employer/employee relationship, and therefore legislation designed to protect employees from abuses of that power has been enacted across the country.

Such legislation includes employment standards legislation, which is important to you as a small-business owner and employer because it sets certain minimum legal standards for things such as wages, hours of work, vacation pay, overtime, and termination. Moreover, it applies to every employment contract into which you enter, regardless of whether or not you and your employees agree that it does. In other words, you cannot contract out of employment standards legislation. The standards it sets are standards you must adhere to or exceed. Thus, any employment contract into which you enter — whether oral or written — is deemed by the law to include (in addition to anything else to which you might have agreed) the provisions of the applicable employment standards legislation. Only when a provision of an employment contract exceeds the standard set by the legislation does the contractual provision take precedence (e.g., you agree to provide two weeks' advance notice of termination and the legislation requires only one).

However, employment standards legislation is not the same throughout the country. It varies greatly between provinces. In part, that is because of the vast differences among provincial economies and hence among labour markets. Differing attitudes about the value and nature of certain types of work also play a role in creating differences in employment standards legislation. Finally, such legislation is subject to frequent change by politicians according to their particular economic and political agendas.

In addition to employment standards legislation, federal and provincial human rights legislation also exists. It is designed to ensure the fair and equal treatment of all people in terms of employment, and it specifically prohibits discrimination against an employee or potential employee on the basis of race, ancestry, place of origin, colour, ethnic origin, citizenship, creed, sex, sexual orientation, age, record of offences (e.g., a criminal record), marital/family status (e.g., whether or not someone is divorced or pregnant), or disability. As is the case with employment standards legislation, human rights legislation also varies between provinces, and not every province lists the same grounds of discrimination.

Because of this, any sort of detailed analysis of employment standards, human rights, and other types of legislation in Canada is difficult to provide. It is, however, possible to highlight some of the important legal issues such legislation raises. Furthermore, we can also look into the principles of employment law developed at common law. Finally, we can examine other legislation affecting the employer/employee relationship and consider the purely contractual concerns it involves, all with a view to determining the practical implications for you as an employer and small-business owner.

b. Your Rights and Obligations When Hiring an Employee

The hiring process is perhaps the most crucial stage in any employer/employee relationship. Not only does it set the tone for what follows, but it also lays the foundation for any legal issues that may develop during employment. For that reason, you should take the time to consider the following issues when hiring your employees.

1. Advertising for an Employee

You can advertise for an employee in several ways. Placing an advertisement in the classified section of a newspaper is one way; simple word-of-mouth advertising is another. Regardless of which means you choose, you should be aware that every province has human rights legislation that prohibits you from discriminating in your job advertisements.

For example, you cannot advertise for a "male Class A mechanic" for your garage. To do so would allow an equally qualified female Class A mechanic to lodge a complaint with the relevant governing human rights body. If successful, the complaint could lead to significant fines and require your business to compensate the person complaining.

However, there are exceptions to this rule. For instance, an employer looking for a locker-room attendant for a girls' fitness centre may legitimately advertise for a female to fill that position. Or the publisher of a Danish-language newspaper may legitimately advertise for a

Danish-speaking journalist. The relevant question is whether or not the grounds for discriminating reflect a legitimate requirement of the job. It should not matter to the employer advertising for the Danish-speaking journalist that an applicant is male or female (or even Danish for that matter) as that, presumably, would have no bearing on whether or not the applicant could do the job.

2. The Application and Interview Process

If your advertisement is successful, you will (with any luck) attract one or more candidates for employment. The next stage is to determine which of them is best capable of fulfilling your business needs. That is usually done by requiring them to fill out an application, submit a rÉsumÉ, attend an interview, or any combination of these things. Again, regardless of which method you choose to determine who will ultimately get the job, you must remember the equal-treatment requirements of human rights legislation.

If you require an application form to be filled out, everyone who applies for the job should be allowed to fill out the form and submit it to you for consideration. To not allow this is to suggest that there is some reason apart from job skills to deny a particular person access to the job. If that is not the case (and it should not be), then everyone who wishes to apply for the job should be granted the opportunity to tell you (by filling out the required application form) how he or she is able to meet the position's requirements.

In addition, you must ensure that your application form does not require any information that can be used to discriminate. This is always a tricky matter, as something as simple as a name (Robert versus Roberta) will often advise you of a person's sex. Again, the issue you must consider is whether or not the information requested on your application form is legitimately required for purposes of doing the job. Someone's level of education and previous job experience can have a definite bearing on that person's suitability for the tasks to be assigned. You should, therefore, inquire into those matters. Yet how important is a person's religious background or ethnic makeup to the performance of those tasks? Probably not important at all. Asking about such things can lead only to trouble.

Which brings us back to the issue of requiring something as simple as a name on an application form. On the one hand, it is important to require that it be filled out on an application for purely administrative purposes. After all, if you wish to interview the person, how do you know who to call? But on the other hand, knowing a person's name is — in most cases — equivalent to knowing their sex.

There are two ways out of this dilemma. The first is to follow the common sense approach and ask for a name. You should ask for a home address and telephone number as well. You may even inquire into a person's age, if the position might attract applicants who may not meet the legislative minimum age requirements (see below). But when making the decision about whom to hire, be certain not to allow any of these factors to influence you. In that way, the possibility that you may have discriminated on the basis of sex, for example, is negated by the fact that you did not discriminate on that basis. Of course, you may find yourself having to prove this in front of a human rights tribunal. However, provided you did not discriminate and have an objective basis to support your contention (e.g., by referring to the winning applicant's previous work experience), you should prevail in any dispute.

The second way to avoid the potential discrimination issues raised by application forms is simply to forego them and have job candidates to submit a résumé instead. A résumé is simply a person's written account of reasons for why he or she believes he or she is suited for employment with you. A résumé usually lists a person's education and work experience. It also lists other information the candidate has determined is relevant to your assessment of him or her. Thus, in accepting résumés, you allow the candidates to speak for themselves and you thereby avoid the risk of posing any discriminatory questions. Of course, this does not mean that you can discriminate on a basis of the information they have provided to you. For example, while the advantage of a résumé is that virtually every candidate will voluntarily provide you with his or her name (and, hence, indication of sex), you are still not allowed to use that information to discriminate on the basis of sex, regardless of the fact that you did not request that information.

An interview is another way to determine whether a potential candidate is right for the job being offered. You can interview candidates in addition to or instead of having them submit a written application or résumé. Interviews can also be done after you have reduced the number of suitable candidates on review of the applications or résumés submitted to you. Whatever the case, be sure to follow these guidelines during the interview process:

- *Tell the candidate about the job*. Outline its skill and knowledge requirements, the employee's duties, the rate of pay, the hours of work, and any other relevant information. Stay away from personal matters, both yours and the candidate's. If you wish to engage in small talk, as you perhaps should to help make the candidate feel at ease, confine it to neutral subjects not involving politics, sex, or religion. Talk about the weather offends no one, as Oscar Wilde noted, and always tells you more about a person than the subject matter would suggest.

- *Ask questions designed to elicit information from the candidate that bears directly on his or her ability to do the job*. Do not ask personal or irrelevant questions. What is personal or irrelevant depends, in large part, on whether or not it serves as a basis for discrimination on the grounds outlined above. Again, use common sense. If, for whatever reason, talk shifts to some personal matter relating to the candidate that may, if you consider it when making your decision to hire, constitute discrimination (e.g., if a candidate for a clerical position volunteers to you that she is two months' pregnant), simply explain to the candidate that the matter is not relevant in your decision regarding whom to hire.

✤ *Make notes.* Record what you discussed during the interview and, in particular, how a candidate does or does not fit the job description. These notes should be kept in a safe place so that any alleged contravention by you of the equal-treatment requirements under human rights legislation can be countered with documented evidence. Another way to help you remember what was said and, indeed, obtain further input regarding whom to hire is to have another employee sit in on the interview with you. That person should take notes too and ask the candidate questions relevant to the position. Because discrimination is often based on personal prejudices, having another person present during the interview (or to review any applications or résumés) will help you rebut any claim that your hiring decision was based on your personal prejudices.

To help you with the application and interview process, Samples 12 and 13 show a sample application for employment and list of interview questions you can refer to when preparing your own application form or conducting an interview.

3. Preliminary Considerations in Hiring an Employee

Once you have decided whom to hire, you must make the actual job offer. If the candidate accepts, an employment agreement will have been created at law. Therefore, you should be particularly careful about what you tell an employee at this stage. However, there are some legal issues you must consider even before the offer is made.

(a) Immigration

Under Canadian immigration legislation, Canadian citizens and permanent residents are legally entitled to work in Canada. A permanent resident is a person who is in Canada legally but is not a Canadian citizen. A person who is not either a Canadian citizen or a permanent resident is legally entitled to work in Canada only if he or she has employment authorization from Immigration Canada. No other person is legally entitled to work in Canada. If anyone other than a person legally entitled to work in Canada is caught working, the employer may be liable to a fine or imprisonment or both.

(b) Minimum Age

The employment standards legislation in each province sets a minimum age at which a person may be hired as an employee. That age ranges anywhere from 12 years in British Columbia (with a parent or guardian's written consent) to 17 years in Yukon and Northwest Territories. Note that there are exceptions in certain types of industries (e.g., newspaper routes) and for family members.

(c) Minimum Wage

Employment standards legislation sets minimum wage requirements as well. The minimum wage is the lowest hourly wage rate an employer can pay its employees. With few exceptions, all full-time and part-time employees are entitled to receive minimum wage.

As with the minimum age requirements, there are exceptions to the minimum wage requirements, particularly in the case of students under 18 years of age, employees who serve liquor, and commission salespersons.

(d) Hours of Work

Employment standards legislation provides that no person can be required to work more than an 8-hour workday. In addition, no person can be required to work more than between 40 and 48 hours in any week (depending on the province). Any time worked over and above these hours is (with few exceptions) subject to overtime pay.

You may require your employees to work more than the daily or weekly limit only if an emergency occurs (such as machine breaks down and you have an order to fill) or you obtain a permit from the relevant director of employment standards in your province.

4. The Offer

An offer of employment can take one of two forms. First, you can simply offer the job to the person verbally, telling the person about the job (if you haven't already done so) and advising the person that the job is his or hers if desired, and that person can accept it verbally.

Second, you can make the offer in writing. This is not as difficult as it sounds and is well worth the small effort it requires of you. Simply prepare a letter to the candidate setting out the relevant terms of employment, which the candidate should then sign to indicate his or her acceptance of those terms. If accepted, that agreement becomes a contract — your employment contract — on which you both can rely should there be any dispute. The letter should describe the duties; hours to be worked; wage, salary, and any other remuneration; vacation entitlement; and other relevant matters, such as dress code. Sample 15 shows a letter confirming employment, which you can use with the necessary modifications in your small business.

Of course, you can, if you wish, make a job offer verbally and then follow it up in writing. However, what you say about the job must match what you put in the written offer. In addition, both should match what you said in the job advertisement or at the interview. If there have been changes, let the candidate know before you make the offer. That way you can be assured that there is no misunderstanding.

After the offer has been made and accepted, the employee is ready to begin work. This brings you to the next stage in the employer/employee relationship.

c. Your Rights and Obligations during Employment

Both employer and employees have obligations to each other during the period of employment.

1. The Employer's Obligations to its Employees

Your legal obligations to your employees during their employment are many and varied. They derive from several sources, including the common law, legislation, and your employment contract.

(a) Common Law

You should be aware of the following common law obligations an employer has to its employees:

* *Safety.* An employer is obligated to ensure that employees have a safe work environment, which includes having access to safe tools and equipment. An employee may lawfully refuse to work if his or her employer breaches this obligation.

* *Payment.* Because an employer usually withholds payment to the employee until the work is done, the common law implies a duty on the employer to pay the employee. The employer must not only pay the employee his or her wages but must also reimburse the employee for any expenses the employee had to incur in the course of his or her duties (e.g., the employee's use of his own car) and pay over any gratuities that the employer has received on the employee's behalf (e.g., if a customer adds a tip to a bill in a restaurant and pays the total on a credit card). These common-law obligations are implied in every employment contract.

* *Fairness.* There is a growing body of law that suggests that employers have a common-law obligation to deal fairly

with their employees. Although not yet fully recognized in Canadian law, the duty of fairness implies — as its name suggests — that employers must accord employees fair treatment in connection with such matters as performance reviews and termination. Of course, what is fair depends on the circumstances. It should, however, be viewed as a corollary of the employee's duty of good faith toward his or her employer. (See Section c.2. below.)

(b) Legislation

It would take a book of several hundred pages to outline and discuss all the statutory obligations imposed on employers regarding their employees. But it is worth it to consider some of the more important of these.

* *Meals and breaks*. Employment standards legislation requires that employees receive meal breaks during the workday. In most cases, these must occur if an employee is being asked to work more than a certain number of consecutive hours (e.g., five hours). The breaks usually must last at least one half-hour, and the employer is not required to pay the employee during that time. By the same token, the employee is free to do as he or she wishes with the break. Some employment standards legislation provides for additional mandatory break periods; however, the employees usually must be paid during these times.

* *Overtime*. With few exceptions, employees cannot be required to work overtime. Overtime is typically defined in employment standards legislation as any time worked by an employee that exceeds the maximum number of hours per week an employee may work under the legislation. As a rule, employers must pay overtime to their employees at a rate equal to one-and-a-half times the regular hourly wage.

* *Manner of payment of wages*. Employees must be paid in cash or by cheque at the employee's workplace. As well, there are provisions relating to the frequency with which employees must be paid (usually no less than every two weeks) and the information the employee must be given regarding the pay (the period it covers, source deductions, and so on).

* *Vacation*. Employees must be given an annual vacation after they have been employed by you for a period of 12 months. The length of time allowed for vacation is up to you but cannot, in most cases, be less than two weeks. You, as employer, have the right to decide when employees can take vacation. Employees must be paid while on vacation, generally at a rate equal to some percent of their wages. Vacation pay usually must be paid at the time employees take the vacations.

* *Public holidays*. Provided employees meet the qualifications under the relevant employment standards legislation, they are entitled to a paid day off on days designated as public holidays. You can require those who do not qualify to work on public holidays. If a qualifying employee is asked to work on a paid public holiday and he or she agrees, then the employee usually must be paid on that day and be allowed to take another day off with pay in lieu of the public holiday. If the employee does not take another day off, he or she is entitled under some legislation to one-and-a-half times the regular wage for the number of hours worked on the holiday. There are exceptions to these rules and they apply mostly to tourist and entertainment businesses such as hotels, motels, resorts, and restaurants.

* *Maternity and parental leave*. Provided an employee meets the qualifications of the relevant employment standards

legislation, she is entitled to maternity or pregnancy leave. The length of the leave varies with each jurisdiction; however, it usually lasts about 17 weeks. Both full- and part-time employees qualify for pregnancy leave. In some cases, parental leave is also allowed. Each employee taking pregnancy or parental leave is allowed, under the law, to return to his or her job at the end of the leave. If, during the time of the leave, a new benefit became associated with the job (e.g., the hourly wage went up), the employee is entitled to that benefit.

* *Sick leave*. Most employment standards legislation does not require you to give your employees sick leave. Whether you do so is up to you. That said, terminating someone's employment because they became ill or unable to work is fraught with potential liability. Among other things, it might be considered a violation of human rights legislation insofar as it can be said to amount to discrimination on the basis of a disability. Furthermore, the law tends toward the position that an employee is entitled to paid sick leave. If this matter should arise in the operation of your small business, seek the advice of a lawyer.

* *Minimum wage, minimum age, hours of work*. See Section b. above.

* *Workplace health and safety*. Each province has legislation regulating the prevention of workplace accidents. This legislation provides for health and safety standards applicable to specific industries, and for the duties and obligations of the employer in maintaining and enforcing workplace health and safety, compensating those who have suffered a workplace accident, and penalizing employers who fail to comply with their legislative obligations. You should consider whether or not such legislation applies to you and ensure that you have registered your business with the appropriate workplace health and safety authorities in your jurisdiction.

* *Equal pay for the same work or for work of equal value*. Some provinces have enacted pay equity legislation or added pay equity provisions to other legislation to ensure that men and women receive equal pay for the same work or for work of equal value. Of course, what constitutes work of equal value is not easy to determine. Generally, if one job requires the same level of skill, effort, and responsibility as another job, those jobs can be said to be of equal value. Thus, a factory worker placing labels on the front of a bottle should, all things considered, be paid the same wage as one who places them on the back of the bottle.

* *Employment insurance (EI)*. The *Employment Insurance Act* is a federal statute designed to provide an insurance system for those who find themselves unemployed. For the employer, the first concern is whether or not its employees fall within the definition of persons engaged in "insurable employment." (Most employees of small businesses do.) If so, the employer is required under the legislation to make certain deductions from the employees' pay and remit them to Revenue Canada. In addition, the employer is also required to make contributions on behalf of each its employees engaged in insurable employment. Further information should be obtained from your local Revenue Canada office. Note that a sole proprietor is entitled to make employment insurance contributions on his or her own behalf.

* *Canada Pension Plan (CPP) contributions*. The Canada Pension Plan covers employees in every province except Quebec and

was established to provide a pension to each employee on his or her retirement or disablement. Again, the employer is obligated to take the required deductions from each employee in "pensionable employment" and remit it to Revenue Canada. Moreover, the employer is also required to make contributions on behalf of pensionable employees. A sole proprietor may make CPP contributions on his or her own behalf.

🍁 Income Tax Act *deductions*. Under the federal *Income Tax Act*, employers are required to withhold a certain portion of each employee's salary, wage, bonus, commission, or similar payment and remit the withheld money to Revenue Canada. How much to withhold depends on a variety of factors. Be sure to consult the appropriate government publications available at your local Revenue Canada office.

🍁 *Human rights violations*. The restrictions against employer discrimination under human rights legislation apply throughout the period of employment.

(c) Contract

An employer is legally bound by the terms of the employment contract. The question is, what are those terms?

First, the terms of the employment contract consist of whatever terms you and the employee have agreed to. Setting those terms down in writing (in the form of an employment agreement) will, of course, resolve any dispute in that regard.

Second, the terms of an employment agreement, whether oral or written, may be amended by legislation. As noted earlier, employment standards legislation sets out certain minimum employment standards requirements that cannot be waived or contracted around. If the legislation requires you to give an employee two weeks'

advance notice of termination, then regardless of whether or not you and the employee agree that only one week is necessary and regardless of whether or not you do so in writing, you are still required to give two weeks' notice. To give less is to violate the legislation.

However, if the legislation requires you to give two weeks' advance notice of termination and you and the employee agree (either verbally or in writing) that you will give three weeks', then you must give three weeks' advance notice. Remember, employment standards are minimum standards.

Finally, certain terms may be implied in your contract. This can occur in several ways. As already mentioned, it is implied in the common law that employers have certain obligations as part of every employment contract. Some legislation — notably, employment standards legislation — does the same. Yet your actions, too, can imply certain terms in an employment contract. For example, if your employees are allowed to close shop one hour early every Friday, then unless there is something to indicate otherwise, they may take that as a term under their employment contract. Accordingly, you must clearly distinguish an employee's duties (e.g., to work until regular closing hours) from gratuitous favours (e.g., granting the privilege to close early on certain days).

2. The Employee's Obligations to the Employer

Of course, employees have obligations to their employers. These obligations also have their source in the common law, legislation, and the employment contract.

(a) Common Law

Two common law duties are implied in every employment contract: Duty of good faith and fiduciary duty.

(i) Duty of Good Faith

At common law, every employee owes his or her employer a duty of good faith: the employee must serve the employer honestly and faithfully. This obligation is broad enough to encompass a wide range of employee behaviour and has been interpreted by the courts as a catch-all provision implicit in every employment contract.

Types of employee behaviour that may constitute a breach of the employee's duty of good faith include:

* *Dishonesty*. Employees cannot act dishonestly in dealing with their employer's money and property. For example, an employee cannot sell your products at a price higher than that for which you believe they are being sold and pocket the difference. It is also dishonest if an employee lies to you about an employment-related matter; for example, whether the employee was ill or hurt and so was unable to perform his or her duties.

* *Disclosing your trade secrets or confidential business information*. An employee is not free to disclose your confidential business information or trade secrets — information that gives your business a commercial advantage because it is not known by others. Thus, your employees owe a duty of good faith to you not to disclose or make use (other than for your business purposes) of confidential business information such as customer lists, secret recipes, formulae, financial and marketing information, and supplier accounts.

* *Competing with your business*. Your employees are not allowed to engage in activities that compete with your business, either during work hours or on their own time. This is true, in particular, if an employee makes use of your confidential business information or trade secrets. The chef you employ in your restaurant cannot operate her own catering service on the side (unless, of course, you agree otherwise) and, in particular, cannot use your award-winning secret recipe for Wiener schnitzel in her business.

* *Theft*. Clearly, theft, vandalism, arson, and other types of criminal behaviour by an employee, when perpetrated against the employer, constitute a breach of the employee's duty of good faith.

(ii) Fiduciary Duty

In addition to their duty of good faith, top management and key employees also owe their employer a fiduciary duty. The term refers to a special duty of loyalty that increases in direct proportion to the position of trust an employee occupies in a business. Thus, a fiduciary duty does not usually affect low-level employees but applies to those in positions of power or having special knowledge of the affairs of the business.

Employees subject to a fiduciary duty are forbidden, in essence, to put themselves in a position of conflict of interest with their employer. The employee cannot serve (or try to serve) his or her personal interests at the expense of the interests of the employer. Examples of behaviour creating a conflict of interest include the following:

* *Appropriating benefits that belong to the employer*. Suppose your development company hires an employee to find lands suitable for industrial development. The employee comes across a prime location being offered at a bargain-basement price. It would constitute a conflict of interest if the employee did not convey that information to you but instead used it for his or her own benefit by buying the land and then "flipping" it. In sum, an employee is not allowed to divert the employer's business to himself or herself.

* *Kickbacks*. Your employees cannot accept a kickback, commission, or any other type

of benefit from a person or entity with whom you do business if that benefit might disadvantage you, the employer. For example, your supply manager cannot choose from whom you will purchase your supplies based on whether or not the supplier will offer him or her some sort of personal benefit.

Such opportunities do not present themselves to every employee in an organization but they are often encountered by employees whom the employer has entrusted with a certain responsibility that, if not carried out faithfully, could seriously harm the employer's business. It is to these employees that a fiduciary duty applies.

(b) Legislation

There are relatively few statutorily entrenched obligations of employees to employers. Such legislation exists primarily for the protection of employees. However, most employment standards legislation imposes an obligation on employees to give their employers minimum notice of termination. The amount of notice generally increases with the number of years an employee works for the employer. In some provinces, there are exceptions to this requirement (for example, if the employer breaches the terms of the employment contract). For the most part, however, employees cannot simply leave you in the lurch; they must inform you in advance if they wish to quit.

Legislation other than that covering employment standards also imposes specific requirements on employees. For example, health and safety legislation requires that employees carry out their duties in a safe and careful manner.

(c) Contract

Every employee is legally bound to comply with the terms of his or her employment contract, provided the contract is legally enforceable and no particular term of the agreement violates the employee's statutory rights. For example, regardless of what the employment contract says, an employee is not bound to give you three weeks' advance notice that he is quitting his job if the relevant legislation says that only two are required. Of course, any such term probably would not render the entire agreement unenforceable but would simply be struck from the agreement. The rest of the terms would be enforceable.

If the employment contract requires the employee to start work at 8 a.m., that is when the employee must begin work. If it requires the employee to wash dishes as part of his or her duties, the employee must wash the dishes. If it requires him or her to wear a uniform, the employee must wear a uniform. Because an employment agreement is just that — an agreement — the employee must do what he or she has agreed to do. That is the legal effect of a contract (see Chapter 9, Contracts).

Nonetheless, an employment agreement by its very nature can lead to certain obvious points of contention between the employer and employee whenever a dispute arises between them. The one that most frequently occurs is disagreement regarding what the actual terms of the contract were. Does hiring someone as a waiter in your restaurant mean that person will also have to clean dishes or bus tables? An employer and employee may disagree on that matter. In fact, what they are disagreeing about are the terms of the employment contract; specifically, whether the duties of a waiter include washing dishes or bussing tables. Again, the importance of a written employment agreement over a verbal one is apparent.

Disputes also often develop if an employer unilaterally changes the terms of the employment contract. Suppose, for example, your flower shop is adding a delivery service. You now require those of your employees with driver's licenses to begin making deliveries as part of their jobs. Have you unilaterally changed the terms of the employment contract? That depends on whether or not the new duties of the employee are such that would ordinarily form part of the duties of an employee in similar circumstances. If not, you may not be able to require your employees to take on those new duties without giving some further consideration to the employee — for example, a higher wage. To do otherwise would be to risk breaching the employment agreement. Of course, if the new duties are the kind that would ordinarily form part of the duties of an employee in similar circumstances, the employee is contractually bound to perform those duties.

Thus, along with the common law and statute, your employment contract will play a role in determining your employees' obligations to you. The issue you as an employer must next consider is what to do if an employee refuses to meet those obligations.

d. Your Rights and Obligations When Firing Employees

Suppose an employee is not working out, or you simply no longer require that employee's services. If the employee wishes to leave on his or her own accord (quit), he or she must give you the appropriate notice of termination, and you must fulfil whatever obligations you have remaining to that employee (e.g., payment of final wages, vacation pay).

But what if you wish to terminate the employee's employment with you; that is, fire him or her? What are your obligations? That depends on the manner and reasons for termination.

1. Termination without Cause

In most cases, you may end an employee's employment at any time provided you comply with the relevant statutory termination notice and payment requirements. Exceptions to this rule include the following situations:

* The employment contract has a specific term — for example, two years — in which case to terminate employment before that time, you must pay in full

the wages (and any other benefits) the employee would have received had the contract been carried through to its term.

* The employee is on maternity or parental leave.

* The employee seeks to enforce his or her rights under the applicable employment standards legislation.

Otherwise, an employer may — without reason or cause — simply fire an employee. This is known as termination without cause or termination with notice. However, you must meet certain statutory requirements, the most important of which is providing notice of termination to the employee. Notice of termination refers to the notice you must give that informs an employee that his or her employment is ending permanently. That notice usually must be in writing. Sample 15 is an example of a notice of termination, or dismissal letter.

Although there are significant legislative differences among jurisdictions regarding the specifics of how to provide notice of termination, the employee must almost always be given due notice; that is, notice of termination in accordance with the minimum period of advance notice required under both the applicable legislation and the common law.

The longer an employee has worked for you, the longer the period of advance notice. For example, an employee who has worked for your Ontario business for one year or more but for less than three years is entitled under Ontario employment standards legislation to two weeks' advance written notice of termination. Therefore, the employee must receive notice of termination on or before June 1 for termination to take effect on or after June 15. This allows the employee to prepare for the loss of his or her job.

The length of due notice may be increased beyond that required by employment standards legislation based on factors such as the employee's ability to find work elsewhere, the status of the employee's position, the employee's contributions to your business (including the quality of the employee's work while employed with you), the employee's age, and whatever else might seem customary or reasonable in the circumstances.

It is also worth noting that during the notice period (the period between the time the employee was given notice of termination and the time termination actually takes effect), the employer is not allowed to change the terms of the employment contract. You cannot lower the employee's wages during the notice period or change the employee's hours.

Perhaps most important, however, employers should be aware that instead of providing due notice, an employer may simply terminate the employment effective immediately and provide the employee with termination pay (or, as it is sometimes called, pay in lieu of notice).

In the simplest terms, termination pay is the pay to which the employee would have been entitled during the notice period, had he or she continued to work for you during this period: the amount of termination pay to which the employee is entitled is equal to what the employee would have received during the relevant notice period. If someone is entitled to two weeks' advance notice of termination, you may simply terminate the person's employment effective immediately and provide him or her with a cheque for two weeks' pay. This is a useful course of action when you wish to be rid of the employee right away, especially if you fear that he or she might disrupt the work environment during the notice period.

When choosing this route, the employee's benefits must continue throughout the notice period. In addition, any vacation pay and other entitlements due to the employee must take this period into account.

Discovery

Regardless of whether or not you choose to provide notice of termination or payment in lieu of notice when terminating an employee, the employee is entitled to his or her vacation pay, wages, and benefits (e.g., bonuses), if any, usually within a certain number of days after the date of termination.

In some cases, an employee may be entitled to severance pay, compensation for their years of service to the business. This entitlement usually applies only if the employee has worked a significant period for you (e.g., five years) and meets the other tests set by the law.

As a final matter, you are generally exempt under employment standards legislation from having to give notice of termination or termination pay in the following cases:

- The employment contract has expired (i.e., if it has provided for a specific term of employment and that time has elapsed). Be aware, though, that if there is no specific evidence of this, such as a written agreement, courts will infer that the term of an employment contract is indefinite.

- The employee is engaged in certain seasonal industries, such as construction.

- The employee has been in your employ less than three months. (The law sometimes considers this three-month period a probationary period.)

- You are temporarily laying off the employee (see Section d.4. below).

- The employment contract is frustrated by some unexpected event such as the business premises being burned down or a flood.

* You are firing the employee for just cause, such as wilful misconduct, disobedience, or wilful neglect of duty.

2. Termination for Cause

Termination for cause is also commonly referred to as "summary dismissal." Simply put, it means immediate termination of employment: termination on the spot.

Summary dismissal is justified in the following circumstances:

* *Serious misconduct*. This includes behaviour ranging from competing with your business to verbally or physically assaulting another employee. The issue is whether the misconduct is serious, which is always to be decided on the facts. However, the law has developed in such a way as to suggest that to be truly serious, misconduct cannot refer to an isolated incident, especially if the employee is remorseful or has taken steps to augment his or her behaviour. A single incident of misconduct will usually constitute serious misconduct only in exceptional circumstances in which something truly grievous has occurred (e.g., theft or sexual harassment).

* *Habitual neglect of duty*. A consistently late employee, an employee who habitually refuses to show up for work, or an employee who spends an inordinate amount of time engaged in personal matters throughout the workday may be terminated for cause. Of course, the employee's neglectful actions must be habitual, occurring frequently, and suggest evidence of a specific pattern of behaviour.

* *Incompetence*. To constitute just cause for dismissal, employee incompetence must be substantive. You cannot summarily dismiss someone you have hired

as a secretary because he or she is not familiar with the particular workings of your fax machine, especially if this is knowledge he or she can easily acquire in the course of employment. The standard of competence required in any given situation always depends on the nature of the duties to be performed and the representations the employee has made about his or her capabilities. In short, an employee cannot be summarily dismissed simply because he or she failed to live up to expectations.

* *Disobeying work rules*. Before an employee can be summarily dismissed for disobeying work rules, the employer (to avoid a wrongful dismissal suit) must be able to show that the rules were made known to the employee, that the rules were consistently enforced with the employee and others in the business to whom the rules apply, that the rules are reasonable, and that any breach of the rules by the employee is serious. Forgetting to wear one's Hungry Hippo cap while waiting tables at a restaurant of that name is not enough to justify termination for cause, unless, of course, it is habitually or deliberately being done in violation of work rules.

* *Conduct incompatible with the employee's duties or that prejudices the employer's business*. Examples include an employee working for a competitor or divulging your trade secrets. This kind of behaviour does not necessarily have to take place during business hours; an employee in your fur boutique may be prejudicing your business if he or she is also publicly engaged in animal rights activities.

* *Wilful disobedience of an employer's reasonable request involving the employee's duties*. An employee must do the job he or she agreed to do. Your requests, provided

they are reasonable and form part of the employee's duties, must be obeyed by the employee, failing which you have just cause to summarily dismiss him or her.

Of course, in each case the facts will ultimately determine whether dismissal was just or wrongful. This is not an exhaustive list of all grounds for justifiable termination for cause. In general, an employer may summarily dismiss an employee if the employee can be said to repudiate the employment contract: the employee, either by speech or conduct, must have effectively treated the employment contract as at an end.

Summary dismissal need not be done in writing nor must there be any advance notice of termination (hence, the "summary" in summary dismissal). Furthermore, you do not have to explicitly state that the employee is terminated. Your actions may suffice to convey that message. For example, you may refuse to allow him or her onto the premises.

Regardless of how you choose to summarily dismiss an employee, bear in mind that he or she is still entitled to his or her wages, vacation pay, and any other benefits accrued up to the time of dismissal: the employee must be paid for all the time he or she has worked for you, right up to the time of dismissal, and any vacation pay and benefits must be accounted on that basis.

3. Wrongful Dismissal

Wrongful dismissal by an employer occurs whenever an employee is terminated —

* without cause and without either due notice of termination or pay in lieu of due notice of termination,

* with cause, and the cause (the reason for termination) is not justified,

* through constructive dismissal (see Section c. below), or

* contrary to applicable legislation.

In each case, the employee can bring a legal claim against the employer that, if successful, may entitle the employee to a variety of remedies, including an award of damages. For that reason, it is worth carefully considering the bases of a wrongful dismissal claim.

(a) Dismissal without Due Notice or without Pay in Lieu of Due Notice

If there is no justifiable cause for terminating a worker's employment, you may not dismiss him or her without providing either due notice of termination or pay in lieu of such notice. To do so is to wrongfully dismiss the worker.

(b) Dismissal without Justifiable Cause

Dismissal without justifiable cause is the basis for most wrongful dismissal claims, because most employers and employees differ in their interpretation of the extent and nature of the conduct said to be the reason for dismissal. An employee summarily dismissed for physically assaulting another may contend that he had been provoked or that the assault amounted to little more than a touch. The question then becomes whether or not the firing was legally justifiable. Employers should consider the following principles.

Behaviour said to justify summary dismissal must be serious. Minor or isolated instances of misconduct will not be enough to support the summary dismissal of an employee. You must be certain you are able to judge the actions of the employee fairly and objectively.

Unless the employee's behaviour was of such a serious nature as to justify immediate dismissal, the employee should be given a second chance. When doing so, however, be sure that you let the employee know exactly what he or she did wrong. Also, make the employee aware of the standards of behaviour you expect him or her to follow while in the workplace and that repeated acts of misconduct will result in the termination of employment. Just as important, be sure to make written notes of what you say to the employee so that you are able to show evidence of having given him or her a second chance. You should also make notes of what the employee says to you in response and, in particular, any comments he or she may have regarding the misconduct. Make those notes part of the employee's file.

Condoning misconduct and then firing a person on a basis of that misconduct can support a claim for wrongful dismissal. If, for example, you regularly allow your employees to come to work drunk, you cannot fire one of them on that basis when the mood suits you.

Take mitigating factors into account. An employee who is habitually late for several weeks after a close relative has died cannot reasonably be terminated for cause on that basis. Nor can an employee who strikes another in the course of being sexually harassed or otherwise assaulted. In the former case, understanding is needed. In the latter case, it is important to speak with both employees about their conduct and advise them that it is unacceptable. Again, notes should be made and files kept.

The employer must be fair in dealing with the employee. While this obligation is not etched in stone, the law appears to be developing in this direction. For example, an employee may argue that he or she has been wrongfully dismissed since he or she was not given an opportunity to provide the employer with an explanation for his or her misconduct. What is "fair" is always open to interpretation. However, should the matter ever come before a court, it must be plain that you acted rationally in deciding to dismiss the employee and with the best interests of the business and the other employees in mind. "Fair" in this case would suggest that the employee in question — along with any witnesses — be given an opportunity to provide an explanation of the misconduct.

(c) Constructive Dismissal

Constructive dismissal is a type of wrongful dismissal that occurs whenever an employer unilaterally and fundamentally changes a significant aspect of the employment arrangement in a manner that shows the employer's intention to end its relationship with the employee. Behaviour that may constitute constructive dismissal include situations in which an employer —

- significantly reduces an employee's wages, salary, or other remuneration;

- requires an employee to change work locations;

- significantly changes an employee's duties, title, responsibilities, or job description; or

- significantly changes an employee's work conditions (e.g., a job that was formerly performed indoors is now required by the employer to be performed outside).

Courts will usually take the side of the employee in a constructive dismissal action if it appears that changes to the employment arrangement were made simply in an attempt to force the employee out. After all, an employer cannot be allowed to do indirectly what he or she is not allowed to do directly — namely, summarily dismiss an employee without cause. However, courts remain aware that changes in the workplace are often necessitated by legitimate economic and commercial considerations. Tax or bylaw concerns may make it necessary for you to relocate your business across town. Provided you deal with your employees fairly and your reasons for the change are legitimate, you should have no need to fear a claim of a wrongful dismissal action due to your proposed move. "Fairness" is, of course, based on the particular facts of a situation. A good way to arrive at an understanding of what it means to be fair to your employees is to question how the change will affect them and to seek ways to alleviate their concerns.

(d) Dismissal Contrary to Legislation

As noted, legislation exists at both the federal and provincial level that sets out a wide variety of employee rights. Terminating an employee for exercising those rights could result in a successful wrongful dismissal claim being brought against you. For instance, you could not fire a person because of his or her religion. That would violate the provisions of human rights legislation applicable in the employment setting. Nor could you fire someone for becoming pregnant or for seeking to enforce his or her rights under employment standards legislation. That, too, would constitute wrongful dismissal.

Bear in mind that you cannot get around this type of claim simply by choosing to give the employee due notice of termination or pay in lieu of such notice. For example, if the employee can prove that the motive behind your actions was contrary to the employee's right not to be discriminated against due to his or her religion, any technical compliance with the notice or pay provisions of employment standards legislation will not protect you from a wrongful dismissal action.

(e) Restitution

Courts have the power at common law to award compensation and damages in the case of a successful wrongful dismissal claim.

In granting an employee compensation for wrongful dismissal, the court's intent is to put the employee in the position he or she would have been in had he or she not been wrongfully dismissed. Doing so is no simple task. While it may be possible to account for lost earnings or benefits, it is considerably harder to quantify things such as promotions the employee might have received, overtime the employee might have worked, experience the employee would have gained, and loss of the employee's standing in the industry.

Moreover, a wrongfully dismissed employee may recover damages for such things as breach of contract, mental distress, damage to reputation, or economic losses occasioned by the wrongful dismissal such as the costs associated with having to relocate to a new job. Whatever the case, quantifying the amount of damages is never easy.

Punitive damages are rarely awarded in wrongful dismissal cases. Such damages apply only in cases in which the employee has been treated in a particularly callous manner and the court wants to deter the employer from such behaviour in future.

Employees usually do not have a right at common law to be reinstated — to get their job back. That right applies only to certain public sector jobs. In the private sector, no court would order that an employer and employee be forced to engage in a relationship in which trust has been destroyed.

Finally, an employee is under a legal obligation to mitigate his or her damages. He or she cannot obtain compensation for losses that could have been reasonably avoided. An employee who believes he or she has been wrongfully dismissed cannot simply retire and expect that the former employer will be required to compensate him or her forever after. Under the law, the employee must seek a new job. The employee must also take whatever steps are necessary to ensure that he or she does not suffer more from the loss of employment than circumstances would reasonably dictate. Any compensation or damages awarded by the court would then take the employee's attempts at mitigation into account and, where applicable, reduce compensation or damages accordingly.

4. Temporary Layoff

You may find that your business experiences slow periods during which you do not require the services of all your employees. Rather than fire them, you are entitled to temporarily lay them off. As the term implies, temporary layoff means that you reduce an employee's hours of work or temporarily stop their work without actually terminating their employment (i.e., without permanently laying off the employee).

To prevent abuses of this right, there are several rules you must follow when temporarily laying off someone:

- The temporary lay-off can last for a certain period only (e.g., in Ontario, no more than 35 weeks every 52-week period), after which time the employment will be considered terminated and the employee entitled to the termination rights that entails (e.g., termination pay).

- You will have to provide termination pay to the employee after a certain period from the time of layoff, as defined in the relevant legislation.

- The employee may work for himself or herself or someone else during the layoff period.

- The employee must be recalled to work once the layoff period is over. If the employee refuses to return within a reasonable time of being called back, he or she may not, in some circumstances, be entitled to termination pay.

e. Independent Contractors

As noted earlier, an employee is someone who works for you under a contract of service. An independent contractor, on the other hand, works for you under a contract for services. The distinction is a subtle but nonetheless important one.

First, an independent contractor is not subject to the same obligations as an employee. Specifically, a contractor is not under a general duty to provide you with his or her service. Rather, an independent contractor is usually engaged (as opposed to hired) to provide you with specific services or expertise that you require on a short-term (as opposed to an indefinite) basis.

Therefore, at law, an independent contractor is typically distinguished from an employee by the following:

- An independent contractor has the right to set his or her own hours of work, including any vacation time, subject to any agreement you may have with him or her.

- An independent contractor uses his or her own tools, equipment, and (often) premises in providing his or her services.

- Because of his or her independent status, an independent contractor cannot be restricted by you from providing his or her services to other businesses.

- An independent contractor is subject to his or her own control over how the services are to be performed.

Before engaging an independent contractor, you will need to have an independent contractor agreement, whether verbal or written. This agreement is not subject to employment standards legislation; there are no legislative requirements imposed on employers for things like minimum wage, hours of work, and notice of termination. The parties are at liberty to decide these things between themselves.

Employers sometimes favour the independent contractor relationship over the employment relationship because of the limited legal rights (outside of those contained in the independent contractor agreement) conferred on the contractor. In fact, many employers will insist to certain people wishing to work for them that they agree to do so as independent contractors, despite the fact that the independent contractor agreement effectively subjects the person to the same obligations that would ordinarily apply to an employee.

To help prevent this type of abuse, courts faced with the question of whether a person is an employee or independent contractor will usually resolve any ambiguities in favour of finding employee status. In other words, for an independent contractor to be considered so at law, a court must have clear evidence that the person satisfied all of the indications set out above, regardless of what the parties may have agreed to and despite what is contained in an independent contractor agreement.

The distinction between an employee and a independent contractor is especially relevant when source deductions are concerned. As noted earlier, an employer must make certain deductions and remittances from the salaries and wages of its employees for amounts owing for employment insurance (EI), the Canada Pension Plan (CPP), and income tax. In addition, the employer must also make employment insurance and Canada Pension Plan payments on behalf of all employees. In the case of an independent contractor, an employer is not required to make either any source deductions or contribute anything on the contractor's behalf. This situation provides a further incentive to employers to engage independent contractors rather than hire employees.

Yet difficulties sometimes arise for small-business owners when Canada Revenue Agency (CRA) becomes aware of an independent contractor situation, as often happens when a contractor is terminated or the contract ends and the contractor applies for employment insurance benefits. Despite what the independent contractor might have agreed to with you, to obtain employment insurance he or she will often describe himself or herself as having been your employee. It is then up to you to prove that such was not the case. In other words, the legal assumption will be made that he or she was your employee.

As a consequence, it is likely that you will be assessed by Canada Revenue Agency for amounts owing under EI and CPP legislation, on the premise that the person who you say was an independent contractor was really your employee. Moreover, you will be required to pay to CRA both the amount you should have deducted from the "employee's" salary and the amount you should have contributed on his or her behalf. That can come to quite a bit of money. Moreover, if you are unable to pay it immediately, you will be required to pay interest and penalties until the time you have paid it in full.

To challenge the assessment, you may need to go to tax court and appeal the decision. At that point you must be able to prove the independent contractor status of the person who, at law, will be assumed to have been your employee. As you might expect, this can often be difficult.

How then should you deal with people who truly are independent contractors? There is no simple answer to this question. In certain industries — hairstyling, for example — legislation exists that makes every hairstylist an employee of the hair salon, regardless of any other agreement between the parties. Such legislation aside, your only course of action is to ensure that the person satisfies the legal indicia of an independent contractor. In addition, a written independent contractor agreement is a must. It should explicitly require the independent contractor to make EI, CPP, and income tax payments on his or her own behalf and indemnify you if he or she doesn't.

Sample 16 is an example of an independent contractor agreement. You may refer to it in preparing your own agreements. However, to minimize your potential liability, I strongly recommended that you obtain qualified legal advice whenever engaging an independent contractor.

f. Summary

Employment law tends to develop at an astonishing pace. Keeping up with what you are obligated to do to comply with the law requires some effort on your part. Contact the employment ministry in your province to determine any specifics; the ministry will have brochures and pamphlets to assist you. You should also contact your lawyer if faced with a problem or issue that you are uncertain how to resolve.

Discovery

References

Unless you have agreed to do so, you are not under any legal obligation to provide a reference to a departing employee. However, should you choose to do so, it is important that you be aware that any misstatement on your part about the employee can have dire legal consequences. If you unfairly criticize or recklessly misrepresent an employee's performance, he or she may bring a legal action against you for defamation, libel, or slander. But if you overstate the employee's strengths and abilities, the new employer may sue you for negligent misstatement. This quandary is made worse because your refusal to give a reference when requested by a new employer may be interpreted as a negative opinion about the employee.

It is good policy to refuse to provide a reference for any employee, regardless of whether the reference would be a positive or a negative one. You should be sure to convey to your employees that you do not provide references. Furthermore, should a new employer request a reference, you should advise him or her that you do not give out references for any former employees. Make it clear that this policy applies across the board for your former employees, so that the employer will not draw any negative conclusions from your refusal to provide a reference. Finally, if you do decide to provide a reference, be sure to be fair in your assessment. What is fair is, of course, open to interpretation. The best approach is to comment only on those things you can objectively validate. For example, time-punch cards provide objective evidence of the hours an employee worked and whether he or she consistently showed up for work on time. The key thing to remember is that you do not legally owe a new employer a reference for a former employee. Choosing to give one can open a virtual pandora's box of liability.

Sample 12
Application for Employment

Position applied for _____ Date available _____

Last name   First name(s)

Street address   City   Province   Postal code

Telephone (including area code)   Fax   Email

Are you applying for: ❏ Full-time   ❏ Part-time   ❏ Temporary

Hours available: Mon _____ Tue _____ Wed _____ Thur _____ Fri _____ Sat _____ Sun _____

Work experience (Please list most recent first)

1
Position _____ Date of employment _____
Employer _____ Address _____
Supervisor _____ Telephone _____ Email _____
Beginning pay _____ Ending pay _____
Reasons for leaving _____ May we contact this employer? ❏ Yes ❏ No
Responsibilities _____
_____

2
Position _____ Date of employment _____
Employer _____ Address _____
Supervisor _____ Telephone _____ Email _____
Beginning pay _____ Ending pay _____
Reasons for leaving _____ May we contact this employer? ❏ Yes ❏ No
Responsibilities _____
_____

3
Position _____ Date of employment _____
Employer _____ Address _____
Supervisor _____ Telephone _____ Email _____
Beginning pay _____ Ending pay _____
Reasons for leaving _____ May we contact this employer? ❏ Yes ❏ No
Responsibilities _____
_____

List other relevant work experience _____
_____
_____
_____

Education/training

List secondary and post-secondary education including course of study, and degree or diploma received (highest level achieved first)

_____

_____

_____

_____

List other relevant training (most recent first)

_____

_____

_____

_____

Other activities

List volunteer work, leadership positions, or other activities that you feel may be relevant to this application

_____

_____

_____

Personal references

Please provide three reference contacts other than family members or people you have previously worked with

_____
Name   Telephone   Occupation

_____
Name   Telephone   Occupation

_____
Name   Telephone   Occupation

Is there anything else you would like to tell us about yourself?

_____

_____

_____

_____

_____

I certify that all information provided in this application is accurate and complete to the best of my knowledge, and I understand that intentionally providing false information could result in refusal of employment or discharge. I also authorize the employers, schools, organizations, or persons named above to provide information regarding my employment, education, character, and qualifications.

_____   _____
Signature   Date

Interview Questions/Interview Summary

Interview Questions

Educational background and work experience

1. In your post-secondary education, what was your main course of study? Why did you choose that field?

2. What skills, relevant to the position applied for, have you gained and developed from your educational experience and/or other training?

3. Describe your duties and responsibilities in each of the three most recent jobs you've held.

4. What were some of your major accomplishments in jobs previously (or currently) held? What were some disappointments and how did you overcome them?

5. How have you benefited from previous employment in terms of your skills and personal development?

6. What are your interests outside of work and why?

7. What accomplishments have you had in activities outside of work and school?

Personal qualities

1. Think about one of the jobs you've had recently that you feel has been significant in your life. What did you like and dislike about this job and why?

2. Why are you applying for this position? Why do you want to work for our company?

3. What are your strengths and weaknesses (list three or four of each)? How are you working to overcome your weaknesses?

4. *(Interviewer: take an opportunity to bring up something particular about your company and its business environment and give the interviewee the opportunity to comment and ask further questions.)*

Subject to discuss:

Interpersonal qualities and communication skills

1. Describe a situation in which you had difficulty with a coworker or supervisor, such as a personality conflict or misunderstanding. How did you handle it?

2. Consider a job in which you had contact with customers or clients and think of a time when a customer or client came to you with a complaint. Describe what happened, how upset the person was, and how you dealt with the situation.

Organizational skills

1. Thinking of a job in which you worked reasonably or completely independently, explain how you organized your workload.

2. Consider this hypothetical situation: If several people depend on you to do certain tasks for them and someone needs you to do something else on top of your regular workload, what would you do? If you've taken on the extra project and it's so time consuming that you know you'll have problems finishing either it or your regular work, how would you handle the situation and why?

3. Describe an instance when you've changed or attempted to change the way a certain task was done. What kinds of changes became more productive? What changes didn't?

Technical/mechanical skills

1. Do you have experience in (*name relevant computer applications*)? How much experience do you have with these applications and in what ways have you worked with them?

2. What experience do you have with other types of office and computer-related equipment? Specify exact machines and models if possible.

3. *Interviewer: Ask about the applicant's experience with equipment specific to your business. Also consider asking if the applicant knows how to handle technical problems, do repairs, or can perform certain jobs manually if necessary.*

List equipment to be discussed:

Closing the interview

Always give the applicant the opportunity to ask questions, request further clarification of job duties, or make additional comments about his or her experience, qualifications, or character. Finish the interview by explaining the next step in the job selection process (e.g., when he or she will hear about your decision, if you will have time to notify each applicant), arrange a time for further contact (a second interview perhaps), and thank the applicant for his or her interest and time.

INTERVIEW SUMMARY

Interview Summary

Name of applicant _____ Interviewer _____

Position applied for _____ Department _____

Interview date _____ Hiring deadline _____

Summary of relevant work experience and education

_____

_____

_____

Rating the applicant

Rate the applicant on a scale of one to five for the following qualities and skills, one meaning the applicant has little or no ability in this area and five meaning he or she has excellent abilities and qualities.

Personal qualities		Interpersonal qualities		Communication skills	
Appearance	5 4 3 2 1	Confidence	5 4 3 2 1	Listening	5 4 3 2 1
Punctuality	5 4 3 2 1	Assertiveness	5 4 3 2 1	Verbal expression	5 4 3 2 1
Dependability	5 4 3 2 1	Amiableness	5 4 3 2 1	Writing ability	5 4 3 2 1
Enthusiasm	5 4 3 2 1	Flexibility	5 4 3 2 1	Understanding	5 4 3 2 1
Integrity	5 4 3 2 1	Teamwork	5 4 3 2 1	Developing ideas	5 4 3 2 1
TOTAL	_____	TOTAL	_____	TOTAL	_____

Organizational skills Technical/mechanical skills

Prioritizing tasks	5 4 3 2 1	Office equipment	5 4 3 2 1
Time management	5 4 3 2 1	Computer literacy	5 4 3 2 1
Multi-tasking	5 4 3 2 1	Computer knowledge (list specific programs and applications)	
Efficiency	5 4 3 2 1	_____	5 4 3 2 1
Accuracy	5 4 3 2 1	_____	5 4 3 2 1
TOTAL	_____	TOTAL	_____

Other skills needed for the position (list)

_____ 5 4 3 2 1

_____ 5 4 3 2 1

_____ 5 4 3 2 1

_____ 5 4 3 2 1

_____ 5 4 3 2 1

_____ 5 4 3 2 1

TOTAL _____

Checklist

- ❏ Permission to check employment and personal references
- ❏ Date available confirmed
- ❏ Meets educational requirements
- ❏ Meets work experience requirements
- ❏ Recommend for follow-up interviews
- ❏ Recommend for hiring

Other Comments

_____

_____

_____

_____

_____

_____

_____

_____

_____

Sample 14
Letter Confirming Employment

Dear _____:

I am pleased that you have accepted the position of _____ at our company, starting on _____. You shall perform the following duties and have the following responsibilities:

Please note that these duties and responsibilities are not exhaustive and that you may be expected to perform other reasonable duties and responsibilities should the need arise.

Subject to statutory holidays, your working hours are from _____ to _____ , _____day through _____day, with a _____ minute lunch break and _____ minute coffee break. You are entitled to _____ days of ordinary unpaid vacation(s) per calendar year after your first year of employment, and 6 days of paid/unpaid sick leave per calendar year.

Your starting salary/wage is _____You will be on probation for _____ during which time we may terminate your employment at any time without notice or payment in lieu of notice. If your employment is continued, we may only terminate your employment without cause on two weeks' notice or payment in lieu of notice; however, we reserve the right to terminate your employment at any time without notice or payment in lieu of notice for good cause.

Your performance and salary will be reviewed after a period of _____ and a performance and salary appraisal will then occur annually in _____.

The company offers a benefit package which will be outlined to you by our Human Resources Manager on your first day. Other policy and procedure details are contained in the Personnel Manual which will also be given to you at this time.

Your supervisor is _____. Please see him/her on your first day and he/she will help you get settled.

I look forward to working with you. If you have any questions, please do not hesitate to contact me.

Yours truly

(Name)
(Title)

Sample 15
Dismissal Letter

June 20, 20--

Dear _____:

Re: Termination of employment

I regret to inform you that your employment with _____ will be
terminated effective _____ for the following reason(s):

Your severance package will be administered according to company policy, and you will receive
a statement detailing accrued benefits. Please also refer to the policies outlined in the company
personnel manual covering applicable insurance benefits.

_____ is available to discuss with you
these details as well as any other questions or concerns you may have. Please contact him/her
at your earliest convenience, and he/she will arrange termination matters with you.

I sincerely regret that this action is necessary, and wish you success in your future employment
endeavours.

Yours truly,

cc: _____   [person named above as liaison]

_____   Personnel Department

Sample 16
Independent Contractor Agreement

[YOURCO LETTERHEAD]

[*insert date of letter*]

Delivered by Hand

[*insert Name
and Address of Contractor*]

Dear [*insert Name of Contractor*]:

This letter will confirm your agreement to provide computer consultation and related services to Yourco on the following terms:

1. During the term of this Agreement, you agree to serve Yourco and perform any and all computer consultation and related services as Yourco may require in connection with Yourco's recent adoption of a new computer-based accounting system, including [*insert specific duties; e.g., conduct technical component examinations, prepare reports*], at such times as may be agreed upon.

2. You will be paid at the rate of $_____ per [*hour, day, week*] for services rendered in accordance with this Agreement. You will invoice Yourco on a monthly basis, which invoices shall include GST and shall set forth the time spent and work performed and which shall be payable within thirty (30) days of receipt by Yourco. You shall be required to provide Yourco with your GST registration number.

3. Both you and Yourco agree that the relationship created by this Agreement is that of independent contractors and not that of employer and employee. Nothing in this Agreement shall be interpreted to constitute a party as the partner, employee, or agent of the other nor shall either party have any authority to bind the other in any respect, it being intended that each is and shall remain independent of the other and responsible only for its own actions.

4. As an independent contractor, you will be responsible for the payment of any and all taxes levied against you, including, without limitation, all federal, provincial, and local personal and business income taxes; employment insurance, health and benefit fees; GST and any other taxes; and business license fees or expenses as required in connection with the provision of your services under this Agreement.

5. You agree that any information received or uncovered by you during any performance of your obligations under this Agreement including, without limitation, any [*list specific items of confidential business information; e.g., technical reports, accounting data*] will be treated by you in full confidence and will not be revealed by you to any other people, firms, or corporations unless otherwise directed in writing by Yourco or required by law.

6. This Agreement will take effect on _____ and will end on _____, provided that either party may terminate this Agreement, at will, at any time, with or without cause, by giving written notice of termination to the other party not less than thirty (30) days prior to the effective date of such termination. Termination of this Agreement, with or without cause, shall not relieve any party from liabilities owing and accrued to the other party at and up to the time of termination.

7. You shall be liable for and you hereby agree to indemnify and save Yourco harmless from and against any and all liability, damages, demands, claims, actions, proceedings, suits, judgments, and expenses (including lawyers' fees) that may be brought against or suffered by Yourco as a result of or arising out of: (i) any action or omission by you in connection with the provision of your services under this Agreement; (ii) your negligence or wilful misconduct; and (iii) your failure to comply with your obligations under this Agreement.

8. You may not assign, sub-contract or delegate your rights or obligations (or any part of them) under this Agreement without the prior written consent of Yourco.

9. This Agreement constitutes the entire agreement of the parties to this Agreement and all prior oral or written understandings by and between the parties shall be deemed to have been superseded by reason of this Agreement.

10. The terms of this Agreement may be amended only in writing signed by both parties.

11. Time is of the essence of this Agreement.

12. This Agreement is governed by the laws of the Province of [*insert province here*] and the laws of Canada applicable therein.

Would you please indicate your agreement with the terms and conditions set forth in this Agreement by signing and dating the duplicate copy of this letter in the space provided below and returning it to Yourco, whereupon this Agreement shall constitute a valid and binding obligation of each of the parties to this Agreement.

Yours truly,

[*insert name and signature of Yourco's signing officer*]

I confirm my agreement with and acceptance of the terms of this Agreement.

Dated this _____ day of _____ 20--.

_____   _____
Witness   [*signature of consultant*]

13
Resolving Disputes

No matter how well you run your small business, chances are you will find yourself involved in the occasional dispute. That dispute could involve anyone from an employee to the government.

Knowing how to resolve disputes in a cost-efficient and timely manner is among the most important skills you can acquire. This chapter looks at the types of disputes — in particular, legal disputes — your small business may be involved in and the steps you can take to resolve them.

a. What Is a Dispute?

What is a dispute? At first glance, the answer seems obvious: when people disagree about a matter, there is said to be a dispute.

From a legal perspective, however, things aren't quite that simple. Legally, a dispute is more than a simple disagreement. For example, you and I might disagree about whether or not Wayne Gretzky — as the greatest hockey player that ever lived — should also be the highest paid. Having expressed our opinions, we could each go our separate ways. Moreover, we could leave the matter unresolved without really affecting anything of importance (except possibly our opinion of each other's hockey knowledge).

But suppose that I were Gretzky's agent and you were the general manager for the hockey team trying to sign him up for the coming season. Suppose further that we are trying to negotiate his contract. Our disagreement about whether Gretzky should be the highest-paid player now takes on real significance because it affects our respective interests. How we resolve the issue of what Gretzky should be paid has a direct bearing on things that matter to us (and Gretzky). And if we don't resolve that issue, Gretzky may not be paid anything at all (and your hockey team won't have the benefit of his services).

The element of conflicting interests is what turns a simple disagreement into a true dispute.

This distinction is important where the law is concerned because the law exists in part to decide matters of conflicting interest, rather than mere disagreements. That is, the law exists to determine whose interests, in any given dispute, should prevail, and in making that determination, it focuses on the legal rights those interests engender. When those rights conflict, a legal dispute — as opposed to any other type of dispute — arises.

Discovery

As the owner and operator of a small business, you may be involved in any number and type of legal disputes involving a broad variety of individuals and institutions. For example:

- You and an employee may dispute the terms of employment.

- A supplier may dispute your claim to have paid him for the delivery of raw materials to your factory.

- A customer may dispute the accuracy of claims you made about a product you sold her.

- Revenue Canada may dispute the amount you remitted for income tax.

Such disputes often take a great deal of time and energy to resolve. Moreover, they are not always resolved to the mutual satisfaction of the disputing parties, frequently destroy both business and personal relationships, and can cost you money — sometimes lots of it.

b. Reducing the Likelihood of Being Involved in a Dispute

From a business perspective, the ideal is to avoid becoming involved in disputes whenever you can. Of course, that is more easily said than done.

Still, there are steps you can take to reduce the likelihood of becoming involved in a legal dispute. The most important of these is not to infringe the rights of others or unfairly prejudice their interests. In the legal context, that means don't breach a contract, don't fire someone because they become pregnant, don't unlawfully withhold payment of your taxes, don't misrepresent your products or services, and don't engage in any other type of illegal behaviour. That alone will ensure that you are never involved in a legal dispute.

In addition, you can correct your infringement of someone's legal rights as soon as the infringement is brought to your attention; ensure that the parties' respective legal rights and obligations are clearly set out in writing (e.g., in a contract) if they are not otherwise provided for by the law; and ensure that you know your own legal rights and obligations and are acting within their scope.

Yet it is not always clear where another person's legal rights end and yours begin. Avoiding a legal dispute may not be an option. If that is the case (as it sometimes is), you really have no choice; you must resolve it.

c. How Can You Resolve Your Disputes?

1. Resolving a Dispute Yourself

Resolving a dispute yourself is rarely a simple matter. To arrive at a mutually satisfactory resolution in a non-legal dispute, you must make full use of your people skills and business judgment.

However, when the dispute involves a legal matter, resolution becomes that much more difficult because it requires a knowledge of the law. Of course, not everyone knows the law, but everyone has a certain degree of common sense. Everyone has an idea of what it means to think and act reasonably. And everyone recognizes the difference between fair and unfair behaviour. That being the case, most people have at least a preliminary understanding of the approach the law takes to resolving disputes, for the law is ultimately guided by the intuition attendant to common sense and the clarity of thought achieved through reason to arrive at what, taken from the broadest perspective, will be a fair and just outcome. By taking the same approach to resolving any legal disputes in which you become involved, you can ensure that the outcome will accord with the demands of the law.

Thus, when faced with a legal dispute — for instance, whether or not you paid a supplier for the delivery of goods (as required under sale of goods legislation) — the first step is to analyze the situation. Seek the answers to the following questions:

* What is the issue? Is the supplier claiming that I did not pay him? That I paid him only part of what I owe him? That payment was late?

* What are the facts? Did I, in fact, pay? Is the cheque in the mail? Did the cheque bounce?

* What evidence do I have to support the facts? Is there an invoice? A receipt? Did anyone see me pay?

* What are our (my and the other person's) respective legal rights and obligations? Is there a contract (oral or written) setting out the payment terms? If not, is there a law governing our rights or obligations?

These are the questions that a lawyer would ask — and a judge as well — should the dispute ever proceed that far. Yet you may be able to avoid going to court by first conducting your own investigation. Once you have the information you need, you can begin to weigh the strength of your side in the dispute against the other side. Consider the following questions:

* Who do the facts support?

* Who does the evidence support?

* Who — viewed rationally and legally — is really in the right?

Again, these are the questions that a lawyer and judge would consider in trying to resolve your dispute. Of course, because you may not know the law, it may be difficult for you to determine who

is legally in the right. But as mentioned earlier, the law is based on what is fair, reasonable, and accords with common sense. Provided you take the same approach in your analysis of the dispute, you can arrive at a good estimate of how the law will see it as well.

Once you have finished your analysis and determined — given the facts, the evidence, and your understanding of the law — whose position in the dispute is the stronger one, you should take steps to resolve it.

If you determine that you are clearly in the wrong, try to correct that situation in a manner that both satisfies the other person in the dispute and is fair to yourself.

If you determine that the other person is in the wrong (and he or she agrees), that person should then correct the situation. Of course, getting that person to agree that he or she is in the wrong may be difficult, especially if you do not have any evidence to support your position. (Again, you should take note of the importance of keeping accurate records of all your business transactions.)

If you cannot determine who should prevail in the dispute or have determined that the other person is in the wrong but cannot get him or her to agree either to accept your determination or to correct the situation, you may have no choice but to take up the matter with your lawyer or, either with or without the assistance of a lawyer, go to court.

A final word before you take either of those steps: An important part of resolving any dispute is deciding if the matter is worth fighting. Court and lawyer costs are expensive. They also consume much time and energy. You must, therefore, consider whether in any given instance it will cost you more to pursue the resolution of a dispute — even when you are clearly in the right — than simply to let it go. It may be that in some circumstances the best resolution is just to chalk the situation up to experience and perhaps seek some other form of redress. For example, you might choose to stop doing business with the other person, if only to avoid any future disputes. The fact is, few unscrupulous businesspeople are capable of staying in business very long and, all things considered, that may be redress enough.

2. Taking the Dispute to Your Lawyer

You should be sure to bring any legal dispute to the attention of a lawyer if you are uncertain of your legal rights and obligations, if the dispute involves a complex legal issue, or if you may be sued or are considering suing. Your lawyer can advise you of your legal rights and those of the other person involved in the dispute, provide you with a legal analysis of the dispute in light of the available facts, give you his or her opinion about the strength of your case and the likelihood that it will be resolved in your favour, and let you know how the law can help you to resolve the dispute.

Most important, your lawyer can act as your advocate. In other words, your lawyer can present your position to the other side in a clear and forceful manner based on a thorough understanding of the law. This is particularly useful if the dispute involves a complex legal issue. It may also be of great assistance when the person on the other side is represented by a lawyer: your lawyer can ensure that what you are told about the law by the other lawyer is accurate. Your lawyer can also help you respond to any claims made by the other side and argue your case with the other lawyer on your behalf.

To save yourself both time and money, come to your lawyer's office equipped with detailed notes setting out the answers to the questions outlined above in Section c.1. If your lawyer thinks you have a good case, he or she will then (on your instructions) contact the other person in the dispute (or that person's lawyer) to present your position. This is usually done by sending a letter.

In some cases, a letter from a lawyer will be enough to show the other side that you mean business. It is not uncommon for a lawyer making a demand in a letter (e.g., to receive payment for an outstanding account) to note that unless the demand is met by a certain date, the client (you) will "take all actions necessary to enforce his [or her] legal rights, including bringing a legal claim against you without further notice." In effect, your lawyer is saying that if the other person fails to comply with your demand, you may sue that person.

Having said that, a good lawyer will try to resolve a dispute without taking it to court. A letter of the sort just mentioned is in many ways an invitation to talk, especially if it is not clear in whose favour the dispute should be resolved or whether or not any mitigating circumstances exist. It is hoped that the person receiving the letter (or that person's lawyer) will write back to provide you with his or her account of the events leading up to (and resulting in) the dispute. Armed with that information, both you and your lawyer will be in a better position to determine the strength of your case and how it might be resolved.

It may also help you to better understand the opposing party: Is this person acknowledging fault but simply stalling for time? Is that person's business in financial trouble? Can he or she afford to defend or pursue, as the case may be, a lawsuit? This information can be of value to you in seeking a resolution.

After both you and the other person had the opportunity to state your cases through a lawyer and evaluate the relative merits of your positions, you can try to resolve the dispute between yourselves: that is, with the assistance of your lawyers but without going to court.

Sometimes that may mean one party agrees to meet the demands of the other (e.g., for payment of an outstanding account). Other times it might mean agreeing to some of the other person's demands but not to all of them. For example, you might agree to pay the $500 you owe the other person, but only if you can do so in installments of $100 each over a mutually acceptable period. That kind of give-and-take is known as "settling" a dispute and, for reasons to be discussed below, is sometimes recommended even when you are clearly in the right.

3. Taking the Dispute to Court

If the other party either does not agree to meet your legitimate demands or refuses to settle the dispute on terms acceptable to you, and assuming that you are determined to pursue the matter to its conclusion, your only option is to take the dispute to court.

Anyone thinking of taking a dispute to court should know something about the Canadian court system. After all, the decision of a court — whether for or against you — has the force of law.

d. Canada's Court System

The first thing to know about Canadian's court system is that there is not just one court system in Canada but several. To begin, each province has its own court system, established by provincial statute. The territories have their respective court systems as well. Then there is the tax court system, the federal court system, and the Supreme Court of Canada.

In addition to the various court systems, there are tribunal and other quasijudicial systems established under federal, provincial, and territorial legislation that may be relevant in resolving a dispute. Human rights tribunals may be used to resolve human rights disputes, and municipal board hearings may be set up to hear municipal by-law disputes.

There are significant similarities between these various systems. There are also many differences. As a small-business owner, any one of these systems may become relevant to you in a given set of circumstances, so it is worth it to consider each of them.

1. Provincial and Territorial Court Systems

Courts established under provincial legislation generally have the broadest jurisdiction in Canada. They are empowered to hear and determine almost any dispute brought before them, whether it involves a breach of contract or an act of criminal fraud. Any disputes you have will most likely be heard by a provincial court.

Most provincial court systems are structured in roughly the following manner.

(a) Small Claims Court

At the lowest level, there is the small claims court. The term "lowest level" is not meant to indicate that disputes brought to small claims court are in any way inferior to other disputes nor the decisions regarding them less important. It merely indicates that while a case may be argued in small claims court and appealed to higher level (usually county or district court), there is no level of court that can make an appeal to small claims court. Small claims court is the first (in the sense of lowest) in a strict hierarchy of courts within the provincial court system.

Small claims courts are distinguishable from other courts in the provincial system in a number of ways. First, there is usually a limit on how large a monetary claim can be adjudicated before a small claims court. In some cases, it can go as high as $50,000 but is usually less. Second, while there are formal rules of court to be observed by the parties in the dispute, the judge, and others, the rules tend to be less complicated than those established in higher-level courts and, as a result, hearings tend to be more informal. Third, because of this tendency to informality, the parties to the dispute need not be represented by a lawyer, though they can be. And finally, there are certain types of disputes that small claims courts are not empowered to hear — those involving cases of libel or slander, for example. Furthermore, one judge hears and decides the case.

(b) Provincial Courts

The next level of courts are the provincial courts. These courts have two purposes: they serve as the court of appeal for small claims court decisions, and they stand on their own as first-level trial courts in each province.

In many ways, provincial courts are like small claims courts, except that the proceedings are more formal (and therefore a lawyer is usually required to argue your case); the limit, if any, on the amount of the claim to be adjudicated is much higher; and they can hear a broader spectrum of disputes.

In general, a provincial court decision can be appealed to the next level of court (that is, district or county court) or directly to a superior court.

(c) District or County Courts

In some jurisdictions, there are district or county courts, empowered to hear appeals from small claims or provincial courts and serving as trial courts in their own right. Again, there are fewer restrictions on the types of matters that may be heard in a district or county court than in a small claims or provincial court and often a higher limit (if any) on the amount of the claim to be adjudicated.

(d) Superior Courts

Each province has a set of superior courts empowered to hear almost any dispute (except those exclusively within the jurisdiction of other courts). Moreover, there are no restrictions on the amount of any claim to be adjudicated. As a consequence, most major disputes are heard in a superior court.

In addition to serving as a trial court, superior courts often serve as the court to which decisions of small claims, provincial, county, or district courts must be appealed. They also serve to review decisions of administrative boards and tribunals.

As you might expect, the rules governing the conduct of superior court trials and appeals are complex, and navigating them requires the assistance of a lawyer.

You are usually able to appeal any decision of a superior court to a provincial court of appeal.

(e) Court of Appeal

The court of appeal is the highest-level court in a provincial or territorial court system. As its name implies, it is not empowered to conduct trials but only to hear appeals. These courts decide questions of law and do not adjudicate on questions of fact.

Generally, three judges sit on a court of appeal, and decisions are based on majority rule. Only lawyers are qualified to appear before a court of appeal. Once a court of appeal has made a decision, it binds all courts below it within that jurisdiction for all future cases involving the same legal issue. The only way to change that decision is for the court of appeal to do so on another occasion, or for legislation to be enacted overriding the decision of the court, or for the matter to be appealed and won in the Supreme Court of Canada.

2. The Supreme Court of Canada

The Supreme Court of Canada is the highest court in the country and represents the final word on any dispute brought before it.

Cases come before the Supreme Court of Canada from provincial courts of appeal (and, in some cases, provincial superior courts) and the federal court of appeal. In civil matters, the Supreme Court hears appeals at its discretion (i.e., if the Supreme Court agrees the case merits its attention, it will grant "leave to appeal" and will hear the case).

Few commercial law cases (i.e., those affecting your small business) make their way to the Supreme Court of Canada, owing to, among other things, the cost involved in taking a case that far and the fact that commercial matters are less likely to be socially and politically relevant than, say, human rights matters — which are the issues usually brought before the Supreme Court.

But the Supreme Court does hear commercial cases, and because every lower court (regardless of jurisdiction) is required to follow the decision of the Supreme Court on the same issue, you should be aware of Supreme Court decisions. The best way to learn about those decisions is from the news or the business section of your newspaper.

3. Federal Courts

The federal court system in Canada was established to hear cases regarding matters regulated exclusively by federal law, including copyright, trademark, and patent registration matters.

There is both a trial division and an appeals division of the federal court. These are, generally speaking, subject to rules of conduct similar to those established under provincial court systems and require you to be represented by a lawyer in any case brought before them.

4. Tax Court of Canada

The Tax Court of Canada was established in 1983 to hear appeals of assessments made under a variety of tax and tax-related legislation, much of which is relevant in the context of small-business ownership. Such legislation includes the *Income Tax Act, Employment Insurance Act*, and the *Canada Pension Plan Act*. (See Chapter 14, Taxes.)

Unlike other court systems in Canada, the Tax Court of Canada has only a trial division. Any appeal of a decision of the trial division must be made to the Federal Court of Canada.

e. Going to Court

In the commercial context, a dispute comes before a court when one person sues another. To sue someone means to bring a legal claim against that person to obtain some type of relief (such as an award of money, or damages) for losses you

have suffered. That claim is often referred to as a lawsuit or, simply, a suit.

1. Initiating a Lawsuit

A lawsuit is initiated when a person — the plaintiff — files a legal claim with a court and subsequently serves that claim on the person being sued — the defendant. Filing a legal claim involves preparing a written statement of claim (or similar document), registering it with an office of the court in which the claim is to be brought, and then having it delivered, usually through a special form of personal legal service, to the defendant. The defendant then has a certain amount of time (usually 20 to 30 days from the date on which he or she was served with the statement of claim) to file a statement of defence with the court. In some cases (e.g., small claims court), the court will provide the plaintiff with a copy of the statement of defence. Most often, however, the defendant is required to serve the plaintiff with a copy of the statement of defence after it has been filed.

If the defendant does not file a statement of defence within the time allowed, "default judgment"— a declaration that the plaintiff has won the case and is entitled to the relief he or she is seeking — may (and likely will) be ordered by the court against the defendant without notifying the defendant of the fact that it is about to occur. An order for that relief (usually payment of some amount of money) will then be made against the defendant.

2. Deciding Whom to Sue

Whom do I sue? That question is often difficult to answer, as you may not always be aware of the exact circumstances giving rise to the dispute. For example, the person who backed his delivery truck into your store's front window may be employed by a company engaged as an independent contractor by the sole proprietor you engaged to provide you with delivery service. Who is legally responsible to make good the losses you suffer as a result of the accident?

When in doubt, contact a lawyer to help you determine who the various potential defendants to your claim might be.

Your lawyer may simply advise you to choose to sue everyone reasonably connected with your claim. The various defendants are then left to work out among themselves who should ultimately bear responsibility, and in what proportion, for the losses you have suffered. Claims frequently involve allocating responsibility, or liability, among several people in proportion to their actual contribution to the circumstances giving rise to the claim. In the earlier example, the driver may be 50 percent responsible for the damage to your window, but his employer 50 percent responsible for allowing him to drive an unsafe vehicle.

In addition, a defendant may sue another person (who you may or may not have named in your lawsuit) as the person ultimately responsible for making restitution. That action involves making what is sometimes referred to as a crossclaim: a statement of claim made by a defendant against a third party to the suit, who would then have to file a defence to the crossclaim.

You can also be countersued. That occurs where the person you are suing sues you in response. To do so, he or she typically files a statement of defence and counterclaim with the court and has it served on you. You must then file a defence to the counterclaim and serve it on the person whom you were (and still are) suing. In the case of the earlier example, a countersuit might arise if you had not shovelled the previous night's snow from your driveway and the delivery truck suffered damage because the driver could not properly control it due to the snow on your driveway.

It will be relatively clear in some cases who is at fault. This will often be apparent from the surrounding facts. For example, a contract might set out who is at fault or a particular person might admit liability.

Finally, it should be noted that any legal entity may be sued — an individual, sole proprietorship, partnership, corporation, or government ministry. Furthermore, any legal entity may bring a lawsuit, though, in some circumstances, sole proprietorships and partnerships may not sue in their own name if that name has not been registered with the appropriate government authority. (See Chapter 4, Choosing a Business Name.)

3. Choosing the Court in Which to Bring Your Lawsuit

As noted, not every court can hear every type of claim. There are access restrictions based on the amount of damages sought and the nature of the issue disputed. Accordingly, you do not always have a choice as to which court you may bring your case; the law sometimes makes that decision for you.

Most commercial disputes involving small businesses are brought before either a small claims or provincial court, depending on the nature of relief being sought. If the case is a simple commercial dispute in which the only relief sought is an award of money, then provided the award of money is less than the relevant threshold, the most appropriate place to bring the dispute may be small claims court. Any dispute seeking other types of relief — for example, an injunction (see below) — should (and often must) be brought in provincial court.

The chief advantage of suing in small claims court is that you are allowed, and often encouraged, to handle the suit yourself. That includes everything from preparing your statement of claim (or statement of defence) to arguing your case before the judge. Doing so can save you the cost of legal fees.

4. Preparing a Statement of Claim

A statement of claim describes the factual background and the plaintiff's reasons behind his or her claim for relief. The statement of claim is the primary document to which the court will refer when considering whether or not to grant the plaintiff the relief sought. It is also the basis on which the defendant must present a defence.

Therefore, if you are preparing a statement of claim, draft it so as to convince the court of your point of view. That means clearly and concisely, setting out the following:

(a) *The plaintiff's position.* (For example, it may be your position as a plaintiff that a client has not paid you for some service you provided.)

(b) *The relief being sought.* (You are therefore seeking payment of the amount that client owes to you.)

(c) *The grounds for claiming that relief.* (The client has signed a contract stating the price and terms of payment and indicating that the money is due and owing.)

(d) *All relevant facts.* (You have provided your services, rendered an account, and made several demands for payment — both oral and written — but have not received any money from the client.)

A statement of claim is often a standard form document created under a particular jurisdiction's rules of civil procedure. The only thing you (or your lawyer) need to fill out are the relevant facts as you allege them. In most cases, the text contained in the standard form advises the defendant that a civil action has been started against him or her by the plaintiff; that to defend the action, the defendant must file a statement of defence within a certain period (usually less than a month); and that if the plaintiff does not file a statement of defence within the time stipulated, default judgment may be awarded to the plaintiff.

If the case is a relatively straightforward matter that will be brought in small claims court, you may wish to prepare your statement of claim yourself. If, however, the claim involves some complex legal issue or for some other reason must be brought elsewhere than in small claims court, you should seek the assistance of a qualified lawyer in preparing it. Of course, that can be costly, but you can reduce that cost by coming to your lawyer with an outline of the relevant information set out above, thereby giving your lawyer a valuable head start on your case.

A statement of claim is typically structured as a series of numbered paragraphs setting out (usually in chronological order) the relevant facts of your case. A statement of claim should not contain arguments. It is your (or your lawyer's) job to present your arguments in court based on the alleged facts set out in your statement of claim. In Sample 18, an example of a statement of claim for a fairly common type of commercial dispute — a failure to pay for work performed — the facts themselves are ordered in such a way as to lead to a conclusion favouring the claimant's position in the dispute — thereby effectively functioning as an argument.

Discovery

Pleadings

All pleadings, whether a statement of claim or a statement of defence, should —

(a) set out the relevant facts — and only the facts — as alleged by a particular party,

(b) set out the alleged facts in a logical and easy-to-follow order, and

(c) make clear what each party is requesting from the court.

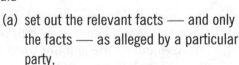

Do not underestimate the importance of well-drafted pleadings, as they form the very foundation on which your case will proceed. It is important to ensure that any pleadings are drafted specifically to address the particular circumstances of your case. In addition, I strongly recommended that you engage the services of a qualified litigation lawyer whenever you plan to sue or are being sued.

5. Preparing a Statement of Defence

The statement of defence serves one purpose: to defend against the allegations made in the statement of claim (i.e., to deny the claim). To do this, you, as the defendant, must set out the relevant facts as you allege them to be true. Write the statement of defence in such a way as to convince the court of your position. It should set out in a clear and concise matter:

(a) *What, if anything, is true in the plaintiff's statement of claim.* (For example, it may be true that the plaintiff provided services — say, painted your living room — rendered an account, and made several demands, both verbal and written, for payment.)

(b) *What, if anything, the plaintiff has said in the statement of claim that is not true or of which you have no knowledge.* (It is not true that you have not paid her. In fact, you provided the plaintiff with a cheque on the day she finished the work.)

(c) *The grounds for denying the plaintiff's claim for relief.* (The cheque represented full payment of the amount owed to the plaintiff for her services.)

(d) *Any relevant facts not mentioned by the plaintiff.* (The cancelled cheque was returned to you by your bank indicating that it had been cashed.)

Like a statement of claim, a statement of defence is a standard form document created under the rules of a particular jurisdiction's civil procedure. Again, the only thing you (or your lawyer) need to fill out are the relevant facts as you allege them.

You may be able to draft your statement of defence yourself, provided the matter is a relatively simple one and the case is being brought in small claims court. Alternatively, you can and should seek the advice of a litigation lawyer if the case involves a complex issue or is being brought somewhere other than small claims court.

Again, like a statement of claim, the statement of defence is not the place to argue your case; that takes place in court. However, a well-drafted statement of defence will let the facts speak for themselves, thereby serving as a kind of argument.

Sample 18 at the end of this chapter is a statement of defence, offering a defence to the claim made in Sample 17, the statement of claim.

6. Pre-Trial Matters

Once the statement of claim and statement of defence — the pleadings — have been filed and served on the opposing parties to the suit, you (or your lawyer) must take certain steps to prepare for trial. These steps vary according to jurisdiction and level of court. However, certain steps are generally applicable.

(a) Exchange of Relevant Documentation

Opposing parties to a legal dispute will typically request and have the right to review the other party's documentation relating to the dispute, including any relevant documentation bearing directly on the subject of the dispute, such as correspondence, business records, contracts, notes, receipts, and accounts in the possession or control of the other party.

In this context, "relevant"means that the document in question must be material to the matter in dispute. Therefore, a plaintiff may see a defendant's cancelled cheque if that cheque is the basis of the defendant's claim to having paid the plaintiff the amounts he or she is seeking. It does not, however, grant the plaintiff unrestricted access to the defendant's financial records. Nor does a party have a right to access the other party's communications (whether written or otherwise) with his or her lawyer. Those are privileged and need not be disclosed.

For a document to be in the "control"of a party means that while the document may not be in the party's possession, the party can nonetheless gain access to it. A document might be in the control of a party if it is lodged in a safety-deposit box or held by some third party (e.g., a trustee, accountant, or doctor) who may legally be compelled to release it.

The exchange of documents takes place through an affidavit of documents. A party lists the documents relevant to the dispute in his or her possession or control, attaches those documents to the affidavit, and delivers it to the other party.

An exchange of documents does not typically occur in the small claims setting (although there are rules of court that allow for it in special circumstances). Rather, the parties are requested to attach any relevant documentation to the pleadings themselves.

(b) Examination for Discovery

Once the parties have had the opportunity to review each other's documentation, they then engage in a process known as "examination for discovery."Simply put, examination for discovery means interviewing the other party to (ostensibly) get the other side of the story; that is, to obtain any information that the other side's pleadings and documents have not revealed.

Of course, the real purpose behind an examination for discovery is to find weaknesses (factual and otherwise) in the other party's case. It also serves to give the other party a chance to trip themselves up on their own words and allows you to uncover any information of which you might not already be aware. Finally, it lets you assess the kind of witness the other person will make at trial if called to the witness stand to testify. Is the

person nervous? Believable? Smug? Uncertain? Unctuous?

So an examination for discovery can serve an important strategic function. It typically begins by the plaintiff requesting that the defendant (or, if the defendant is not a person but a company or partnership, a representative of the defendant) attend the offices of an official examiner to be interviewed by the plaintiff's lawyer. A mutually convenient time and location is arranged for the interview, and both parties and their lawyers attend. The defendant is sworn to tell the truth by the examiner, and the plaintiff's lawyer begins asking questions relevant to the dispute. This is recorded and transcribed by the official examiner, who then, on completion of the examination, provides both sides with transcripts. The contents of that transcript can be used by either party at trial.

The entire procedure is then repeated, this time with the plaintiff answering the defendant's lawyer's questions.

With few exceptions, small claims court procedure does not involve examinations for discovery.

(c) Pre-Trial Motions

Pre-trial motions, or "interlocutory proceedings"as they are known in some jurisdictions, are used primarily to resolve any technical disputes that may develop before trial. They are in many ways like a trial themselves and involve the preparation of motion records and other documentation designed to put forward a party's point of view. The motion is then brought before a judge who decides the issue and awards costs.

A pre-trial motion may be brought by either party and typically involves disputes such as disclosure of relevant documentation in affidavit of documents, whether or not the other party should be required to answer a question he or she may have refused to answer during examination for discovery, or whether the pleadings may be amended to reflect a change in circumstances since they were first filed.

As they usually involve technical matters relating to the conduct of the dispute, pre-trial motions are often argued by lawyers knowledgeable about those matters.

(d) Pre-Trial Hearings

Once the exchange of affidavits of documents has taken place and the examinations for discovery have been conducted (and in the absence of settlement), the parties sometimes must attend a pre-trial hearing. If pre-trial hearings are not required, they can sometimes be requested.

A pre-trial hearing is essentially a dress rehearsal for the trial that the lawyers and (if they wish) the parties to the dispute may attend. Few of the formalities of an actual trial are followed; no witnesses are called and it is not held in a courtroom. Rather, a pre-trial hearing usually takes place in a judge's chamber. The parties' lawyers are asked to set out their respective cases, and the judge gives his or her opinion on how the matter will be resolved at trial. The parties then decide, on that basis, whether they will go to trial or seek some alternative resolution to the dispute, such as settlement. The judge conducting the pre-trial hearing cannot conduct the actual trial itself.

(e) Settlement Discussions

Settlement discussions can occur at any time during a dispute. However, they often don't take on any real urgency until the matter is about to go to trial. By that point, everyone has a pretty good idea where they stand and what the likely outcome of the dispute will be. Taking the dispute to trial may simply prove meaningless to a party, not to mention costly.

This is why parties frequently attempt to settle their disputes. What few people realize is that settlement — by definition — implies an element of give-and-take. If you, as the plaintiff, expect to get everything in settlement that you are asking for at trial, then you are not asking for a settlement, and the defendant might as well take his or her chances at trial. After all, what has the defendant got to lose?

However, if you are willing to forego some things in return for the certainty that the defendant will give you the rest of what you are demanding, then you are contemplating settlement.

Of course, the real question is, "What do I have to give to get what I want?" That question will ultimately be determined through negotiations with the other side. Those negotiations often take place between the lawyers on their clients' behalf. It is important to note that your lawyer cannot decide to settle a matter, nor to accept or reject a settlement offer, without your instructions to do so. Those matters are entirely within the client's discretion.

But a lawyer can and should advise you on whether or not he or she thinks a settlement offer is a fair one. Your lawyer may also suggest appropriate counteroffers. Whatever the case, the final decision is yours. And if you find that a suitable settlement arrangement cannot be reached, you may have no choice but to proceed to trial.

7. Trial, Appeal, and Resolution

Contrary to what you might see on television, legal trials are relatively prosaic affairs, and those involving commercial disputes all the more so. And well they should be: after all, the point of a trial is not to stage a theatrical event but to resolve a dispute within the framework established by the law.

Most cases brought before a court present few surprises and therefore little drama. Both parties generally know everything that will be said in court and who will say it. The plaintiff (or the plaintiff's lawyer) usually states his or her case first, to be followed by the defendant. Each side may call witnesses and enter evidence into court to support the case. Both the witnesses and the evidence may be challenged by the other side. Witnesses are challenged through cross-examination, a process of questioning.

Once all evidence has been presented and closing arguments made by each side, the judge can decide the case. The case may also be heard and decided by a jury, if either of the parties wish to proceed that way. The judge's role is primarily to ensure that the rules of the court are observed and to explain to the jury the legal issues to be resolved and the options available to the jury in resolving those issues.

Depending on the complexity of the case, a judge or jury may not make its decision immediately. However, once a decision is made, whether by judge or jury, it has the force of law and becomes binding on both parties.

The trial concludes when the judge informs the parties of his or her (or the jury's) decision and an order is made for relief. At that point, the dispute has been resolved. If it has not been resolved to a party's satisfaction, that party may appeal the decision to a higher court. To do so, a notice of appeal must be filed with the court within a certain number of days from the date of the trial decision and then served on the other party.

Appealing a case, of course, adds more cost and effort to resolving the dispute. You will need to measure the potential gains associated with an appeal against the losses suffered at trial.

Perhaps the most important point worth noting about an appeal is that while it may result in the reversal of the trial decision, an appeal can be launched only on the basis of an error in the application of the law committed at trial, not on the basis of a finding of fact. In other words, you cannot appeal your case on the basis that the trial judge found as a fact that the cancelled cheque you offered as evidence of payment of the amount claimed was a forgery. You can, however, appeal on the basis that the judge failed to properly apply the law in determining what a forged cheque is. The distinction is often subtle but nonetheless important.

It is important to obtain the advice of a qualified litigation lawyer whenever you consider appealing a case.

Checklist 3 outlines a set of helpful rules to remember whenever you are taking a dispute to small claims court.

8. Enforcement of Order

The dispute has been resolved. Nothing remains but for the defendant to meet the terms of the court's order (assuming an order is made against the defendant) and, where ordered, pay the plaintiff restitution. Usually that involves an award of money (damages). However, it sometimes also includes legal fees and interest, usually calculated from the moment the circumstances giving rise to the dispute occurred to the date of judgment. The defendant may also be ordered to pay post-judgment interest, especially if it is clear the defendant will not be paying the plaintiff for some time.

Whatever the case, being ordered to pay restitution and actually doing so are two different things. Unfortunately, not everyone who is ordered to pay restitution does so. Various collection options are available to judgment creditors — people owed money under a court order.

(a) Garnishment

Garnishment is a statutory proceeding available to any judgment creditor. It allows the judgment creditor to compel a third party in possession of the judgment debtor's (the person against whom judgment has been rendered) money or property to apply that money or property to satisfy the debt. For example, if a judgment debtor is employed, a notice of garnishment can be served on the employer requiring the employer to withhold a portion of the judgment debtor's wages and remit it to the sheriff of the relevant jurisdiction.

On receipt of that money, the sheriff will distribute it to the judgment creditors according to the priority of their claims and in proportion to the debts owed them.

Among the things that can be garnished are —

* salaries, wages, and fees owed to a judgment debtor;

* bank accounts of a judgment debtor; and

* contractual debts owed to a judgment debtor, such as rent payments.

As you can see, garnishment can be a powerful tool and must be exercised with great care. In particular, it is important that anyone pursuing garnishment proceedings strictly comply with the rules established under applicable laws. The slightest technical defect can result in having the garnishment proceedings cancelled.

(b) Writ of Seizure and Sale

Some orders can be enforced by a writ of seizure and sale, which allows a judgment creditor to institute proceedings granting a sheriff the right to enter the premises of a judgment creditor and take possession of certain types of property. That property can then be publicly auctioned and the funds obtained from the auction applied to satisfy the debt owed to the judgment creditor.

The types of property that may be seized and sold include most types of motor vehicles and interests in real estate. However, the following are generally exempt from seizure and sale:

* Clothing

* Household furniture, appliances, utensils, and food

* Tools of the judgment debtor's trade

Again, because of the intrusive nature of this remedy, it must be exercised with a close eye to ensuring strict compliance with all of the relevant legislation.

(c) Examination in Aid of Execution

An examination in aid of execution is in many ways like an examination for discovery, with the exception that its primary purpose is to help a judgment creditor determine what, if any, assets a judgment debtor has and where they are located.

As is the case with an examination for discovery, an examination in aid of execution is conducted under oath before an official examiner who records and transcribes the examination. The information collected can then be used in connection with garnishment and writ of seizure and sale proceedings.

A judgment debtor who fails to attend an examination may be held in contempt of court. A judgment debtor may also be found to be in contempt of court if he or she fails to answer legitimate questions or otherwise tries to mislead the judgment creditor.

Obtaining an order for contempt of court against a debtor usually entails bringing a motion before the court. If the court finds that the judgment debtor is in contempt, it can make an order for, among other things, a fine to be paid by the judgment debtor, payment of the judgment creditor's costs, or in some cases, imprisonment.

Because of the information an examination in aid of execution can provide, it is usually undertaken by a judgment creditor before garnishment or seizure and sale proceedings are pursued. Consequently, the examination must be properly conducted to discover where the judgment debtor might be "hiding" assets. You should seek the assistance of a qualified lawyer in any examination in aid of execution you wish to have conducted.

9. Other Types of Hearings

Those who wish their disputes resolved by an independent third party have alternatives to court.

(a) Arbitration

Arbitration is a form of dispute resolution often sought by parties to a commercial dispute. It involves engaging a mutually acceptable, independent, and neutral third party to conduct a hearing (in much the same way a court trial is conducted) and render a decision.

Discovery

Because they tend to be less expensive than court, arbitration hearings are becoming a popular form of commercial dispute resolution. These are some other advantages:

- *Speed*. Arbitration hearings can be obtained much more quickly than court hearings, resulting in speedier resolution.

- *Privacy and confidentiality*. By choosing arbitration over court, the parties are able to resolve their dispute privately and confidentially.

- *Expertise*. In an arbitration, the parties to a dispute can choose the person (or people) who are to hear and decide the case. The parties can therefore choose people who are knowledgeable in a particular industry and able to provide insights and bring an understanding to a dispute that a judge might not.

These advantages and others have resulted in many small businesses choosing to make provision in their contracts that any dispute will be settled by arbitration.

Several types of arbitration are available and can involve one arbitrator or more. The decision the arbitrator renders may be binding or non-binding on the parties to the dispute. The hearing may be held according to the terms agreed to by the parties to the dispute or as provided under statute.

In binding arbitration, the parties agree that the decision of the arbitrator will be binding on the parties to the dispute. In non-binding arbitration, the decision of the arbitrator is not binding on the parties but can serve as a guide to resolution.

Most jurisdictions in Canada have enacted legislation regarding the arbitration of disputes. You should discuss that legislation with your lawyer to determine the various rights and obligations of the parties in an arbitration hearing.

(b) Mediation

Mediation is in many ways like arbitration and shares its advantages. The most important distinction between the two is that mediation does not confer any decision-making power on the independent third party who has been asked to hear the dispute. Rather, it is the mediator's job merely to assist the parties to negotiate and come to a mutually satisfactory resolution of their dispute, based in part on the mediator's impartial recommendations.

In both arbitration and mediation, the parties to the dispute may (unless they otherwise agree) be represented by and seek the advice of their lawyers. Most litigation lawyers have some experience in arbitration and mediation matters.

(c) Board/Panel Hearings

As noted earlier, certain kinds of disputes are required by law to be heard by special tribunals, boards, or panels created by legislation specifically for that purpose. These include legal disputes relating to labour and employment matters; municipal law matters; and health, safety, and other public regulatory matters.

Each of these types of tribunal, board, or panel hearings are subject to their own specific sets of rules of conduct. For that reason, anyone involved in a matter to be heard by a public tribunal, board, or panel should seek the assistance of a lawyer qualified to handle such affairs.

(d) Tax Disputes

Tax disputes are particularly relevant to small-business owners because they can develop in any number of situations in the course of owning and operating a small business. For example, a tax dispute may arise in which the Minister of National Revenue contends that an employer has not made the appropriate Employment Insurance or Canada Pension Plan remittances to CRA on behalf of its employees (see Chapter 14, Taxes). The employer would then be assessed by the minister and required to pay any outstanding amounts. A tax assessment could also arise if a sole proprietor has filed an income tax return with CRA and the minister determines that it does not accurately reflect amounts due and owing CRA. Whatever the case, CRA will provide you with a notice of assessment informing you of the minister's decision and the amounts in dispute.

To formally challenge the minister's decision, a taxpayer (in this case you as the employer or proprietor) would have to file a notice of objection to an assessment with the minister. That document is much like a court pleading in that it sets out your position regarding the assessment and any relevant facts on which your position is based. There are few formal requirements regarding the notice of objection other than that it must be set out in writing and filed within the stipulated time (90 days after the date the minister mailed the assessment).

Thus, provided that you are sufficiently comfortable with your understanding of the issue in dispute, you may prepare and file your own notice of objection to an assessment. Be sure to follow the rules described earlier regarding the techniques to be used in drafting pleadings. Alternatively, you may, and in most cases should, seek the advice of a tax lawyer or accountant.

Once the notice of objection is received by the minister, the minister, through an appeals officer, will then either confirm, vary (i.e., change), or vacate (i.e., abandon) his or her assessment. If the assessment is not vacated, the minister will reassess the taxpayer and either confirm or vary the original assessment.

If the reassessment varies the original assessment, then the taxpayer has 90 days from the day after the date of mailing to dispute the reassessment. Again, disputing requires filing a notice of objection with the minister. The minister will then either (again) vacate its reassessment or reassess the taxpayer, either confirming or varying the original reassessment. There is generally nothing to be gained by filing another notice of objection, as the first appeal officer has already examined the issues.

If an assessment or reassessment is confirmed or reassessed at any point by the minister after a notice of objection, and a taxpayer wishes to dispute it, the taxpayer's next step is to appeal the matter to the Tax Court of Canada. That involves filing a notice of appeal with the court. The minister must then file a reply to the notice of appeal, setting out his or her position regarding the assessment or reassessment and the facts on which that position is based, and deliver it to the taxpayer. Some time thereafter, the dispute will go to trial in the Tax Court of Canada.

The Tax Court of Canada operates under two sets of procedures or rules of conduct for handling tax appeals. There is the "general" procedure, under which the court must observe certain technical rules in conducting the hearing. Then there is an "informal" procedure, which does not bind the court to observe those rules and operates, in many ways, like small claims court. The informal procedure applies in limited circumstances, including situations in which the aggregate of federal tax and penalties for non-payment (or late payment) in issue for each taxation year is equal to or less than $12,000.

Although a taxpayer may appear in tax court represented by an accountant, or even without any representation, it is usually worthwhile to spend the money to consult a tax lawyer, even if only at the early stages, to develop a strategy.

Regardless of which route is chosen, a court must ultimately decide whether the appeal will be allowed (i.e., decided in favour of the taxpayer) or dismissed (i.e., decided in favour of the Minister of National Revenue). Any appeal from that decision must go to the Federal Court of Appeals, and if appealed even further, to the Supreme Court of Canada, whose decision in the matter is, of course, final.

Note, finally, that as with any other legal dispute, tax disputes can be settled before going to trial. A taxpayer may, therefore, wish to pursue that option with the minister in the appropriate circumstances.

f. Summary

The ability to avoid business-related disputes and to resolve those that do arise is crucial to the smooth operation of your business. Not only will you save time and energy — which you can then devote to other aspects of your small business — but resolving disputes can also have a positive outcome on your bottom line. And that's something worth fighting for.

Statement of Claim

1. The plaintiff claims —

   (a) the sum of $2,140 for work provided to the defendant (which sum includes applicable Goods and Services Tax);

   (b) prejudgment and postjudgment interest on that sum at the rate of [*insert rate*] as set forth in the services agreement between the plaintiff and the defendant. [*Note: If there is no agreement between the parties setting out the rate of interest payable on overdue amounts, you may wish to claim prejudgment and post judgment interest at the rate allowable under the relevant legislation in your jurisdiction. Be sure to discuss this with your lawyer.*];

   (c) costs of these proceedings, including applicable Goods and Services Tax.

2. The plaintiff is a corporation, incorporated under the laws of the province of Ontario, engaged in the business of floor refinishing.

3. The defendant is an individual, residing at all material times at 679 Dover Court, Toronto, Ontario, Canada, M5G 2L2 (the "Premises").

4. On or about January 20, 20--, the parties entered into a written services agreement (the "Agreement"). Pursuant to the Agreement, the plaintiff agreed to sand, polish, and finish the hardwood floors (the "Services") located at the Premises at an agreed price of $2,140, the ("Price") inclusive of applicable Goods and Services Tax.

5. On or about January 25, 20--, the plaintiff completed the Services in accordance with the terms of the Agreement. At that time, the plaintiff requested payment for the Services from the defendant. The defendant refused payment.

6. Despite several subsequent requests for payment by the plaintiff, the defendant has refused to pay anything on account of the Price.

7. Pursuant to the Agreement, interest on overdue amounts payable under the Agreement is calculated at a rate of [*insert rate*] per annum.

Sample 18
Statement of Defence

1. The defendant —

   (a) admits the allegations contained in paragraphs 3, 4, 6, and 7 of the statement of claim;

   (b) denies the allegations contained in paragraph 5 of the statement of claim to the extent of the completion of the Services (as defined in the statement of claim) but admits the remainder of the allegations contained in paragraph 5 of the statement of claim;

   (c) has no knowledge of the allegations contained in paragraph 2 of the statement of claim; and

   (d) denies that the plaintiff is entitled to the relief claimed in paragraph 1 of the statement of claim.

2. Pursuant to the terms of the Agreement (as defined in the statement of claim), the Services included, "the sanding, polishing, and finishing of all hardwood floor surfaces, including the stairs leading to the second floor" (the "Stairs").

2. The plaintiff did not sand, polish, or otherwise finish the Stairs. Further, the polish was not properly applied to those other areas of the Premises (as defined in the statement of claim) required to be sanded, polished, and finished under the terms of the Agreement.

3. Upon each request by the plaintiff for payment, the defendant advised the plaintiff that the Services had not been properly performed, and that until such time as they had been properly performed, the defendant would not tender payment on account of the Price (as defined in the statement of claim).

4. The defendant requests that the plaintiff's claim be dismissed with costs in this matter to be awarded against the plaintiff.

Your Day in Court: Ten Rules to Follow in Small Claims Court

1. COME TO COURT PREPARED

The better you know your case, the better able you will be to present it to the judge and convince the judge of your point of view. For that reason, you must come to court prepared, and that means both knowing what you want to say and actually being able to say it.

That process involves three steps. The first step is to know the issue in dispute. In other words, you have to know why you are in court. For example, you may be in court over a dispute about whether or not you have been paid for work you did for the defendant. The second step is to be able to tell the court why the dispute should be resolved in your favour. In the demand letter in Sample 11, the dispute should be resolved in your favour because you did the work, yet the cheque the defendant gave you in payment was returned to you marked "nonsufficient funds" by the bank. The final step is to be able to say exactly what it is you want from the court, which in this case is to be paid in full by the defendant. You may not win your case simply by taking these steps but you are at a greater risk of losing if you don't take them.

2. PROVIDE EVIDENCE TO SUPPORT YOUR CASE

It is one thing to tell the judge that you were not paid for your services by the defendant; it is quite another to show the judge both a contract saying that the defendant would pay you for those services and the cheque marked nonsufficient funds. With the evidence in hand, the judge no longer has to worry about whether or not to believe you or the defendant; he or she has objective and independently verifiable proof in support of your position and can rely on that in making a decision. Therefore, it is always important that you provide the judge with whatever tangible evidence you have to support your case.

3. PRESENT YOUR CASE IN AN ORDERLY FASHION

When presenting your case to a judge, think of it as telling the judge a story — the story of what happened between you and the defendant. And just as you would start a story at its beginning (rather than in the third chapter), so too should you present your case according to its proper sequence of events. Most of the time, that means simply recounting the facts in their chronological order. For example, you could say, "On May 5, I repaired the defendant's car. On May 6, the defendant picked up his car and gave me a cheque in payment for the repairs. And on May 8, the defendant's cheque was returned to me marked 'nonsufficient funds' by my bank." Such a statement is both clear as to what occurred and easy to follow. At other times, information can be summarized for the judge. For example, you could say, "I phoned the defendant on each of May 10, 11, 13, and 15, advising him of the returned cheque and requesting payment. On each of May 10, 11, and 13 he advised me that a new cheque was on its way. However, on May 15 he told me no cheque was on its way and that he decided not to pay for the repairs." This, too, is clear and represents an orderly (albeit not chronological) re-telling of events. The point is that no matter how you wish to present your case to the judge, make sure that — as with any good story — it is told in a clear and orderly fashion.

4. **LISTEN TO THE JUDGE**

The judge is there to resolve a dispute and knows what information is needed to accomplish that task. Listen to what the judge says and shape your arguments around the judge's concerns. If the judge asks you whether or not the defendant first offered to pay you in cash before giving you a cheque, you should answer that question even if it seems irrelevant to you. The judge may have his or her own reasons for asking (e.g., perhaps he or she wants to determine whether or not the defendant ever had the intention of paying you — as evidenced by his willingness to part with hard cash instead of a cheque). By answering the judge's questions, remaining silent when the judge asks you to remain silent, or focusing on matters that the judge has specifically raised for discussion, you are helping the judge in his or her quest for the truth. And — if you are in the right — that can only help you.

5. **LISTEN TO THE OTHER PARTY TO THE DISPUTE**

People love to talk. Especially those with something to hide. Listen to the other party presenting his or her case to the judge and make notes about any inconsistencies or obvious flaws in that person's reasoning or account of the facts. Then, when it's your turn to speak, draw the court's attention to those inconsistencies. For example, if the defendant wished to argue that he does not owe you any money because the repairs were never properly carried out, you might wish to point out to the court that (i) had the repairs not been properly carried out, the defendant would have known it at the time he came to pick up his car (because, after all, the repairs involved fixing a flat tire); and (ii) the defendant never once mentioned that the repairs had not been properly carried out during any of the phone conversations you had with him about the bounced cheque. Indeed, you had heard nothing about the quality of the repairs until receiving the statement of defence. By really listening to what the other party has to say in court, you are in a better position to counter his or her arguments and advance your own.

6. **STICK TO WHAT IS RELEVANT AND SPEAK TO THE ISSUES**

You are trying to recover an unpaid debt owed by the defendant to your auto repair shop. It is relevant that the cheque the defendant presented to you in payment was returned marked "nonsufficient funds" by the bank, and that should be drawn to the judge's attention. That information helps to resolve the issue in dispute. That the defendant cheats on his wife, double parks, or has poor taste in neckties is, however, not relevant. Moreover, raising such matters not only diverts attention from what is important but also will likely anger the judge (who has precious little time or interest to waste on personal grievances). In sum: speak to the issues, nothing else.

7. **BE CLEAR AND CONCISE**

There is nothing more difficult than to be both clear and concise when speaking. Public speaking isn't easy, and even seasoned lawyers often get flustered. Therefore, before you go to court, practise what you are going to say in front of someone who is unfamiliar with the dispute and see if that person is able both to follow what you are saying and be convinced that you are in the right. If so, then your chances in front of the judge improve. If not, ask the person to point out any parts of your argument (or the facts) that are not clear and then work to clarify them. The better you are able to communicate with the judge, the more likely it is that the judge will understand and appreciate your point of view in the dispute.

8. **ADMIT THE OBVIOUS, EVEN IF IT IS NOT IN YOUR FAVOUR**

There is nothing to be gained by hiding relevant facts from the court or denying the truth. If you do so and are found out, the judge may draw the conclusion that you are being dishonest, and on that basis, choose not to believe anything else you may say. However, it is not your job to argue the other side's case. Yes, you should openly acknowledge that the defendant painted your fence — albeit a week after he said he would. However, it is not your job to point out to the court that it was raining every day of that week prior to that day. After all, you don't know if that is the reason the defendant didn't show up. Presumably, only the defendant knows of the reason for the delay. It is up to him or her to make his own argument.

9. **AIM TO PERSUADE**

Arguing a case before a judge means trying to persuade him or her of your point of view. While this does not mean you should ever lie or overstate your case, it is important that the judge get the sense that you are in the right and that he or she should decide the dispute in your favour. By appealing to the judge's reason and sense of fair play, you will have gone a long way to reaching that goal. Most important, never appear difficult, smug, arrogant, patronizing, insolent, or insulting — either to the court, the other party, or anyone else connected to your case.

10. **APPEARANCES COUNT**

Do not underestimate the importance of appearances in a court of law. The way you dress, carry yourself, speak, and your ability to maintain eye contact all say a lot about the kind of person you are and whether or not you can be said to have any credibility; that is, whether or not you can be believed. Remember that good judges work by intuition. Most have heard it all and seen it all; after all, most commercial disputes generally involve the same cast of characters involved in similar (if not the same) sets of circumstances. Thus, it is the judge's job to read between the lines of any dispute. It should be your goal, therefore, to show the judge — both in manner and dress — that you are honest, forthright, and to be believed.

14
Taxes

This chapter examines the tax implications of owning and operating a small business. It focuses on how the form in which you carry on business affects your tax liability. In addition, it explores your obligation to collect and pay the federal goods and services tax and the provincial retail sales tax.

a. Our System of Taxation

Canadians and their businesses are subject to a variety of different taxes, including taxes on income. Income taxes represent a primary source of government revenue and are levied by both the federal and provincial governments against the income earned by individuals and corporations resident in Canada.

Federal income taxes are imposed under the *Income Tax Act* (Canada) (often referred to simply as the ITA) and its regulations. Furthermore, each province has its own income tax legislation, which usually applies to any individual or corporation with a permanent establishment in that province.

In some provinces (Ontario, for example), the income tax applicable to individuals is overseen and administered by the federal government. Individuals do not, therefore, need to file separate

federal and provincial income tax returns when declaring their income for a given year.

The income tax applicable to a corporation is, however, usually overseen and administered on a provincial basis, so a corporation must file separate federal and provincial income tax returns declaring its income for a given fiscal year.

Both federal and provincial income tax apply to your total world income (your income regardless of where in the world that income — or any portion of it — originates).

Individuals and corporations are taxed differently under income tax legislation. Individuals are taxed at progressive rates, meaning the tax rates imposed on them increase with the increase in their income. Corporations, however, are usually taxed at a flat rate on each dollar of income, regardless of how much income is earned.

The Canadian tax system is self-assessing. It is up to the taxpayer to determine how much tax he or she owes. In addition, our tax system is a self-reporting one, meaning that the taxpayer must also file the appropriate tax return and pay any income tax owed. A failure to do these things when required can lead to stiff fines, penalties, and possible imprisonment. (See Chapter 13, Resolving Disputes, for a discussion of tax appeals and assessments).

How much income tax your small business has to pay — and who is responsible for paying it — will, in part, be determined by the business form under which you operate.

b. Tax and the Sole Proprietor

The tax implications of doing business as a sole proprietor are relatively straightforward: any income your business (your sole proprietorship) earns or any losses it incurs in any year must be included with your income earned or losses incurred from other sources during that year, in addition to any employment or investment income you may have earned. The total is then subject to income tax at the rate applicable to individuals.

If, for example, you have a full-time job that earns you a salary of $30,000 per year and you operate a sole proprietorship fixing leaking basements on weekends, you must apply the losses or income resulting from your weekend job to your salary in calculating your total taxable income. And because a sole proprietor is taxed at the progressive rates attributable to individuals under the ITA, any income above your $30,000 salary (any income you earn in your sole proprietorship) could be taxed at a higher rate if the total exceeds a certain threshold under the ITA.

By the same token, you could decrease the rate at which you pay income tax — and hence the amount you will actually have to pay — if your sole proprietorship creates losses. A loss is created if, for example, you purchased certain assets to carry on your sole proprietorship (e.g., a computer, software, buckets, boots, or machinery) and the fall in value or depreciation of those assets for a given year (through wear and tear) exceeds the income you earned from your business during that year. The types of assets you may depreciate, the rate at which you may depreciate them for income tax purposes (the rate at which you can claim

their fall in value), and the period over which you can do so is determined by the ITA.

Therefore, your total income in a given year would be your $30,000 salary plus your income and minus your losses (including any depreciation of your business assets) arising from your sole proprietorship. Because it is not a separate entity at law, a sole proprietorship is not taxed separately from the sole proprietor himself or herself. For that reason, accountants and lawyers will frequently recommend that you carry on business as a sole proprietor (as opposed to as a corporation) if you —

❧ plan to carry on your business alone;

❧ have other income; for example, from employment; and

❧ expect your business to lose money for the first few years.

That way you can use the losses from your business to reduce the income you earn from other sources (e.g., your regular job) and hence the amount of income tax that you will have to pay.

As a sole proprietor, you must calculate the income tax you owe, if any, on the basis of any income you earned or losses you incurred during the calendar year immediately preceding the year in which you file your return. The ITA allows you to deduct the business losses that you incur in any one year and which exceed your income for that year against income you have earned in the three preceding years and the next seven years.

If, for example, your business losses exceed your salary from your regular job in any given current year (and if your job and your business are your only sources of income), the portion of those losses exceeding your salary can be applied to reduce your salary (or any other income) either in the three preceding years or the following seven.

Note, finally, that because a sole proprietor is subject to the filing requirements applicable to an individual, you must file your income tax return by April 30 of each year for the preceding calendar year.

c. Tax and Partnership

Like a sole proprietorship, a partnership is not a taxable entity. This is true for both general and limited partnerships. Any income or losses created by the business of the partnership is determined at the partnership level and allocated among each of the partners. Each partner's share of that income or loss must then be included along with that partner's income or losses from any other sources (e.g., employment or investments) in calculating that partner's income for tax purposes.

Determining whether any income or losses have been created at the partnership level means looking to whether the partnership itself (as opposed to the partners) has earned income or incurred losses (e.g., through the depreciation of partnership assets) in carrying on its business. Those earnings or losses are then allocated among the partners in proportion to their share in the partnership (or however else the allocation may have been determined by the partners) for use in calculating each partner's individual income.

If, for example, a partnership consisting of five partners has a net loss of $10,000 in a given year, that loss would be allocated (presumably) equally among the partners so that each had $2,000 to deduct, or "write off," against their other income. Perhaps one partner might be able to reduce his salary earned from regular employment by $2,000. Similarly, another partner could reduce the amounts she has earned through investments by $2,000.

This ability to flow the losses of a partnership through to the partners makes partnership an attractive business form for those wishing to shelter their income from other sources. (To shelter your income means to reduce it through deductions created by, among other things, business losses.)

However, where tax shelters are concerned, general and limited partnerships are not equal. That is because a partner, whether in a general or limited partnership, cannot deduct more than his or her "at risk" amount — the amount that partner has invested or committed to the partnership — from his or her income.

In the case of a general partnership, a general partner is "at risk" to lose both his or her investment in the partnership and, because of the partner's unlimited liability, is further committed to satisfy any debts or obligations of the partnership out of his or her personal assets. A partner in a general partnership, therefore, has an unlimited at-risk amount.

The at-risk amount of a limited partner, though, is limited to the amount he or she has invested in the limited partnership. A limited partner enjoys limited liability for the debts of the limited partnership and, therefore, is not committed to contributing anything beyond his or her investment.

For those willing to accept the risk of personal liability, participation as a partner in a general partnership may — because of the potentially larger deductions it allows — serve as the better tax shelter.

A partnership is therefore sometimes recommended as the form under which to carry on business if you —

* plan to carry on business with someone else;

* have other income; for example, from employment; and

* expect your business to lose money for the first few years.

As a partner, you can then use the losses from the business of the partnership to reduce your income from other sources and hence reduce the amount of income tax you will have to pay.

When calculating that tax, you must, as was the case with a sole proprietor, include any income earned or losses incurred during the calendar year immediately preceding the year in which you file your return. Also as was the case with a sole proprietor, you can deduct your share of the business losses that the partnership incurred in any one year and which exceed your income for that year against income you have earned in the three preceding years and the next seven years.

Nevertheless, remember that a corporation can also be a partner in a partnership. A proportionate share of any income the partnership earns or losses it incurs will accordingly be allocated to the corporation and taxed at the corporate rate. A partner who is an individual would, of course, be subject to tax at the individual rate.

Again, as with the case of a sole proprietor, an individual partner must file his or her return by April 30 each year for the preceding calendar year. A corporate partner may file its return within six months of its fiscal year-end (see below).

d. Tax and the Corporation

Unlike either a sole proprietorship or a partnership, a corporation is a taxable entity. Its owners — the shareholders — are subject to tax as well. This situation has several implications for you as a small-business owner carrying on business through a corporation.

1. Corporation

(a) General Principles of Taxation

As an entity distinct from its shareholders, a corporation is subject to both federal and provincial income tax. That means that the income or loss of a business carried on by a corporation is both determined and taxed at the level of the corporation itself. Unlike a partnership, losses cannot be flowed through to the shareholders and taxed at that level. Instead, any losses of the business belong exclusively to the corporation and can

therefore be applied only against the corporation's income.

As noted earlier, corporations are subject to tax at a flat rate on each dollar of income. Individuals are taxed at progressive rates. When an individual's annual income reaches approximately $55,000, the rate at which that individual's income is taxed begins to exceed the rate at which a corporation's income is taxed. Therefore, from a tax perspective, you may — assuming your income will be less than $55,000 — be better off doing business as a sole proprietor or as a partner in a partnership rather than through a corporation. The exception is if the corporation through which you carry on your small business (or plan to do so) qualifies as a Canadian Controlled Private Corporation (see below).

At present, the federal income tax payable by a corporation is set at a rate of 38 percent. This figure is, however, subject to a corporate surtax and federal abatement. The abatement allows for provincial income tax to be imposed and it applies only to corporations earning income attributable to a province or territory in Canada.

Provincial income tax on corporate income is imposed under various provincial corporate taxation statutes. In general, a province will impose income tax on a corporation with a permanent establishment or fixed place of business in that province. The rates at which corporate income is taxed vary between provinces. Furthermore, many provinces impose surtaxes and offer abatements or reductions based on, among other things, your type of business.

In addition to income taxes, most provinces impose capital taxes on a corporation with a permanent establishment in that province. A "capital tax" or "paid-up capital tax" is a tax levied on the paid-up capital of a corporation. Paid-up capital refers to the money or property paid into a corporation in exchange for shares in that corporation. You should, however, note that the definition of paid-up capital varies between provinces. Usually, though, corporations with total assets and gross revenues of $1 million or less each do not have to pay any capital tax. Capital tax, therefore, does not often apply to small businesses.

What may apply is the manufacturing and processing reduction available to any corporation carrying on a manufacturing or processing activity in Canada. It reduces the net rate of federal tax on manufacturing and processing income and should be investigated by anyone carrying on those types of business.

Every corporation must file the appropriate federal tax return and pay any income tax, if owed. In most provinces, CRA collects both federal and provincial income taxes, and you need file only one return. Alberta, Ontario, and Quebec require corporations to file a separate provincial income tax return.

After a corporation's income tax has been calculated, it must file its income tax return(s) within six months of its fiscal year-end — the last day of its fiscal period. A fiscal period is the corporation's taxation year; that is, the 52-week period a corporation is allowed to select under the ITA as the basis on which to calculate its income taxes. A fiscal year does not need to begin and end on the same days as a calendar year (i.e., January 1 and December 31), but can begin on any day the corporation selects — June 11, for example — and end (52 weeks later) on June 10 of the following year. That period will constitute the corporation's fiscal period unless the corporation subsequently changes it. Any change will, however, require the consent of CRA. A corporate income tax return must be filed for the fiscal period immediately preceding the year in which the return is filed.

(b) Canadian-Controlled Private Corporation

A Canadian-Controlled Private Corporation, or CCPC, is, as its name suggests, a private corporation resident in Canada and not controlled, either directly or indirectly, by a public corporation, non-resident, or combination of the two. The term private corporation means that the shares of the corporation are not listed on a stock exchange. The restriction on control requires that no more than 50 percent of the voting shares in the corporation can be held by a non-resident or public corporation (or combination of the two). Based on this definition, it should be apparent that most small businesses in Canada qualify as CCPCs.

This is important from a tax perspective because a CCPC is entitled to a tax deduction on its first $500,000 of business income earned in Canada in a year, for each year in which it carries on business. This "small business deduction," as it is commonly known, reduces the income tax a small business has to pay so that — in the case of Ontario, for example — the rate of income tax applicable to a corporation on its first $500,000 of income is cut in half. This makes the small business deduction among the most important ways for a small business to reduce income tax. There is a strong incentive to incorporate your small business if it will qualify as a CCPC.

2. Shareholders

Most shareholders of incorporated small businesses are also employees of the business. This owner-manager status gives rise to the question of what is the most tax-efficient way for you to be remunerated. In other words, how can you — as both a shareholder and employee of your incorporated small business — arrange to receive income from that business in a manner that minimizes the income tax you have to pay?

One way is to receive income through dividends. A dividend, you will recall from Chapter 3, is a distribution of the profits of the company to its shareholders. As the owner-manager of your corporation, you have the right — acting in your capacity as director — to declare a dividend and remunerate yourself in that way. That dividend must then be included in your income from other sources.

For purposes of calculating your income, the ITA requires that you add one-quarter of the amount of the dividend to the actual amount of the dividend itself. This is called "grossing up" your dividend, and it means that you are required to pay income tax on an amount equal to one and one-quarter of the dividend you receive.

However, to help offset that liability, the ITA provides for a dividend tax credit. That credit is designed as a "progressive" measure to ensure that high-income earners pay more income tax on their dividends than low-income earners. That said, the dividend tax credit should, in most cases, at least equal the "gross up" amount and therefore provide you, as a shareholder, with a favourable tax result.

As an alternative, you may wish to forego declaring a dividend in favour of paying yourself a salary as an employee of your small business. That salary will then be subject to income tax at the rate applicable to individuals under the ITA. If you pay yourself a small salary, the amount of income tax you will have to pay will also be relatively small.

Moreover, it is worth noting that in some cases a corporation can deduct from its income the salaries it pays out to its employees. If a corporation pays out all its income in the form of salaries, the corporation will not have to pay any income tax. However, because the shareholders will have effectively received the income of the business as a salary, that income will be taxed at the rates applicable to individuals. As noted above, that rate is, up to a certain level, less than it is for a corporation in certain circumstances.

It may also be worthwhile to pay yourself a salary as opposed to a dividend if you have unused personal credits or tax deductions that you can use to reduce your personal income. The ITA provides that a certain portion of your salaried income can be earned free from federal income tax. This may entail paying yourself a salary up to

that limit and then giving yourself the rest of that income in the form of a dividend.

The point is, as an owner-manager of an incorporated small business, there are a number of tax-planning strategies available to you by which you can minimize your income taxes. It is up to you to discuss those options with your lawyer and accountant to determine which are best suited to meet your particular needs.

Finally, regardless of whether you received remuneration in the form of a salary or dividend, you must file your income tax return by April 30 of each year for income earned during the preceding tax year.

e. GST

With few exceptions, every business is required to collect and remit GST, the goods and services tax imposed under the federal Excise Tax Act on goods and services consumed in Canada. The current rate of GST is 5 percent of the amount paid for the goods or services supplied. "Supplied" in this context means when property or services are provided and includes any sale, transfer, lease, or disposition of property.

The scheme of the GST is such that goods and services are taxed whenever they are supplied. At the same time, however, the GST is fully recoverable by every person paying it in the course of their business activities, except for a non-commercial user or supplier of the goods and services. Thus, only the ultimate consumer bears the GST. The collection scheme is set up in this way so that business is responsible for collecting and remitting the GST on behalf of the government.

Goods and services are either subject to GST at the prescribed rate of 5 percent, subject to GST but are zero-rated, or are exempt from GST. Zero-rated goods and services are subject to GST but at a rate of 0 percent; they are effectively exempt from GST.

Goods and services that are subject to GST at the prescribed rate include cars, soft drinks, furniture, dance lessons, accountants' and lawyers' fees, taxi fares, restaurant meals, and hotel accommodation.

Goods and services subject to GST but zero-rated include basic groceries (milk, bread, vegetables), prescription drugs and dispensing fees, and medical devices (hearing aids, eyeglasses, thermometers).

Goods and services exempt from GST include most health, medical, and dental services provided by licensed physicians or dentists; educational services; and most services provided by financial institutions, such as arrangements for a loan or mortgage.

As a small-business owner, you should do the following to ensure your compliance with your obligations under GST legislation.

1. Register Your Business

Every person engaged in a commercial activity in Canada with annual sales and revenue of GST-taxable goods and services of more than $30,000 is required to register with CRA, Customs and Excise. The term "person" includes any individual, business, partnership, or corporation.

You are not required to register if your annual sales of taxable goods and services do not exceed $30,000.

You can register by filling out the appropriate form, available from any CRA office. Once you are registered, you are eligible to receive a credit for the GST you have paid on all business purchases. This credit, known as the "input tax credit," can result in a refund to you from CRA if the credit exceeds the amount of GST you are required to pay.

At the time you register, you will be advised of the frequency with which you will have to file a GST return — a statement of the amount of GST you have charged and the amount you have paid in a given reporting period. Filing frequency can be monthly, quarterly, or annually, depending on the value of your annual sales volume of taxable goods and services, as indicated on your registration form. The higher the value of your annual sales and revenues, the shorter (usually) your reporting period will be and hence the more frequently you will need to make filings.

2. Keep Records

You must maintain written records of how much GST your small business has charged (the tax you collected) and how much it has paid. The difference between these two amounts represents the amount you must remit to CRA or the amount of your refund.

To support your claim for a refund, you must keep invoices of your business purchases. Although you do not have to file these with your GST return, CRA excise auditors may ask to see them at some later time. Anyone providing you with a GST-taxable supply should provide you with an invoice stating, among other things, his or her GST registration number.

3. Collect the GST

It is your responsibility, as the seller of your goods or services, to charge, collect, and remit GST to CRA, Customs and Excise.

GST is supposed to be a visible tax. Therefore, if the price of your goods and services includes the GST, you are required to inform your customers of that fact. Placing signs around your business is one way to do so.

Discovery

GST should be calculated on the price of your goods and services before any provincial sales tax is added.

4. Calculate the GST You Owe (or Your Refund)

You are responsible for calculating how much GST you owe (or how much should be refunded to you). To do so, simply determine the GST you have charged, calculate your input tax credit (how much you are required to pay), and remit the difference or claim your refund on your GST return.

Note that you may have up to four years to claim your input tax credit from the date your GST return is due for the reporting period in which the tax on the purchase was paid or payable.

5. File Your GST Return

The final step in the process is to file your GST return. Everyone who is required to collect the GST must file a return, even if there is no refund owed to you or money due to CRA. That means that you do not need to file a return if your annual sales of taxable goods and services do not exceed $30,000, provided you have not been collecting GST on those sales.

Discovery

Canada Revenue Agency will charge you interest and penalties if you don't remit GST on the date it is due.

Regardless of your assigned filing frequency or the size of your business, you must use the Goods and Services Tax Return for Registrants form to make your filings. Instructions on how to complete the form and where to file it are available with the form.

f. Retail Sales Tax

With the exception of Alberta, every province in Canada imposes retail sales tax, or RST, on the retail sale of tangible personal property or goods and certain specific services. The reference to "tangible" is meant to exclude things like a sale of shares in a corporation or other security. (See Chapter 6 for a discussion of the meaning of "security.")

A retail sale is one that is not made for resale. Unlike the GST, RST must only be collected from the ultimate consumer. Payment of RST is made at the time the consumer purchases the taxable goods or services and is collected by you, the seller. You must collect tax from your customers on the total selling price of the taxable goods or services, excluding any GST. You are then required to remit the RST you collected to the relevant provincial taxing authority, usually at the end of each month. This is done by completing and filing the appropriate return.

As you are ultimately responsible for determining the amount of RST payable, it is once again important that you keep records of all your retail business transactions.

Each province lists items that are exempt from RST. These include things such as items sold for resale purposes, certain kinds of vehicles (e.g., forklifts), inventories, ships or aircraft, gasoline, medical and related expenditures, children's clothing, and books.

Every business that sells RST taxable goods or services to consumers must be registered with or obtain a vendor's permit from the relevant provincial taxing authority. A registration form and instructions on how to complete it can be obtained from that authority.

Provincial sales tax rates vary between provinces. Moreover, in Newfoundland, Nova Scotia, and New Brunswick, the GST has been harmonized with the RST so that a single Harmonized Sales Tax, or HST, of 15 percent is collected and remitted under GST legislation. Quebec also has a HST, but it is administered by Revenu Québec. As of the writing of this book, Ontario has an HST of 13 percent.

g. Summary

In addition to the types of taxes discussed in this chapter, your small business may be subject to any number of other federal, provincial, or municipal taxes. Moreover, you should be aware of any additional taxes you are obligated to collect and remit to the federal, provincial, or municipal taxing authorities. You can investigate these matters by contacting the office of the Ministry of Revenue in your province or CRA. Your accountant and lawyer should also be able to help you.

When discussing taxation with your lawyer or accountant, be sure to get his or her opinion on tax-planning strategies that can help to minimize the tax you must pay. As you will quickly discover, sound tax planning can be an important element in the satisfaction you derive from owning and operating your small business.

15
Professional Advisors

Chances are, you will require the services of a lawyer at some time during the start-up and operation of your small business. You will also probably require the services of a banker and an accountant.

The purpose of this chapter is to assist you in selecting the right professional advisors for your small business. However, as this book is concerned with the legal issues associated with owning and operating a small business, this chapter will focus largely on the role your lawyer should play in your business affairs.

Professional advisors provide you with the specialized advice you may need during the start-up and ongoing operation of your business, usually in connection with some specific financial or legal matter. In those areas, it is in your interests to obtain an expert opinion.

The three professional advisors you will most rely on are your banker, accountant, and lawyer. What those people can do for you is considered in detail below.

a. General Selection Criteria

Any professional advisor you choose to assist you with your business should, of course, be qualified to do the job you are asking him or her to do. That is usually a matter of training and expertise. That is examined later in this chapter, as we consider each of the specific types of professional advisors available to you.

Your more general concerns when choosing a professional advisor are the intangibles. That is, consider the kinds of things that training and expertise don't necessarily provide but which are, in many respects, equally important. That includes interest, personality, and experience.

1. Interest

A good professional advisor should take a real interest in you and your business. It is not enough that he or she simply know about the type of business you do or be familiar with the industry in which you carry on business; rather, your professional advisor should take steps to become informed about your particular business and its place in your industry.

This sort of professional advisor is often easy to identify because such people will take steps to familiarize themselves with what you do and how you do it. Your professional advisor might do the following:

Visit your business premises and ask for a tour. He or she might also ask to take part in any major business transactions by, for example, visiting an office you plan to lease or another business you wish to buy.

Keep you apprised of things that may be of interest to you without your necessarily having requested this. For example, if you operate a restaurant, your lawyer should clip and send you recent articles and other general information regarding things such as changes to municipal smoking by-laws that he or she may come across.

Invite you out to lunch or other non-business related events to get an alternative perspective on the kind of person you are, the needs your business may have, and the ways in which he or she, as your professional advisor, can best fulfil those needs.

It is important that a professional advisor see you as more than just a paycheque. To properly provide you with the services you need to meet your particular business goals, a professional advisor must take an active interest in your small business.

2. Personality

Do not underestimate the importance of getting along with your professional advisors on more than just a business level. Clashing personalities don't often result in a good working relationship, and in the end you will be the one to suffer.

Always carefully consider whether or not a particular advisor is the kind of person you can work with and respect. You should, for example, assess a professional advisor's —

Demeanor. Does this person patronize you? Is he or she a "know it all"? Does he or she accord you respect by taking

the time to explain his or her advice and asking for your input?

Organization. Does this person routinely miss returning your calls? Have sloppy work habits?

Business outlook. Is this person an optimist? A pessimist? Is the person conservative in his or her approach to business? Have a chip on his or her shoulder that may interfere with representing your interests?

Personality differences between you and your professional advisors may not necessarily mean strife. Those differences can often be complementary. For instance, most entrepreneurs tend to be risk takers who rely on their business instincts. Most lawyers tend to be risk avoiders who rely on the certainty of the law and written agreements. Often, different personalities can work together to ensure that every consideration is taken into account where your small business is concerned.

3. Experience

Experience is more than simply having done the same job for a long time. It means having real insight into the job itself. For example, it means the difference between knowing how to prepare a shareholders agreement and how to prepare the right shareholders agreement in the circumstances.

The following are some of the signs of an experienced professional advisor:

He or she is able to consider the "big picture" whenever you ask for advice in connection with a business matter. For example, if you are incorporating a company, your lawyer and accountant should be able to advise you on how to structure the share ownership with a view to the future interests of your spouse and children.

He or she will be able to provide you with a variety of options for achieving the same end.

* He may be connected to others in your industry (e.g., government officials) who can assist you in problem solving.

Experience comes at a price. What you should consider is whether or not the price you pay for an experienced professional advisor outweighs the costs of remedying any mistakes a less experienced advisor might make.

b. Your Banker

A small-business owner will typically go to a bank to obtain the financing he or she needs. A loans officer specializing in small businesses or some other bank professional will meet with you to discuss what kinds of financing are available to you and how you can obtain it. He or she should also be able to provide you with information regarding —

* the bank's loan and other financing options;

* the types of savings, chequing, and other cash-management services the bank can offer your small business; and

* short- and long-term trends in the economy, interest rates, and other factors affecting the success of your small business.

In return, a banker will also be seeking information from you. Usually, he or she will ask you to provide as much information as you can about your business, including its assets and liabilities, how long it has been in operation, who is primarily responsible for its day-to-day management, and what, if any, future plans have been made for it. On that basis, a banker will then determine whether or not the relationship is worth pursuing.

At the same time, you should also be considering whether or not the relationship is worth pursuing, bearing in mind that the banker will be your primary connection to the bank. Thus, the following are some questions for you to ask yourself when selecting a banker:

* Is this person willing to consider my vision for my business and work with me toward realizing it?

* Does this person understand the industry in which I carry on business?

* Is this person going to smother me in paperwork and require me to report on terms that are unacceptable to me?

* What kind of financial services will this person make available to me, and at what cost?

* What kind of security will this person demand when making loans to me? (See Chapter 6, Financing Your Small Business.)

* Will this person be available and accessible to me or will my business constantly be put at the bottom of his or her list of priorities?

You should deal with these questions sooner rather than later, as it will be difficult to change your relationship with a bank once you are indebted to it.

Selecting a banker is as simple as walking into the branch office of your neighbourhood bank and asking to speak with a small-business loans officer or other relevant personnel. That person will, more than likely, be glad to sit down with you and discuss your needs and expectations.

There are probably more than a few different banks in your neighbourhood. You should, therefore, try to visit as many as you reasonably can to find the right fit. Comparison shop to determine who can provide you with the best service and attention at the lowest price.

Finally, it doesn't hurt to advise a prospective banker about any other business (personal or otherwise) you can bring to the bank if it is willing to meet your business needs. A bank, after all, is itself a business and is always looking for ways to profit from a relationship.

c. Your Accountant

An accountant's primary role as a professional advisor is to provide you with expert advice on the tax and accounting issues affecting your business.

An accountant is not a bookkeeper. A bookkeeper enters information — usually in the form of sales and expenditures figures — into the books or financial records of your small business. It is the accountant's job to properly categorize and analyze that information and then provide you with an accurate picture of your small business's profits and losses.

Your accountant should also be able to —

* indicate ways for you to improve your profitability (e.g., your accountant might show you how you can reduce costs by spending less on overhead),

* prepare and file tax returns and related documentation on your behalf,

* prepare your business's annual financial statements,

* provide you with tax-saving advice regarding your business,

* help you to apply for and obtain government and other business-related grants and financing, and

* help you arrange your personal finance goals so as to coincide with your business finance goals.

Sometimes, an accountant can also provide bookkeeping services. However, for many small businesses, that task is — for cost reasons — usually assigned to someone within the business itself.

In selecting an accountant, you should follow the same guidelines as you would use when selecting a banker. In particular, you should be certain that your accountant is knowledgeable about the kind of business you do so that he or she can advise you of industry-specific tax, financing, and related issues that might be important to your business.

Be aware that there are no legal restrictions on who may call themselves an accountant. Consequently, there is the danger of engaging the services of an someone who has little, if any, knowledge of accounting. Your best bet is to search out someone who has obtained a professional designation such as a CA (Chartered Accountant), CMA (Certified Management Accountant), or CGA (Certified General Accountant). These designations indicate a background and training in accounting matters.

Again, it is important to comparison shop when selecting an accountant. Do not be afraid to ask questions about what a particular accountant can do for you and at what price.

d. Your Lawyer

Given the legal issues associated with the start-up and operation of a small business, it is likely that at some time you will require the services of a lawyer.

A lawyer is someone who is legally qualified to practise law in a particular jurisdiction. To become qualified, a person must undergo training as a lawyer, which includes obtaining a Bachelor of Laws degree (LLB) from an accredited university.

An LLB usually requires a person to successfully complete a three-year course of study in a university law program. To be accepted into that program requires that the person meet the admissions criteria, which generally entail successful completion of an undergraduate degree at an accredited university. The average law school graduate will therefore have attended university for some seven years before practising as a lawyer.

Upon graduation, a person who has successfully completed law school will have to undergo a period of apprenticeship known as "articles" before he or she is allowed to practise law in a jurisdiction. Articles can last up to 18 months (depending on the province) and usually involves both classroom study and a practical component in which a prospective lawyer gains hands-on experience working at a law firm.

Once a prospective lawyer has successfully completed the articling process and met the necessary ethical requirements established by the law society of his or her jurisdiction, he or she may then be called to the bar of that jurisdiction. At that point, the person is qualified to practise law and to call himself or herself a lawyer.

1. What Can a Lawyer Do for You?

Your lawyer's job is to provide you with legal advice. Specifically, he or she should be able to identify legal issues that concern your small business, tell you what the law says about how those issues must be addressed, and — on your instructions — help you to address them.

However, this doesn't mean that your lawyer can or should make your business decisions for you. That is perhaps the biggest misconception small-business owners have about their lawyers. Your lawyer may advise you that you have the right to sue someone for a breach of contract, but your lawyer should not (and probably will not) tell you whether or not you should do so. Just as important, he or she cannot act in that regard on your behalf without your instructions to do so.

As part of the job of providing you with legal advice, your lawyer should also be able to —

* advise you of your legal rights and obligations,

* assist you in structuring your business affairs around those rights and obligations, and

* argue your position if a dispute arises in connection with your legal rights and obligations or those of another person.

Checklist 4 lists what your lawyer can (and should) and cannot (and should not) do for you.

2. When Should You Seek the Advice of a Lawyer?

The cautious (and, therefore, recommended) approach is to seek the advice of a lawyer whenever a legal issue arises that involves your small business. Of course, it is not always clear when that might happen. Moreover, it can become expensive to consult a lawyer on all such issues. It is perhaps more helpful to say that you should definitely seek the advice of a lawyer when —

* you agree to do something (either verbally or in writing) that will significantly affect your rights or may result in liability to you if something goes wrong;

* you are asking someone to agree to do something (either verbally or in writing) that you are paying a significant amount of money for or that — if things go wrong — can affect the successful operation of your business;

* you are being sued or are planning to sue someone, and the matter in dispute involves a complex legal issue or a legal issue about which, though perhaps not complex, you know little; or

* you are subject to some sort of government order or other demand that if not complied with can result in fines, penalties, or imprisonment.

These examples are not exhaustive. In general, you should be sure to seek out the advice of a lawyer whenever you are concerned about the legal aspects of a particular business decision. Moreover, the time for seeking the advice of your lawyer is before the decision is made. For example, the time to ask your lawyer's advice about entering into a specific contract is before you actually do so (e.g., before you sign it). That sounds obvious, but few lawyers are surprised at the number of people who walk into their offices with the request to review the fairness of a contract that they have already signed.

3. What Should You Look for in Selecting a Lawyer?

When looking for a lawyer to help you with your business affairs, you should, of course, look for the same qualities you would expect to find in any other person providing you with professional services. As well, your lawyer should have the following qualities:

* *Display a high degree of integrity*. Specifically, he or she should approach any matter you bring to him or her in a forthright and honest manner. Underhanded tactics and "sharp practice" are the marks of a person who cannot be trusted and a lawyer whose services should be avoided.

* *Be knowledgeable in business law matters*. The legal profession is becoming highly specialized. Experts are emerging in every area of law. And while you might not always require the services of an expert, it is important that you engage the services of someone who knows what he or she is doing. Hiring a lawyer who specializes in family or criminal law matters to give you legal advice in connection with a loan does not make sense.

* *Be willing and able to participate in the growth of your small business*. A good lawyer will want to have a successful small-business person remain as a client. However, that involves growing with the client by continuing to offer and provide the types of services your small business will need. An ongoing relationship of this sort will help you cut down on your legal costs because your lawyer will already know most of the relevant background

information whenever you consult him or her on a legal matter.

Lawyers — unlike bankers and accountants — are often required to present opposing points of view to one another on their clients' behalfs. This is particularly true when a dispute has developed between the clients. A good lawyer should, therefore, have excellent oral and written advocacy skills. He or she should be able to present your side in a dispute clearly and concisely. Your lawyer should also be forceful and confident in his or her presentation of your point of view (assuming it is a legitimate one). Finally, your lawyer should have a sense of when a fight is worth fighting and when it may simply be in your best interests to back off. Discretion, it seems, is also the better part of good lawyering.

Selecting a particular lawyer to help you with your business is not always an easy task. Most lawyers find their clients through word-of-mouth advertising. You should canvass other small-business people to see if they can recommend a good lawyer. The law societies of the various provinces can also refer you to business lawyers in your area. A referral, however, is no guarantee of a lawyer's skill or competence.

Once again, comparison shop. Most lawyers are willing to provide you with an initial consultation at no charge. This will give you an opportunity to learn about what the lawyer does and what he or she can do for you. It's also a great opportunity to evaluate the lawyer's demeanor and the extent of his or her operations. Most important, however, is that this consultation gives you the chance to ask some questions.

Discovery

Your relationship with your lawyer differs from that with your banker or accountant in that the law dictates that any communications between you and your lawyer are strictly confidential. You cannot be compelled to disclose those communications (even in a court of law), nor can your lawyer disclose these communications without your authorization (unless you are planning to commit a crime).

4. What Should You Ask Your Lawyer?

What you should ask a lawyer depends on the stage of your relationship with him or her.

(a) When You First Meet

When first meeting a lawyer whom you propose to ask to do some work for you, you should ask these questions (along with any other relevant questions that come to mind):

* What kind of law do you practise? Do you have a specialty? How far can you take a matter — for example, a lawsuit — before it must be turned over to someone with greater expertise?

* What kind of environment do you practise in? Are you a sole practitioner or do others work in your firm with you? Who in your firm will be handling my work?

* Have you done work for others in my industry? What is the depth of your experience?

* What will your services cost? What are your payment terms? (Within 30 days of billing? Certified cheques only?) Do you require a retainer fee?

A "retainer fee" is a fee a lawyer requests up front when taking on a legal matter for you. The lawyer must deposit it into a trust account, and then that fee serves as a source of money to which the lawyer has access to pay his or her bills for the legal work done for you. The lawyer need merely bill you for the work he or she has done and then debit the trust account for that amount. Any fees in excess of the amount deposited in the trust account will be billed to you directly.

Not every lawyer will require a retainer fee. As your relationship grows — and provided you pay your bills — the need for a retainer fee diminishes.

When requesting a retainer fee, a lawyer should also provide you with a retainer letter. That letter will confirm that you have engaged the lawyer to assist you with a particular legal matter and set out the parameters of the services the lawyer will provide. Whenever you review a retainer letter (and you always should), ensure that it accurately describes what the lawyer said he or she would do for you. When taking on a legal matter for you, your lawyer will rely on that letter as evidence of your instructions. It is important that those instructions are, in fact, your instructions.

You must also ensure that the retainer letter accurately sets out any fees or costs the lawyer has quoted you, whether as a lump sum or an hourly rate.

If you discover that the retainer letter does not accurately set out your instructions or raises other issues of concern to you, be sure to contact your lawyer immediately to clear up any discrepancies. Your lawyer should then send you a letter confirming your revisions. Alternatively, you should send your lawyer a letter to that effect. In either case, put it in writing.

Discovery

At present, not every province in Canada allows a lawyer to charge a contingency fee for his or her services. A contingency fee is essentially a fee charged and calculated as a proportion of an award of money a lawyer obtains on your behalf in the resolution of a dispute or the completion of a deal (e.g., the sale of your business).

Contingency fees can allow people who do not ordinarily have the money to pursue legal claims the opportunity to do so, but the fear is that it will encourage lawyers to pursue weak cases and result in "ambulance chasing." Whatever your point of view, it is important

for any small-business owner who agrees to a contingency-fee arrangement to set out in writing the precise amount of the contingency fee, the nature of the dispute to which it relates, and under what circumstances it becomes payable. All this should be acceptable to you before you agree to a contingency-fee arrangement.

(b) During the Course of Your Relationship

If your lawyer is handling a legal matter for your small business, you should, on an ongoing basis, ask —

* to be kept apprised of the status of the matter and any new developments as they occur,

* to be billed on a regular basis so that you are able to address cost issues as they arise, and

* to be provided with a copy of any correspondence that the lawyer sends out relating to your case, so that you can be aware of what he or she is doing for you.

In addition, your lawyer should provide you — at no charge — with recent updates to the law and other items of information he or she may come across that affect your small business.

(c) After Your Lawyer Has Completed a Matter for You

When a lawyer has completed a legal matter for you, he or she is responsible for providing you with a written report on that matter. You should ask the following questions if they are not already answered in the report:

* What did the lawyer do for me in this matter?

* What are the relevant documents (e.g., a promissory note), and what is their significance?

* What should I be aware of going forward from the completion of this matter? For example, are there any payment obligations?

Furthermore, your lawyer should bill you as soon as possible following the completion of the matter. That bill should state in detail any actions the lawyer has taken on your behalf and the cost of these actions. It should also describe any disbursements and other costs. Getting the bill shortly after completion of the matter will enable you to address any concerns at a time when they are still fresh in your and your lawyer's minds.

5. Ethical and Professional Standards Governing Lawyers

The practice of law is governed by the various provincial law societies. Those law societies set the ethical professional standards to which every lawyer practising in the province must adhere. Those standards are similar across the country and affect a lawyer's conduct and relationship with clients, other lawyers, the judicial system, and the public. In addition, the Canadian Bar Association publishes a set of ethical and professional standards to which lawyers practising in Canada must adhere.

A violation of those standards can lead to a disciplinary hearing before a board established by the law society. Furthermore, if found guilty, a lawyer may be suspended or disbarred, meaning that he or she is no longer allowed to practise law in that province. Thus, very few lawyers take their ethical obligations lightly.

The ethical obligations of a lawyer are enough to fill a book. The following are some of the more important obligations bearing directly on the kinds of legal issues about which you — as a small-business owner — may be concerned:

* A lawyer cannot represent both sides in a dispute. This seems obvious but is often overlooked. Remember: the lawyer's job is to act as advocate, not judge.

* A lawyer cannot act in a manner that is likely to cause a conflict of interest unless there has been adequate disclosure and the consent of the clients has been obtained. For instance, a lawyer could not act for more than one shareholder in negotiating and drafting a shareholders agreement unless the shareholders on whose behalf he or she was acting all consented to that arrangement. Moreover, if at some later time a dispute arose regarding the shareholders agreement, the lawyer could act for none of the people he or she represented in preparing it.

* The lawyer should not enter into any business transactions with the client except under the very strict guidelines set by the relevant law society. These usually require the lawyer to take steps to ensure that the client is fully aware of the nature and extent of the involvement of his or her lawyer and that any actions taken by the lawyer regarding the business do not prejudice the client.

6. What Should I Expect from a Lawyer?

You should expect that your lawyer is qualified, skilled, and competent to do the job for which you have engaged him or her. You should expect that your lawyer treat you and your small business with respect and conduct himself or herself with the utmost integrity and honesty. Most of all, you should expect that your lawyer will act in your best interests — whether that means steering you away from unnecessary litigation or negotiating your office lease. After all, your lawyer is there to serve you.

e. Summary

When selecting professional advisors for your small business, be sure to follow the guidelines detailed in this chapter. Above all, comparison shop. Ask questions — lots of them. Remember: what you don't know can hurt you.

Checklist 4
Your Lawyer . . .

CAN (AND SHOULD):

❑ Provide you with legal advice

❑ Represent you in a legal dispute

❑ Advise you of your legal obligations

❑ Aggressively pursue your rights

❑ Keep all information acquired from you strictly confidential

❑ Refuse to provide you with his or her services if he or she is not qualified to do so

❑ Advertise his or her practice

❑ Deal forcefully with an opposing lawyer

❑ Refuse to take your property for safe keeping if he or she is unable to do so

❑ Charge you for his or her services

❑ Assist you with the legal dimensions of your business affairs

❑ Present your case in court in a manner which best advances your cause

❑ Refer you to another lawyer if he or she is unqualified or otherwise unable to handle your concern

❑ Deal with the other party's lawyer

❑ Provide you with conscientious, diligent, and efficient service

CAN'T (AND SHOULDN'T):

❑ Make your business decisions for you

❑ Represent both sides in a legal dispute

❑ Counsel you on how to evade them

❑ Use or threaten to use the criminal law to collect civil debts

❑ Do so if it will prevent a crime from being committed

❑ Withdraw those services after he or she has begun providing them to you unless he or she has a good reason to do so and has given you sufficient advance notice

❑ Do so in a way that detracts from the integrity, independence, or effectiveness of the legal profession

❑ Do so in an unfair or discourteous manner

❑ Neglect to take care of your property if he or she agrees to do so

❑ Charge a fee that is unfair or unreasonable

❑ Borrow money from you or otherwise take an interest in your business affairs unless he or she follows very strict legal and ethical guidelines

❑ Deceive the court or the opposing party

❑ Charge you for that

❑ Deal with the other party, without the consent of that party's lawyer

❑ Be overconfident or too bold in giving assurances on legal questions, especially if the matter is one of opinion

Afterword
The Road to Success

Good business makes for good law. And good law makes for a successful business.

If this book has fulfilled its purpose, you will now have a firm grounding in some of the legal issues affecting your small business. You should know the form under which it would be most advantageous for you to run your small business and where you might get the money to do so. You should know how to deal with your customers so that they continue to be your customers but also in a way that ensures that you are paid for what you do for them. You should know how to solve disputes when you can't avoid them and how to avoid choosing a name for your business that will cause a dispute. You should know what intellectual property is and how to protect yours, how to write a contract, and when it is inappropriate to fire an employee. Armed with that knowledge and an understanding of the other issues covered in this book, you should be able to meet any challenges facing your small business.

But remember: A knowledge of legal issues and even of the law itself can take you only so far down the road to success. In the end, that knowledge must be tempered by reason and intuition and supplemented with a strong understanding of how a small business works.

Though I myself am a lawyer, I come from a long line of small business owners. Most of what I learned about owning and operating a small business I learned from my father while working at one or another of his various small businesses. To this day, I remain in awe of his ability — and the ability of others like him — to use the skill and judgment he gained through years of hard work to meet new challenges and opportunities and never to fail to take decisive action.

It is for people like my father that this book is written.

Good luck.

Download Kit

Please enter the URL you see in the box below in a web browser on your computer to access and use the download kit.

---

www.self-counsel.com/updates/canlegal/17kit.htm

The following files are included in the download kit:

- Bonus chapters: "The Internet Age" and "Privacy Obligations"
- Sample policies and agreements
- — And more!